How to
Master Skills for the

Second Edition

TOEFL® iBT
WRITING Advanced

DARAKWON

How to Master Skills for the Second Edition

TOEFL® iBT

WRITING Advanced

Publisher Kyudo Chung
Editor Sangik Cho
Authors Michael A. Putlack, Stephen Poirier
Proofreader Michael A. Putlack
Designers Minji Kim, Hyeonju Yoon

First Published in December 2007 By Darakwon, Inc.
Second edition first published in March 2025 by Darakwon, Inc.
Darakwon Bldg., 211, Munbal-ro, Paju-si, Gyeonggi-do 10881
Republic of Korea
Tel: 02-736-2031 (Ext. 250)
Fax: 02-732-2037

ISBN 978-89-277-8096-0 14740
         978-89-277-8084-7 14740 (set)

www.darakwon.co.kr

Photo Credits
Shutterstock.com

Components Main Book / Answer Key / Free MP3 Downloads
7 6 5 4 3 2 1   25 26 27 28 29

Table of
Contents

INTRODUCTION

1 Information on the TOEFL® iBT

A The Format of the TOEFL® iBT

Section	Number of Questions or Tasks	Timing	Score
Reading	**20 Questions** • 2 reading passages 　– with 10 questions per passage 　– approximately 700 words long each	35 Minutes	30 Points
Listening	**28 Questions** • 2 conversations 　– 5 questions per conversation 　– 3 minutes each • 3 lectures 　– 6 questions per lecture 　– 3-5 minutes each	36 Minutes	30 Points
Speaking	**4 Tasks** • 1 independent speaking task 　– 1 personal choice/opinion/experience 　– preparation: 15 sec. / response: 45 sec. • 2 integrated speaking tasks: Read-Listen-Speak 　– 1 campus situation topic 　　reading: 75-100 words (45 sec.) 　　conversation: 150-180 words (60-80 sec.) 　– 1 academic course topic 　　reading: 75-100 words (50 sec.) 　　lecture: 150-220 words (60-120 sec.) 　– preparation: 30 sec. / response: 60 sec. • 1 integrated speaking task: Listen-Speak 　– 1 academic course topic 　　lecture: 230-280 words (90-120 sec.) 　– preparation: 20 sec. / response: 60 sec.	17 Minutes	30 Points
Writing	**2 Tasks** • 1 integrated writing task: Read-Listen-Write 　– reading: 230-300 words (3 min.) 　– lecture: 230-300 words (2 min.) 　– a summary of 150-225 words (20 min.) • 1 academic discussion task 　– a minimum 100-word essay (10 min.)	30 Minutes	30 Points

B What Is New about the TOEFL® iBT?

- The TOEFL® iBT is delivered through the Internet in secure test centers around the world at the same time.

- It tests all four language skills and is taken in the order of Reading, Listening, Speaking, and Writing.

- The test is about 2 hours long, and all of the four test sections will be completed in one day.

- Note taking is allowed throughout the entire test, including the Reading section. At the end of the test, all notes are collected and destroyed at the test center.

- In the Listening section, one lecture may be spoken with a British or Australian accent.

- There are integrated tasks requiring test takers to combine more than one language skill in the Speaking and Writing sections.

- In the Speaking section, test takers wear headphones and speak into a microphone when they respond. The responses are recorded and transmitted to ETS's Online Scoring Network.

- In the Writing section, test takers must type their responses. Handwriting is not possible.

- Test scores will be reported online. Test takers can see their scores online 4-8 business days after the test and can also receive a copy of their score report by mail.

2 Information on the Writing Section

The Writing section of the TOEFL® iBT measures test takers' ability to use writing to communicate in an academic environment. This section has two writing tasks. For the first writing task, you will read a passage and listen to a lecture and then answer a question based on what you have read and heard. For the second writing task, you will state and support an opinion in an online classroom discussion.

A Types of Writing Tasks

- **Task 1** Integrated Writing Task

  – You will read a short text of about 230-300 words on an academic topic for 3 minutes. You may take notes on the reading passage.

  – After reading the text, you will listen to a lecture discussing the same topic from a different perspective for about 2 minutes. You may take notes on the lecture.

  – You will have 20 minutes to write a 150-to-225-word summary in response to the question.

- **Task 2** Writing for an Academic Discussion Task

  – You will see a discussion board on a university website that comprises two students responding to a question posted by a professor.

  – You will have 10 minutes to read everything and to write a response to the topic in the online post. It should be at least 100 words.

B Types of Writing Questions

- Integrated Writing Task

  – Summarize the points made in the lecture, being sure to explain how they challenge specific claims/arguments made in the reading passage.
  cf. This question type accounts for almost all the questions that have been asked on the TOEFL® iBT so far.

  – Summarize the points made in the lecture, being sure to explain how they cast doubt on specific points made in the reading passage.

  – Summarize the points made in the lecture, being sure to specifically explain how they answer the problems raised in the reading passage.

- Writing for an Academic Discussion Task

  – Yes or no questions: These questions require you to agree or disagree with a statement.

  – Preference questions: These questions ask you to state a preference between two similar things.

  – Open-Ended questions: These questions ask for your own thoughts or opinions on a broad topic.

C Important Features of Evaluation

- Quality of Response

  In the first task, the quality of the response is about how well you integrate and relate information from the reading and listening materials. In the second task, it is about the relevance and depth of your argument.

- Language Use

  Language use is about the accuracy and range of your grammar and vocabulary. In order to get good grades on the writing tasks, you should be able to use both basic and more complex language structures and choose the appropriate words.

HOW TO USE THIS BOOK

How to Master Skills for the TOEFL® iBT Writing Advanced is designed to be used either as a textbook for a TOEFL® iBT writing preparation course or as a tool for individual learners who are preparing for the TOEFL® test on their own. With a total of twenty units, this book is organized to prepare you for the test by providing you with a comprehensive understanding of the test and a thorough analysis of every question type. Each unit provides a step-by-step program that helps develop your test-taking abilities. At the back of the book are two actual tests of the Writing section of the TOEFL® iBT.

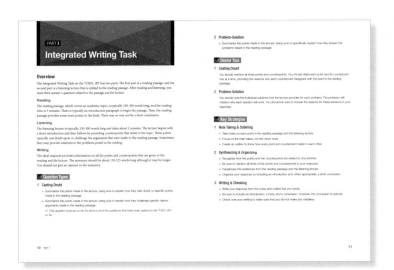

❶ Overview

This section is designed to prepare you for the type of task the part covers. You will be given a full sample question and a model answer in an illustrative structure.

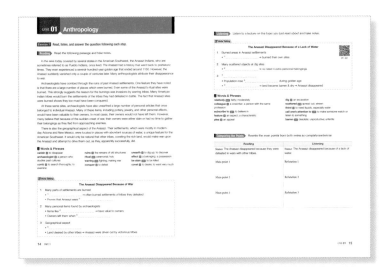

❷ Note Taking & Vocabulary (Integrated Writing Task)

This section provides definitions of difficult words and phrases and also lets you take notes on the passages to make sure that you understand the main points in the passages.

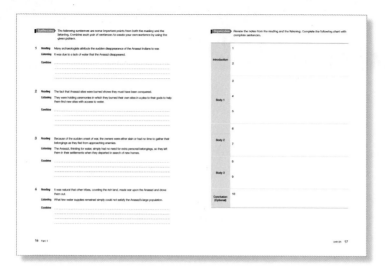

❸ Synthesizing & Organization
(Integrated Writing Task)

This section asks you to combine two different thoughts into a single sentence and lets you organize and write your own essay to make sure that you can respond to the question well.

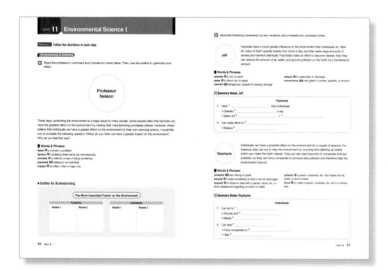

❹ Brainstorming & Outlining
(Writing for an Academic Discussion Task)

This section allows you to brainstorm about the professor's comments and has you complete two outlines to ensure that you understand the responses made by the students.

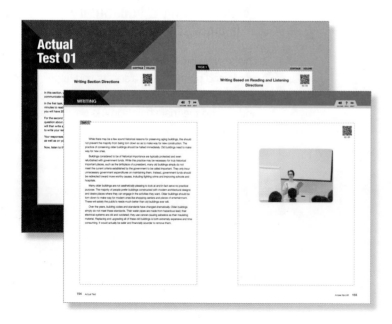

❺ Actual Test

This part will give you a chance to experience an actual TOEFL® iBT test. You will be given two sets of tests that are modeled on the Writing section of the TOEFL® iBT. The topics are similar to those on the real test, as are the questions. This similarity will allow you to develop a sense of your test-taking ability.

PART I

Integrated Writing Task

The integrated writing section consists of one task. You will be presented with a reading passage on a certain topic. Then, you will hear a lecture on the same topic. Typically, the lecture will have a position opposite that of the reading passage. Then, you will be asked a question in which you must write about the arguments made in the listening lecture and the reading passage. You will have 20 minutes to write an essay in response to the question. A typical essay is 150 to 225 words long.

Integrated Writing Task

Overview

The Integrated Writing Task on the TOEFL iBT has two parts. The first part is a reading passage, and the second part is a listening lecture that is related to the reading passage. After reading and listening, you must then answer a question related to the passage and the lecture.

Reading

The reading passage, which covers an academic topic, is typically 230-300 words long, and the reading time is 3 minutes. There is typically an introduction paragraph to begin the passage. Then, the reading passage provides some main points in the body. There may or may not be a short conclusion.

Listening

The listening lecture is typically 230-300 words long and takes about 2 minutes. The lecture begins with a short introduction and then follows by providing counterpoints that relate to the topic. These points typically cast doubt upon or challenge the arguments that were made in the reading passage. Sometimes they may provide solutions to the problems posed in the reading.

Writing

The ideal response provides information on all the points and counterpoints that are given in the reading and the lecture. The summary should be about 150-225 words long although it may be longer. You should not give an opinion in the summary.

Question Types

1 Casting Doubt

- Summarize the points made in the lecture, being sure to explain how they cast doubt on specific points made in the reading passage.
- Summarize the points made in the lecture, being sure to explain how they challenge specific claims/ arguments made in the reading passage.

  cf. This question type accounts for almost all of the questions that have been asked on the TOEFL iBT so far.

2 Problem-Solution

- Summarize the points made in the lecture, being sure to specifically explain how they answer the problems raised in the reading passage.

Useful Tips

1 Casting Doubt

You should mention all three points and counterpoints. You should relate each point and its counterpoint one at a time, providing the reasons why each counterpoint disagrees with the point in the reading passage.

2 Problem-Solution

You should note the individual solutions that the lecture provides for each problem. The professor will mention why each solution will work. You should be sure to include the reasons for these solutions in your response.

Key Strategies

1 Note Taking & Outlining

- Take notes on each point in the reading passage and the listening lecture.
- Focus on the main ideas, not the minor ones.
- Create an outline to show how every point and counterpoint relate to each other.

2 Synthesizing & Organizing

- Recognize how the points and the counterpoints are related to one another.
- Be sure to mention all three of the points and counterpoints in your response.
- Paraphrase the sentences from the reading passage and the listening lecture.
- Organize your response by including an introduction and, when appropriate, a short conclusion.

3 Writing & Checking

- Write your response from the notes and outline that you wrote.
- Be sure to include an introduction, a body, and a conclusion. However, the conclusion is optional.
- Check over your writing to make sure that you did not make any mistakes.

Directions Now you will see the reading passage for 3 minutes. Remember that it will be available to you again while you are writing. Immediately after the reading time ends, the lecture will begin, so keep your headset on until the lecture has ended.

Reading

The factory is a product of both the eighteenth and, even more so, nineteenth centuries. The rise of factories began in England and eventually spread throughout the world. There were three primary reasons as to why this occurred.

Prior to the creation of factories, the majority of work, including making clothes and even metal tools, was done by hand by people in their homes or in small shops. The main technological achievement that enabled the rise of factories was the steam engine. Originally developed in the mid-eighteenth century to pump water out of deep coal mines, the steam engine provided its user with enough power to do the work of many people.

The steam engines people owned, therefore, needed to be centralized in protective buildings to maximize their capabilities. Factories were a direct result of this need. The steam engine and, later, the internal combustion engine, brought about improved transportation thanks to the inventions of the railroad and the steamship. Railroads could transport raw materials to a central point, like a factory, where workers and machines could subsequently transform them into finished products. The railroads and the steamships could then turn around and transport these goods to markets throughout the world.

Another key point in the rise of factories, particularly in England, was property rights. Subsistence farming had been a way of life for untold centuries. However, many people did not own their own land but merely farmed wherever they could. Enclosures, land that was enclosed by hedges and fences and owned by individuals, became dominant features in England. Those without any land became the suppliers of cheap labor in factories. Additionally, laws preventing private property from government seizure encouraged both the development of the land's resources and the further construction of factories.

Listening

Now listen to part of a lecture on the topic you just read about.

> **Script**
>
>
> 01-01
>
> **M Professor**: It's unquestionable that several, uh, unique circumstances in England enabled the rise of factories to occur. But new technology, improved transportation methods, and advances in property laws are not the reasons why this happened.
>
> Steam engines were crucial components of the Industrial Revolution, yet they needed to be built from something. In fact, it was in iron foundries, where the development of strong iron and then steel occurred, that the key aspect in the rise of factories took place. Iron and steel were integral components for parts of steam engines, for making trains and ships, and for building the factories themselves.
>
> Nor can transportation account for the rise of factories. Many factories were built near the resources, such as coal and water, which they required. That's why we've seen many industrial centers spring up near coal mines and rivers. Think of the Ruhr in Germany as an example. In addition, railroads weren't developed until the 1840s and didn't spread around the world until the end of the nineteenth century. Consider that . . . Factories had existed for decades prior to the development of railroads. Additionally, sailing ships were very much in use worldwide even into the early twentieth century, so, well, transportation clearly wasn't that

important to factories.

The rise of individual property rights in England encouraged the development of factories and provided a large labor pool. However, this wasn't the case in many countries. Let me see . . . In Russia, the government and noblemen typically owned factories. And many of the first factories in several countries, including England, were used to make weapons or gunpowder for the military. This production was centralized so as to have exact standards for weapons. In fact, there is very much evidence that the concept of the factory comes from their early usage as buildings for manufacturing arms.

Directions You have 20 minutes to plan and write your response. Your response will be judged on the basis of the quality of your writing and on how well your response presents the points in the lecture and their relationship to the reading passage. Typically, an effective response will be 150 to 225 words.

 Summarize the points made in the lecture, being sure to explain how they cast doubt on specific points made in the reading passage.

Sample Response

Introductory sentence The reading passage's author is convinced there were several reasons why the rise of factories occurred in England, yet the professor disagrees that they were the main reasons why factories became successful.
Relation 1 The first reason the reading ascribes to the rise of factories is the steam engine. The reading mentions that since steam engines could do the work of several men, they had to be put in central locations, which gave rise to factories. **Refutation 1** Meanwhile, the professor believes it was not steam engines but the iron and steel used to make them that were the real important factors, especially since they could also make railroads, ships, and factories. **Relation 2** While the reading passage's author believes the inventions of railroads and steamships enabled raw materials and finished products to be transported quickly worldwide, **Refutation 2** the professor points out that railroads were invented decades after factories and sailing ships were still being used in the twentieth century. **Relation 3** Finally, the reading notes that property rights forced landless people to work in factories and enabled landowners further to develop factories. **Refutation 3** However, the professor claims that it was really the standardized production of weapons, for which factories were often first used, that led to their rise.
Conclusion The reading passage's author and the professor clearly disagree on the reasons why the rise of factories occurred.

Exercise 1 Read, listen, and answer the question following each step.

Reading ▶ Read the following passage and take notes.

In the area today covered by several states in the American Southwest, the Anasazi Indians, who are sometimes referred to as Pueblo Indians, once lived. The Anasazi had a history that went back to prehistoric times. They even experienced a several-hundred-year golden age that ended around 1150. However, the Anasazi suddenly vanished only a couple of centuries later. Many anthropologists attribute their disappearance to war.

Archaeologists have combed through the ruins of past Anasazi settlements. One feature they have noted is that there are a large number of places which were burned. Even some of the Anasazi's ritual sites were burned. This strongly suggests the reason for the burnings was invasions by warring tribes. Many American Indian tribes would burn the settlements of the tribes they had defeated in battle. The fact that Anasazi sites were burned shows they too must have been conquered.

At these same sites, archaeologists have also unearthed a large number of personal articles that once belonged to individual Anasazi. Many of these items, including pottery, jewelry, and other personal effects, would have been valuable to their owners. In most cases, their owners would not have left them. However, many believe that because of the sudden onset of war, their owners were either slain or had no time to gather their belongings as they fled from approaching enemies.

There is also the geographical aspect of the Anasazi. Their settlements, which were mostly in modern-day Arizona and New Mexico, were located in places with abundant sources of water, a unique feature for the American Southwest. It would only be natural that other tribes, coveting the rich land, would make war upon the Anasazi and attempt to drive them out, as they, apparently successfully, did.

📖 Words & Phrases

vanish v to disappear
archaeologist n a person who studies past cultures
comb v to search thoroughly; to examine

ruins n the remains of old structures
ritual adj ceremonial; holy
warring adj fighting; making war
conquer v to defeat

unearth v to dig up; to discover
effect n a belonging; a possession
be slain phr to be killed
covet v to desire; to want very much

📝 Note Taking

The Anasazi Disappeared Because of War

1 Many parts of settlements are burned
   - 1) .... → often burned settlements of tribes they defeated
   - Proves that Anasazi were 2) ....

2 Many personal items found by archaeologists
   - Items like 3) .... → have value to owners
   - Owners left them when 4) ....

3 Geographical aspect
   - 5) ....
   - Land desired by other tribes → Anasazi were driven out by victorious tribes

Listen to a lecture on the topic you just read about and take notes.

Note Taking

The Anasazi Disappeared Because of a Lack of Water

01-02

1   Burned areas in Anasazi settlements
- 1) _____ → burned their own sites

2   Many scattered objects at dig sites
- 2) _____ → no need 4 extra personal belongings

3   3) _____
- Population rose 4) _____ during golden age
- 5) _____ → land became barren & dry → Anasazi disappeared

Words & Phrases

relatively adv fairly; moderately

colleague n a coworker; a person with the same profession

subscribe to phr to believe in

feature n an aspect; a characteristic

plea n an appeal

dig n an excavation

scattered adj spread out; strewn

thirst v to need liquids, especially water

call one's attention to phr to make someone watch or listen to something

barren adj desolate; unproductive; unfertile

Comparing the Points   Rewrite the main points from both notes as complete sentences.

Reading	Listening
Stance The Anasazi disappeared because they were defeated in wars with other tribes.	**Stance** The Anasazi disappeared because of a lack of water.
Main point 1	Refutation 1
Main point 2	Refutation 2
Main point 3	Refutation 3

The following sentences are some important points from both the reading and the listening. Combine each pair of sentences to create your own sentence by using the given pattern.

1   **Reading**   Many archaeologists attribute the sudden disappearance of the Anasazi Indians to war.

        Listening   It was due to a lack of water that the Anasazi disappeared.

        Combine

2   **Reading**   The fact that Anasazi sites were burned shows they must have been conquered.

        Listening   They were holding ceremonies in which they burned their own sites in a plea to their gods to help them find new sites with access to water.

        Combine

3   **Reading**   Because of the sudden onset of war, the owners were either slain or had no time to gather their belongings as they fled from approaching enemies.

        Listening   The Anasazi, thirsting for water, simply had no need for extra personal belongings, so they left them in their settlements when they departed in search of new homes.

        Combine

4   **Reading**   It was natural that other tribes, coveting the rich land, made war upon the Anasazi and drove them out.

        Listening   What few water supplies remained simply could not satisfy the Anasazi's large population.

        Combine

Organization Review the notes from the reading and the listening. Complete the following chart with complete sentences.

Introduction	1 2
Body 1	3 4 5
Body 2	6 7
Body 3	8 9
Conclusion (Optional)	10

Read the following passage for 3 minutes. You may take notes while you read and use your notes to help you answer the question.

Neanderthals were an ancient species of humans that lived from around 130,000 to 50,000 years ago. They primarily resided in the area which is now Europe and Western Asia. While anthropologists do not yet know everything about Neanderthals, many have arrived at the conclusion that Neanderthals were in fact able to speak.

By examining a number of fossilized remains, anthropologists have determined that Neanderthals had large brains. As a matter of fact, Neanderthals had a cranial capacity about ten percent larger than modern humans have. Anthropologists rightly reason that with brains that large, Neanderthals must have been able to communicate through speech.

Slightly over twenty years ago, a hyoid bone belonging to a Neanderthal was found. The hyoid bone connects the muscles between the larynx and the tongue. This bone enables its possessor to move its tongue in a large number of different ways, thereby making the likelihood of speech even greater. This proves that Neanderthals were capable of speech and that they most likely made use of this ability.

In addition, researchers have determined that Neanderthals developed various muscles in their stomach regions. These muscles not only permitted them to control their breathing but also helped them create the sounds necessary for speech. Because of these muscles, which humans also have, they were again more likely to be able to communicate through speech. Accordingly, it is clear that Neanderthals were able to speak and did, in fact, use speech to communicate with others.

Words & Phrases

primarily adv mostly; mainly

reside v to live

anthropologist n a social scientist who studies humans and their cultures

fossilized adj having become a fossil

cranial adj relating to the brain

capacity n capability; ability

larynx n the part of the body where the vocal cords are located

likelihood n a probability; a possibility

permit v to allow; to enable

accordingly adv therefore; consequently

Note Taking

Neanderthals Could Speak

Now listen to a lecture on the topic you read about. You may take notes while you listen and use your notes to help you answer the question.

Note Taking

Neanderthals Couldn't Speak

01-03

Words & Phrases

controversy (n) a debate; an argument

allege (v) to claim or assert without proof

analysis (n) an evaluation; a reasoning

complexity (n) complication; intricacy

remains (n) the leftover part of some creature or object; remnants

guarantee (v) to promise

concede (v) to admit

integral (adj) important; vital

harsh (adj) cruel

engage in (phr) to partake in something; to be able to do something

Writing Summarize the points made in the lecture, being sure to explain how they challenge specific claims made in the reading passage.

Self-Evaluation Check your response by answering the following questions.

	Yes	No
1 Are all the important points from the lecture presented accurately?	☐	☐
2 Is the information from the lecture appropriately related to the reading?	☐	☐
3 Is the response well organized?	☐	☐
4 Are all the sentences grammatically correct?	☐	☐
5 Are all the words spelled correctly?	☐	☐
6 Are all the punctuation marks used correctly?	☐	☐

Exercise 1 Read, listen, and answer the question following each step.

Reading ▶ Read the following passage and take notes.

The dodo was a large flightless bird native to the island of Mauritius in the Indian Ocean. Mauritius was colonized by Dutch settlers in the late sixteenth century, and fewer than one hundred years later, the last dodo disappeared. There is much speculation as to why the dodo disappeared, but experts have narrowed the reasons down to the actions of humans.

There were no humans on Mauritius prior to the Dutch's arrival, so the dodos had no fear of humans and thus were easily hunted. The Dutch also brought other animals, such as cats, dogs, pigs, and various farm animals, and there were many instances in which these animals hunted dodos or destroyed their eggs and nests. The dodo, being flightless, built its nests on the ground in forested areas and laid its eggs in these nests. The eggs and the young dodos therefore had no protection against predators.

When the Dutch colonized Mauritius, they began rapidly altering the land for farming. They cleared forests, which destroyed the dodos' natural habitats. The dodos soon had fewer places to make their nests and lay their eggs. Additionally, since the dodos fed on the tropical fruits native to the island, when the Dutch chopped down the trees, a large part of the dodos' food supply was destroyed.

Some also speculate that the outsiders introduced a disease which proceeded to wipe out all of the dodos. Some diseases may pass from humans to animals or, more commonly, from animal to animal. This would account for the virtually overnight disappearance of the dodos. The introduction of a new species often wreaks havoc on the natives. For example, when the European settlers arrived in America, many Native Americans died due to a lack of immunity to new diseases. The same could have easily happened to the dodo.

📖 Words & Phrases

colonize (v) to take control of; to conquer
speculation (n) an assumption; a theory
prior to (phr) before; preceding
predator (n) a killer; a hunter; an enemy
alter (v) to change
chop down (v) to fell; to cut down

wipe out (v) to eliminate; to kill entirely
account for (phr) to explain
virtually (adv) practically; almost
overnight (adv) very quickly; rapidly
wreak havoc (phr) to destroy; to cause many problems
immunity (n) resistance

📝 Note Taking

The Dodo Disappeared Because of Humans

1   1) _____

  • No humans on the island until the Dutch's arrival ➜ 2) _____
  • Dutch brought many animals ➜ preyed on dodos & their eggs

2   3) _____

  • Dutch cleared forests ➜ 4) _____
  • Many fruit trees were cut down ➜ much of the dodos' food supply disappeared

3   5) _____

  • No immunity ➜ sudden disappearance of dodos
  • Similar case: Native Americans died of European diseases

Note Taking

Humans Were Not Responsible for the Extinction of the Dodo

1 Did not hunt dodos
- *walgvogel* (Dutch name), meaning "1) _____"
- 2) _____ → Dutch did not enjoy the taste

2 3) _____
- Large parts remained unharmed → no serious effect on dodos
- 4) _____

3 Natural disasters killed the dodo
- 5) _____ → destroyed dodos' nests & eggs → dodos were already dying out when Dutch arrived

01 - 04

Words & Phrases

spot (v) to see; to discover

age (n) a very long period of time

disgusted (adj) sickened; appalled; filled with disgust

deforest (v) to cut down large areas of forest

intact (adj) not damaged; still in one piece; unbroken

eliminate (v) to kill; to destroy completely

in decline (phr) a downturn; a period where something is decreasing

massive (adj) very large; huge; immense

remnant (n) the remainder; the leftover

populous (adj) having large numbers or a large population

Comparing the Points Rewrite the main points from both notes as complete sentences.

Reading	Listening
Stance The actions of humans account for the extinction of the dodo.	**Stance** Humans were not the reason why the dodo became extinct.
Main point 1	**Refutation 1**
Main point 2	**Refutation 2**
Main point 3	**Refutation 3**

The following sentences are some important points from both the reading and the listening. Combine each pair of sentences to create your own sentence by using the given pattern.

1   **Reading**   Experts have narrowed the reasons for the dodo's disappearance down to the actions of humans.

  Listening   It is certain that humans did not cause the dodo to become extinct.

  Combine   ....

  ....

  ....

  ....

2   **Reading**   There were no humans on Mauritius prior to the Dutch's arrival, so the dodos had no fear of humans and thus were easily hunted.

  Listening   Yet despite the ease with which they could catch the dodo, the Dutch settlers were disgusted by it and did not hunt it.

  Combine   ....

  ....

  ....

  ....

3   **Reading**   The Dutch cleared forests, which destroyed the dodos' natural habitats.

  Listening   The dodo, which could not fly, did not make its nests in trees.

  Combine   ....

  ....

  ....

4   **Reading**   Some also speculate that the outsiders introduced a disease which proceeded to wipe out the dodos.

  Listening   Massive cyclones struck the island many times in the past, and their high winds may have been responsible for destroying the dodos' nests and eggs while they lay unprotected on the open ground.

  Combine   ....

  ....

  ....

  ....

Introduction	1
	2
Body 1	3
	4
	5
Body 2	6
	7
	8
Body 3	9
	10
Conclusion (Optional)	11

Read the following passage for 3 minutes. You may take notes while you read and use your notes to help you answer the question.

Following so many criticisms since its publication in 1859, Charles Darwin's theory of evolution was attacked once again in 1985 by Fred Hoyle, a British scientist, based on the fossils of a prehistoric bird known as Archaeopteryx. Much of his criticism centered on the London Specimen, the first complete skeleton of the bird, and the Berlin Specimen, which was considered a better specimen than the former since it had a complete head.

The London Specimen was first found in Germany in 1861 and was later bought by the British National Museum of Natural History under the instruction of Richard Owen, a British biologist. Hoyle asserted this specimen was fraudulent, arguing that it was odd that the specimen was discovered only two years after Darwin's theories had been published. He accused Owen of having forged it to support Darwin's theories since Owen was a staunch evolutionist himself.

Hoyle also declared that both the London and Berlin specimens were too perfect to be true, especially when compared to the other fossils of Archaeopteryx known at the time. For example, the two specimens showed detailed evidence of feathers being present; however, the other fossils did not have such feathers. In fact, he believed the fine representations of fossilized feathers were really impressions of feathers made in a thin cement layer and therefore formed the main part of the forgery.

Hoyle's final point rested on the limestone formations where the fossils were discovered. The fossils were found in blocks of limestone that had perfectly split into two pieces. One half of the fossil was perfectly preserved, but the other half was not. In addition, the two halves of the fossil did not match. Hoyle concluded that the perfect half of the fossil was the fake one.

■ Words & Phrases

criticism n disapproval; censure
prehistoric adj occurring a long time ago prior to recorded history
center on phr to focus on
specimen n a sample
skeleton n bare bones

odd adj strange; unusual
fraudulent adj false; fake; phony
detailed adj thorough; minute
forgery n a fake; a counterfeit
limestone n a type of sedimentary rock formed from the decayed bodies of marine animals

📝 Note Taking

Archaeopteryx Fossils = Fakes

Now listen to a lecture on the topic you read about. You may take notes while you listen and use your notes to help you answer the question.

Note Taking

Archaeopteryx Fossils ≠ Fakes

01-05

Words & Phrases

controversy n a debate; an argument

motive n a reason for doing something

advocate n a supporter

risk v to endanger; to jeopardize

impression n an indentation; a mark

astronomer n a person who studies outer space

paleontologist n a person who studies dinosaurs and other prehistoric creatures

confirm v to verify; to show as being correct

yield v to give up

polish v to rub; to hone

Writing Summarize the points made in the lecture, being sure to explain how they challenge specific claims made in the reading passage.

[blank ruled lines for writing]

Reading Read the following passage and take notes.

Starting in 1972, the National Park Service established a policy for forest fires called natural burn. It was acknowledged that some forest fires, such as those caused by lightning, were necessary for forests to maintain balanced ecosystems, so the fires should be allowed to burn. However, an immense fire in Yellowstone National Park in 1988 caused this policy to be abandoned since the fire was initially allowed to burn yet soon raged out of control, destroying much of the park. As a result of the fire, many believed the park to have been severely and irrevocably damaged.

The fire of 1988 destroyed much of Yellowstone, which is the United States' oldest and most beloved national park. Massive areas of vegetation were destroyed, and large empty spaces and acres of burned and blackened trees greeted visitors. Rivers and streams were clogged with ash, and the ecosystem of the park was altered beyond repair.

In addition, great numbers of animals were killed by the fires that burned out of control. The fires were propelled by high winds moving, in some cases, as many as ten miles a day. Many small animals perished in the flames. The fires' rapid advances gave the wildlife little chance to escape. Even today, few of these small forest dwellers have returned to live in the park.

In the years immediately following the fires, the number of visitors declined tremendously. No one was interested in seeing a blackened and treeless park on vacation. Yellowstone had previously been renowned for its marvelous vistas and unique geological formations such as the geyser Old Faithful. But now its reputation as America's wonder is damaged like the park, perhaps even permanently.

📖 Words & Phrases

establish v to create; to start
immense adj huge; enormous
outcry n an objection; a protest
irrevocably adv forever; permanently

vegetation n plant life
clog v to stop up; to block
propel v to push; to drive forward
perish v to die

dweller n an inhabitant; a resident
vista n a view
geyser n a hot spring that shoots up out of the earth

📝 Note Taking

Yellowstone Permanently Damaged

1 1) _____

  • Huge areas of vegetation burned → empty spaces & burned trees
  • 2) _____ → severely changed the park's ecosystem

2 3) _____

  • Small animals 4) _____ → few have returned 2 the park today

3 5) _____

  • People did not want 2 see a treeless park
  • Had once been known 4 its beauty but has now been damaged greatly

Note Taking

Yellowstone Showing Signs of Recovery

01-06

1 Burned vegetation can help a forest
  - Burned material goes into soil → 1) _____
  - Lose many trees → 2) _____

2 3) _____
  - 4) _____ are now appearing in huge numbers

3 Tourist numbers are starting to increase
  - Fewer tourists came after fire because of 5) _____
  - Economy ↑ → more tourists to Yellowstone

Words & Phrases

stance [n] a position; an opinion

on the contrary [phr] in contrast; in opposition

spring up [v] to arise; to grow

penetrate [v] to pierce; to go through

accelerate [v] to speed something up; to make something happen faster

drove [n] a group; a large number

feast on [phr] to eat very much

undergrowth [n] small, thick bushes

endure [v] to experience; to undergo

crisis [n] a disaster; an enormous problem

Comparing the Points Rewrite the main points from both notes as complete sentences.

Reading	Listening
Stance The fire of 1988 destroyed much of Yellowstone and permanently altered it for the worse.	**Stance** Although the fire did severely hurt Yellowstone, the park is starting to recover.
Main point 1	Refutation 1
Main point 2	Refutation 2
Main point 3	Refutation 3

1   **Reading**   As a result of the fire, many believed the park to have been severely and irrevocably damaged.

    Listening   There are numerous signs that the park is recovering while still receiving a great many visitors.

    Combine   ....

             ....

             ....

             ....

2   **Reading**   Rivers and streams were clogged with ash, and the ecosystem of the park was altered beyond repair.

    Listening   Richer soil and more sunlight exist in Yellowstone right now, which is accelerating the recovery process.

    Combine   ....

             ....

             ....

             ....

3   **Reading**   Even today, few of these small forest dwellers have returned to live in the park.

    Listening   Some species that were previously never even a part of the park's ecosystem have found their way to Yellowstone.

    Combine   ....

             ....

             ....

             ....

4   **Reading**   In the years immediately following the fires, the number of visitors declined tremendously.

    Listening   Fortunately, by the mid-1990s, once the economic crisis had passed, the numbers of tourists had risen again.

    Combine   ....

             ....

             ....

             ....

Organization Review the notes from the reading and the listening. Complete the following chart with complete sentences.

Introduction	1
Body 1	2 3 4
Body 2	5 6
Body 3	7 8 9
Conclusion (Optional)	10

Reading ▷ Read the following passage for 3 minutes. You may take notes while you read and use your notes to help you answer the question.

The United States has an extensive national park system that encompasses large areas of the country, especially in western states and Alaska. Currently, the parks charge an admission fee for visitors with the rate depending on the park, the ages of the visitors, and how long they plan to stay. However, these admission fees should be abolished, and all visitors should be allowed entrance to the parks for free.

The most important thing to remember is that they are national parks, meaning that they belong to the country, which really means the citizens of the country. Charging the owners of a place a fee to enter it is simply outrageous. After all, people do not have to pay money every time they enter their own homes. They should not have to do it for national parks either.

Charging admission to national parks also serves to discourage people from visiting them and enjoying their natural beauty. This is especially true for large groups wanting to stay for several days since they are charged exorbitant rates. Because of the high prices, many people are spending their vacations elsewhere and are thus deprived of the opportunity to enjoy their time off in the parks.

Checking every single visitor and collecting admission fees is an additional time-consuming process. There are already long lines at the entrances to these parks, particularly during the summer travel season. People relentlessly complain about these lines, as some of them may have to wait an hour or even longer merely to enter the park. And because park personnel are used to collect these fees, they are unavailable to work elsewhere, which accordingly reduces the quality of services throughout the entire park.

📖 Words & Phrases

extensive adj wide-ranging; very large
encompass v to cover; to include
abolish v to do away with; to stop; to end
outrageous adj offensive; extreme
discourage v to dissuade; to dishearten

exorbitant adj extremely high; excessive
be deprived of phr to be denied; to be without
time-consuming adj taking a long period of time
relentlessly adv continually; continuously
personnel n workers; employees; staff

📝 Note Taking

No Admission Fees 4 National Parks

📝 Note Taking

Admission Fees 4 National Parks

01-07

📖 **Words & Phrases**

strike v to occur

up to date adj modern; recent

federal adj national

overcrowded adj containing too many people or things

head to phr to go to

minimal adj very small; minor

affordable adj inexpensive; reasonable

checkpoint n a place where security personnel can conduct inspections

park ranger n a person who works in a national park, usually in an outdoor capacity

pose v to present

Writing ▷ Summarize the points made in the lecture, being sure to explain how they challenge specific claims made in the reading passage.

Self-Evaluation Check your response by answering the following questions.

	Yes	No
1 Are all the important points from the lecture presented accurately?	☐	☐
2 Is the information from the lecture appropriately related to the reading?	☐	☐
3 Is the response well organized?	☐	☐
4 Are all the sentences grammatically correct?	☐	☐
5 Are all the words spelled correctly?	☐	☐
6 Are all the punctuation marks used correctly?	☐	☐

Exercise 1 Read, listen, and answer the question following each step.

Reading Read the following passage and take notes.

For the past sixty years, fluoride has been added to the public drinking water in the United States. This measure has greatly improved the health of Americans by enhancing their dental health and bone structure. Thanks to this chemical, drinking water has been purified and made safer to drink as well.

The primary reason that fluoride is added to drinking water is to prevent the onset of tooth decay. Fluoride achieves this effect by binding with the enamel on people's teeth, which helps their teeth remain healthy. Studies conducted over several decades in numerous communities have shown that there has been an average of 12.5 percent less tooth decay and 2.25 fewer teeth lost from decay thanks to fluoride. The Center for Disease Control and Prevention also claims that fluoride water treatment can cause a reduction in tooth decay by almost thirty percent.

Additionally, water treated with fluoride is much purer than untreated water. The reason is that fluoride acts as a cleansing agent. It attacks bacteria and other organisms, essentially removing them from the water. On the basis of this reason alone, the World Health Organization (WHO) has called on many developing nations, where clean drinking water is not always readily available, to increase the fluoride content in their water supplies.

Some scientists have even pointed out that there is a great deal of evidence that fluoride helps improve the bone structures of people who drink water treated with it every day. Studies have proven that these people's bone densities have increased, and older women have even shown a tendency to suffer from osteoporosis in smaller numbers if they have drunk fluoride-treated water. Finally, bone fractures from simple falls are less common than in populations of people who do not drink fluoride-treated water.

📖 Words & Phrases

dental `adj` relating to the teeth
purify `v` to make pure; to make clean
tooth decay `n` the rotting of the teeth
enamel `n` the hard white outer layer of the teeth
bacteria `n` microorganisms
organism `n` a creature

readily `adv` easily
density `n` thickness; compactness
osteoporosis `n` a medical condition in which one's bones lose calcium and become more likely to break
bone fracture `n` a break or crack in a bone

📝 Note Taking

Positive Effects of Fluoride in Drinking Water

1 1) ....
   • Binds with enamel on teeth → helps keep teeth healthy

2 2) ....
   • Acts as a cleansing agent → 3) ....
   • WHO wants developing countries 2 put fluoride in water supplies

3 4) ....
   • Increases bone density → 5) .... → fewer bone fractures

✍ Note Taking

Negative Effects of Fluoride in Drinking Water

01-08

1 No need 2 add fluoride 2 drinking water

  • 1) _____

  • European countries don't put fluoride in drinking water → no decline in dental health

2 Has harmful side effects if taken 2 much

  • Discolors water pipes & 2) _____

  • Better water purification methods → 3) _____

3 4) _____

  • Osteosarcomas → a rare form of bone cancer in young boys

  • Skeletal fluorosis → 5) _____

📖 Words & Phrases

cut and dry phr simple
controversial adj divisive; contentious
detrimental adj harmful; dangerous
insert v to put in
abandon v to stop; to leave behind

discolor v to change something's color
monitor v to watch carefully
deem v to consider; to believe
skeletal adj relating to the bones
brittle adj weak; fragile; easily breakable

Comparing the Points Rewrite the main points from both notes as complete sentences.

Reading	Listening
Stance The use of fluoride in drinking water has improved people's dental health and bone structure.	**Stance** Fluoride in drinking water can have some harmful effects on people.
Main point 1	**Refutation 1**
Main point 2	**Refutation 2**
Main point 3	**Refutation 3**

The following sentences are some important points from both the reading and the listening. Combine each pair of sentences to create your own sentence by using the given pattern.

1   **Reading**   This decision to put fluoride in drinking water has greatly improved the health of Americans by enhancing their dental health and bone structure.

        Listening   In fact, many people, myself included, believe that fluoride's effects can be somewhat detrimental to people.

        Combine   ....

                    ....

                    ....

                    ....

2   **Reading**   The primary reason that fluoride is added to drinking water is to prevent the onset of tooth decay.

        Listening   Some, like Sweden and the Netherlands, haven't added fluoride to drinking water for over thirty years, yet they have exhibited no decline in dental health.

        Combine   ....

                    ....

                    ....

                    ....

3   **Reading**   Additionally, water treated with fluoride is much purer than untreated water.

        Listening   While fluoride does purify water, it can still lead to harmful side effects if taken in large amounts since it is a toxic chemical.

        Combine   ....

                    ....

                    ....

                    ....

4   **Reading**   Some scientists have even pointed out that there is a great deal of evidence that fluoride helps improve the bone structures of people who drink water treated with it every day.

        Listening   Fluoride also may cause skeletal fluorosis, a condition caused by excessive fluoride exposure where fluoride is deposited directly into the bones.

        Combine   ....

                    ....

                    ....

                    ....

Organization ▶ Review the notes from the reading and the listening. Complete the following chart with complete sentences.

Introduction	1
Body 1	2 3
Body 2	4 5 6
Body 3	7 8 9
Conclusion (Optional)	10

Read, listen, and answer the question following each step.

Read the following passage for 3 minutes. You may take notes while you read and use your notes to help you answer the question.

A current Internet phenomenon is online pharmacies, which are basically drugstores in cyberspace. Customers go online, select the medicine they need, and order it directly to their homes. They are often cheaper than frequenting real drugstores. Unfortunately, there are myriad problems associated with online pharmacies, and it would be in the public's best interests to ban them from existence.

One major issue is that many medicines and products sold online do not meet Food and Drug Administration (FDA) guidelines for safe products. Particularly worrisome are the herbal remedies and the other untested products that are not considered drugs yet are being used to treat illnesses. Many concoctions made from plant and animal matter are being sold without the benefit of proper testing and approval from the FDA, so they may actually harm unwitting customers.

By purchasing drugs directly from online pharmacies, consumers are bypassing a crucial part of the process. That is, they are not getting consultations from doctors. Many buyers lack important information about their medical conditions because they neglect first to see a doctor and to get a recommendation as to what medicine they should take. In some cases, the medicine they take has unpleasant side effects or even fatal consequences, and by taking improper dosages even of the proper medicine, they may do themselves more harm than good.

Consumers typically have no idea about the origins of many drugs and herbal remedies online pharmacies sell. For example, some of them were manufactured in foreign countries where standards of approval differ from those in the United States. In short, many offer inferior products masquerading as legitimate medicines. Consumers should not trust these medicines even if they have labels and instructions in English. Considering that people's lives are at stake, online pharmacies should be banned from selling their wares.

Words & Phrases

frequent Ⓥ to visit often or repeatedly
myriad adj many; numerous
ban Ⓥ to prohibit
remedy Ⓝ a cure
concoction Ⓝ a mixture; a potion
unwitting adj unknowing; unaware
bypass Ⓥ to avoid; to go around

neglect Ⓥ to overlook; to disregard
masquerade Ⓥ to pretend; to attempt to deceive
legitimate adj real; legal
fatal adj deadly
dosage Ⓝ an amount; a quantity
at stake phr at risk of being lost

📝 Note Taking

Online Pharmacies Should Be Banned

☑ Note Taking

Online Pharmacies Are Beneficial

01-09

📖 Words & Phrases

corner drugstore (n) a small, local pharmacy

restriction (n) a limit

option (n) a choice

abolition (n) a closure; a banning

crucial (adj) very important

deter (v) to prevent; to dissuade

expenditure (n) an expense; the act of spending

await (v) to wait for

competent (adj) experienced; able; capable

consult (v) to ask for advice from; to see

pharmaceutical (adj) relating to drugs or medicine

line the pockets of (phr) to enrich; to make someone richer by paying that person money

Writing Summarize the points made in the lecture, being sure to explain how they challenge specific claims made in the reading passage.

_____

_____

_____

_____

_____

_____

_____

_____

_____

_____

_____

_____

_____

_____

_____

_____

_____

Self-Evaluation Check your response by answering the following questions.

	Yes	No
1 Are all the important points from the lecture presented accurately?	☐	☐
2 Is the information from the lecture appropriately related to the reading?	☐	☐
3 Is the response well organized?	☐	☐
4 Are all the sentences grammatically correct?	☐	☐
5 Are all the words spelled correctly?	☐	☐
6 Are all the punctuation marks used correctly?	☐	☐

Exercise 1 **Read, listen, and answer the question following each step.**

Reading Read the following passage and take notes.

One of the great travelers of the Middle Ages was the Venetian Marco Polo. According to his writings, he journeyed to China in the late thirteenth century and stayed there for seventeen years. However, controversy has always followed Marco Polo's story, and he has been the target of skepticism from his time to the modern day. It appears that the skeptics are correct. Indeed, it is likely that Marco Polo never ventured to China, nor did he engage in any of the actions he took credit for.

There are several supposedly original accounts of his journey. They are written in Italian, Latin, and old French. However, each account differs in its details, which has raised questions about the legitimacy of his journey. One critic, Peter Jackson, a British historian, believes Polo's work was that of a romance writer using the accounts of various travelers who had spent time in the Far East.

Another criticism is that Polo failed to mention many basic facts about China known to have been true during the time he was supposedly there. He never mentioned the practice of binding women's feet or tea drinking. He also never described the Great Wall, one of the world's most impressive structures. And Polo could not speak, read, or write Chinese despite his assertion he had spent seventeen years there.

One of the most telling facts is that Marco Polo's name appears nowhere in the recorded history of China in that period. Considering his claim to have been a close friend of and ambassador to the ruler, Kublai Khan, and a frequent court visitor, this is incredibly surprising. He also wrote about his role in bringing a Mongol princess to Persia, yet this too does not appear in any contemporary history books.

📖 Words & Phrases

skepticism (n) doubt; disbelief
venture to-V (phr) to be brave enough to-V
supposedly (adv) allegedly; apparently
legitimacy (n) truthfulness; authority
account (n) a story; an explanation

impressive (adj) imposing; breathtaking
assertion (n) a statement; a claim
telling (adj) very important
contemporary (adj) of the same time as something else

📝 Note Taking

Marco Polo Never Traveled to China

1 1) ....

  • Written in several languages → different details
  • Could have been written by a romance writer

2 Never mentioned many things about China

  • No mention of 2) ....

  • 3) .... even after 17 years' stay in China

3 4) ....

  • 5) .... → not mentioned

📝 Note Taking

Marco Polo Spent Many Years in China

1 Reason for different versions of accounts of his trip

- First account → written in French by a romance novelist in prison
- Later account → 1) _____ & translated into Latin & back into Italian

2 Did not see many things associated with China

- 2) _____ → not much tea was consumed there
- Entered China from the west → 3) _____

3 4) _____

- Fluent in Persian → was given Persian translators
- Absent from Chinese history → 5) _____

01-10

📖 Words & Phrases

authenticity Ⓝ genuineness; authority
accurate ⓐⓓⓙ precise; correct
account for ⓟⓗⓡ to explain
translate Ⓥ to put into another language; to interpret
manuscript Ⓝ a writing; a document

discrepancy Ⓝ a difference; an inconsistency
consume Ⓥ to eat or drink
erode Ⓥ to wear away
departure Ⓝ a leaving; an exit
merit Ⓥ to earn

Comparing the Points Rewrite the main points from both notes as complete sentences.

Reading	Listening
Stance Marco Polo did not go to China, and his story is unreliable.	**Stance** Marco Polo really did go on the trip to China as he said that he had.
Main point 1	Refutation 1
Main point 2	Refutation 2
Main point 3	Refutation 3

The following sentences are some important points from both the reading and the listening. Combine each pair of sentences to create your own sentence by using the given pattern.

1 **Reading** It is likely that Marco Polo never ventured to China, nor did he engage in any of the actions he took credit for.

Listening Polo indeed traveled to China and then wrote an accurate account of his journey, which became one of the most important books in history.

Combine ....

....

....

....

2 **Reading** Polo's work was that of a romance writer using the accounts of various travelers who had spent time in the Far East.

Listening The first account of his travels was written by a fellow prisoner, a romance writer, who told his tale in Old French.

Combine ....

....

....

....

3 **Reading** Polo failed to mention many basic facts about China known to have been true during the time he was supposedly there.

Listening Polo spent most of his time in the north, where tea wasn't often consumed.

Combine ....

....

....

....

4 **Reading** One of the most telling facts is that Marco Polo's name appears nowhere in the recorded history of China in that period.

Listening As for his absence from any Chinese books, it may be related to the fact that he used a different form of his name in Chinese or Mongolian or simply that he wasn't important enough to merit the honor of being mentioned.

Combine ....

....

....

....

Organization Review the notes from the reading and the listening. Complete the following chart with complete sentences.

Introduction	1
Body 1	2
	3
Body 2	4
	5
Body 3	6
	7
	8
Conclusion (Optional)	9

Exercise 2 Read, listen, and answer the question following each step.

Reading ▷ Read the following passage for 3 minutes. You may take notes while you read and use your notes to help you answer the question.

It is a certainty that the Vikings visited the Americas prior to Columbus's epic voyage in 1492. However, the claim that the Chinese reached America earlier is just as valid. Between the years 1405 and 1433, Chinese Admiral Zheng He led seven great expeditions across the world's oceans. On one voyage, he definitely reached both the east and west coasts of North America.

The evidence is compelling. Off the coasts of the Bahamas is the Bimini Road, an underwater formation that resembles a road. British historian Gavin Menzies believes this was either a dock or a road built by Zheng He's fleet when it visited the Bahamas in 1421. The formation itself appears to have a distinct Chinese pattern as well, and the stones are seemingly arranged on purpose.

The second bit of evidence is the 1970s discovery of over twenty anchors in the waters of the Pacific Ocean off of Palos Verdes, California. These anchors are Chinese in origin. They are made of stone and have holes in the middle, making them uncommon forms of anchor. For thousands of years, the Chinese have used such large, round stones with holes in the middle so as to attach ropes to use as anchors for their ships. These anchors prove that a Chinese fleet, likely Zheng He's, made it to America.

Another sign of this early Chinese expedition is the Newport Tower in Newport, Rhode Island. It is built in the shape of a Chinese lighthouse and is at the same latitude as Beijing, China's capital. It also used crushed seashells as mortar for its bricks, a practice commonly used to construct Chinese lighthouses. The tower's date of construction is unknown to historians, yet carbon dating methods place its creation in the early fifteenth century.

🖥 Words & Phrases

certainty [n] a guarantee
epic [adj] heroic; classic
valid [adj] legitimate; truthful
expedition [n] a long journey
compelling [adj] believable; convincing
dock [n] a pier; a wharf

distinct [adj] unique; particular
anchor [n] a heavy object used to keep a boat from moving at sea
crushed [adj] compressed; flattened
mortar [n] a binder used in construction

📝 Note Taking

Zheng He Visited America in the 15th Century

Now listen to a lecture on the topic you read about. You may take notes while you listen and use your notes to help you answer the question.

Note Taking

Zheng He Never Visited America

01-11

📖 Words & Phrases

credit v to recognize; to acknowledge

competing adj vying; opposing

assure v to promise; to guarantee

utterly adv entirely; totally

supposed adj imaginary

tidal adj relating to the tide

conveniently adv opportunely

barely adv hardly

ancestor n a forebear

bind v to join

Writing ▸ Summarize the points made in the lecture, being sure to explain how they challenge specific claims made in the reading passage.

Self-Evaluation Check your response by answering the following questions.

	Yes	No
1 Are all the important points from the lecture presented accurately?	☐	☐
2 Is the information from the lecture appropriately related to the reading?	☐	☐
3 Is the response well organized?	☐	☐
4 Are all the sentences grammatically correct?	☐	☐
5 Are all the words spelled correctly?	☐	☐
6 Are all the punctuation marks used correctly?	☐	☐

Unit 06 Archaeology

Read, listen, and answer the question following each step.

Reading Read the following passage and take notes.

While the Americas were the last major continental landmass to be inhabited by humans, when these settlements occurred is unknown. The oldest known archaeological site is in Monte Verde, Chile. Some researchers have suggested that humans resided there around 12,500 years ago. However, based on a number of reasons, it is clear that these archaeologists are mistaken and that the site was not inhabited that long ago.

The original settlers of the Americas are known to have been hunter-gatherers who lived off of plants they collected and animals they killed. Farming was unknown to them until thousands of years later. However, excavations at the Monte Verde site have revealed no hunting tools—like spearheads or arrowheads—that would indicate people actually lived there then. The absence of hunting tools indicates no primitive hunter-gatherer society lived at Monte Verde.

Unfortunately, the area around Monte Verde has been used as farmland for many generations, so farmers have damaged the site immensely. By plowing and planting crops on the land, they have compromised any archaeological evidence, thereby making it difficult to tell what actually happened there thousands of years ago. A site typically has its oldest artifacts deep in the ground and its newest ones closer to the surface. However, at Monte Verde, the disturbing of the soil has made it impossible accurately to date any of the artifacts unearthed.

There is also the presence of bitumen, a tar-like substance used for paving roads. This has compromised the site as well. The bitumen has made carbon dating difficult since it can affect the entire dating process. So archaeologists only dated certain objects and did not try to date everything found on the site. This incomplete dating process has led many skeptics to wonder if they were trying to conceal the truth about Monte Verde and its first settlement.

Words & Phrases

landmass [n] a large area of land
reside [v] to inhabit; to live; to dwell
excavation [n] a dig
reveal [v] to show
indicate [v] to show; to suggest; to imply
immensely [adv] hugely; enormously

plow [v] to dig up the land, usually for farming; to till
compromise [v] to make worthless; to make something lose its value
artifact [n] a relic; a manufactured object
unearth [v] to dig up; to uncover
conceal [v] to hide

Note Taking

No One Settled at Monte Verde 12,500 Yrs Ago

1 1) ....

  • Original settlers in Americas = hunter-gatherers
  • Found no spearheads / arrowheads → no early settlers lived there

2 2) ....

  • Plowed land → disrupted soil → 3) ....

3 Presence of bitumen at dig site

  • 2 much bitumen → 4) ....
  • 5) .... → unreliable

Listen to a lecture on the topic you just read about and take notes.

Note Taking

Humans Did Settle at Monte Verde 12,500 Years Ago

1 Ate plants & small animals
- 1) _____ → explain absence of weapons
- No knowledge of how to make weapons

2 Main dig site kept intact
- 2) _____ → never touched by farmers
- Only upper layers of soil were disrupted → 3) _____

3 Thorough enough dating process done
- Some items → 4) _____ → couldn't be dated
- 5) _____ → majority point to a time around 12,500 years ago

01-12

Words & Phrases

uncover v to reveal; to show
peat bog n wet, spongy ground of decaying plant material
consume v to eat; to devour
preserve v to keep; to conserve
rudimentary adj basic; simple
disturb v to upset; to bother

soil n ground; earth
promptly adv immediately
be immersed into phr to be completely involved or absorbed in something
render v to make; to cause to be

Comparing the Points
Rewrite the main points from both notes as complete sentences.

Reading	Listening
Stance There were never any settlers at Monte Verde 12,500 years ago.	**Stance** There was a group of people who lived at Monte Verde around 12,500 years ago.
Main point 1	Refutation 1
Main point 2	Refutation 2
Main point 3	Refutation 3

Synthesizing The following sentences are some important points from both the reading and the listening. Combine each pair of sentences to create your own sentence by using the given pattern.

1 **Reading** It is clear that these archaeologists are mistaken and that the site was not inhabited that long ago.

Listening It has been dated to 12,500 years ago, which therefore proves that this small, yet well-preserved, place was the site of some kind of human settlement.

Combine _____

_____

_____

2 **Reading** The absence of weapons indicates no primitive hunter-gatherer society lived at Monte Verde.

Listening Some archaeologists have also suggested that this group of settlers simply lacked the knowledge of how to make rudimentary weapons, explaining why none was found there.

Combine _____

_____

_____

3 **Reading** By plowing and planting crops on the land, they have compromised any archaeological evidence, thereby making it difficult to tell what actually happened there thousands of years ago.

Listening The main dig site was the bog itself, which the farmers never touched.

Combine _____

_____

_____

4 **Reading** The bitumen has made carbon dating difficult since it can affect the entire dating process.

Listening However, archaeologists did more than twenty-five tests and also used different dating methods to lend them more accuracy.

Combine _____

_____

_____

Organization Review the notes from the reading and the listening. Complete the following chart with complete sentences.

Introduction	1
	2
Body 1	3
	4
	5
Body 2	6
	7
	8
Body 3	9
	10
Conclusion (Optional)	11

The Copper Scrolls are two scrolls made of copper that were found in a cave near the Dead Sea in Israel in 1952. Once they were deciphered, experts learned that the scrolls told the story of a hidden treasure worth more than a billion dollars in today's money. While this story has fascinated mystery buffs and treasure hunters ever since, in reality, it is likely fiction, and no treasure ever existed.

The language of the scrolls presents one of the biggest problems. It is an ancient form of Hebrew for which there are no known documents with which to compare the text. In addition, a close reading of the scrolls shows that someone, either by mistake or on purpose, made some errors in the translations. Debate still rages today as to the exact translation of the scrolls.

What is known is that the scrolls supposedly report that piles of gold and silver were buried in certain locations throughout the area comprising present-day Israel. The amount of treasure as described by the scrolls is so vast that it seems impossible for such a treasure actually to exist. As further evidence, the Qumran sect is believed to have made these scrolls. The Qumran were an ascetic people, neither desiring nor owning worldly possessions. They never would have had such an enormous amount of treasure.

Some scholars and treasure hunters have even determined a few of the locations of the treasure. Yet digs at these places revealed no hordes of gold and silver. In reality, the searchers spent great amounts of money trying to locate these places and then digging around the areas. Whether it is an ancient practical joke or a map to treasures long since recovered, it is certain that the Copper Scrolls will reveal no new treasures.

Words & Phrases

scroll (n) a roll of paper, usually with writing on it

decipher (v) to decode; to translate; to reveal

fascinate (v) to amaze; to wow

buff (n) a person who is very interested in something

compelling (adj) believable; convincing

rage (v) to continue with a lot of arguments

supposedly (adv) purportedly; allegedly

sect (n) a group; a faction

ascetic (adj) living a very simple life; austere

worldly possessions (phr) belongings; property

horde (n) a large amount

Note Taking

Copper Scrolls Are Not Authentic

Now listen to a lecture on the topic you read about. You may take notes while you listen and use your notes to help you answer the question.

Note Taking

Copper Scrolls Are Authentic

01-13

Words & Phrases

hoax (n) a trick; a scam

inaccurately (adv) incorrectly; improperly

tricky (adj) difficult; complicated

deliberate (adj) on purpose; intentional

conclude (v) to determine; to theorize

tidal (adj) relating to the tide

presence (n) occurrence; appearance

scribe (n) a person who records things by writing; a stenographer

correspond (v) to match; to equal

cart away (v) to carry away; to take away

Summarize the points made in the lecture, being sure to explain how they challenge specific claims made in the reading passage.

Self-Evaluation Check your response by answering the following questions.

	Yes	No
1 Are all the important points from the lecture presented accurately?	☐	☐
2 Is the information from the lecture appropriately related to the reading?	☐	☐
3 Is the response well organized?	☐	☐
4 Are all the sentences grammatically correct?	☐	☐
5 Are all the words spelled correctly?	☐	☐
6 Are all the punctuation marks used correctly?	☐	☐

Exercise 1 Read, listen, and answer the question following each step.

Reading Read the following passage and take notes.

In the Tunguska region of Siberia, Russia, in late June 1908, there occurred one of the largest explosions in history. It was a tremendous event with the power of a large nuclear weapon. There have been many theories as to what caused this explosion, including one that states an asteroid struck the ground there. However, the most likely explanation was that this was a large methane gas explosion.

Despite the fact that the first examination of the site was only done in 1927, there have been many expeditions there since then. None of them has shown any evidence of an asteroid strike. No rocks or material from an asteroid have ever been recovered. Asteroid rocks have high concentrations of nickel and iridium and thus would be easily detectable. Finally, no witnesses ever emerged to attest to the fact that they saw an asteroid streaking across the sky.

Known asteroid sites on the Earth leave large impact craters, but Tunguska has none. Some people believe that a lake was the impact crater, yet researchers have found mud silt at its bottom that dates back to more than 5,000 years in the past. However, an area of forest fifty kilometers wide was devastated. Trees were knocked down and stripped of their branches and bark. These effects are more consistent with a gas, like methane, explosion.

Tunguska has many rivers, lakes, swamps, and peat bogs, and it is known for having high levels of methane gas. One extremely believable theory suggests that a high concentration of methane gas built up underground. It was then released, either by humans or naturally, causing it to explode when it was above the forest, thereby destroying many trees. In fact, some eyewitnesses reported seeing lightning nearby, which could have caused the gas to detonate.

Words & Phrases

tremendous adj huge; enormous
asteroid n a mass of rock that moves around in space
concentration n an amount

detectable adj able to be seen or located
attest v to confirm; to state
streak v to move fast
crater n a large, round hole in the ground

silt n deposit; sediment
devastate v to destroy completely; to demolish
detonate v to explode

Note Taking

Methane Gas Explosion Caused the Tunguska Incident

1   No evidence of asteroid strike
    - Many expeditions there since 1927 → 1) ....
    - No eyewitnesses of asteroid streaking across the sky

2   2) ....
    - Nearby lake as possible impact site → turned out 2 have 5,000-yr-old silt
    - 3) .... → supports gas explosion

3   4) ....
    - Gas built up underground → was released and then exploded
    - 5) .... → could have made gas explode

Listening

Listen to a lecture on the topic you just read about and take notes.

Note Taking

Asteroid Strike Caused the Tunguska Incident

1 1) _____

   • Looked like sky had opened → could have been asteroid entering atmosphere
   • 2) _____ → like an asteroid's effect

2 Asteroid explosion in the air

   • Asteroid never hit the ground → 3) _____
   • 4) _____ → similar 2 an asteroid hit

3 Improbability of methane gas explosion

   • Absence of enough gas in that area 4 such a huge explosion
   • 5) _____

01-14

Words & Phrases

debate (v) to argue verbally
atmosphere (n) the air
streak (n) a line; a strip
split (v) to divide in half
shatter (v) to break into many small pieces
quantity (n) an amount

unrecognizable (adj) unable to be identified
conduct (v) to carry out
identical (adj) exactly the same
implausibility (n) improbability
sheer (adj) pure; total

Comparing the Points

Rewrite the main points from both notes as complete sentences.

Reading	Listening
Stance The 1908 explosion at Tunguska was most likely caused by a methane gas explosion.	**Stance** An asteroid strike is the most likely cause of the Tunguska explosion.
Main point 1	Refutation 1
Main point 2	Refutation 2
Main point 3	Refutation 3

The following sentences are some important points from both the reading and the listening. Combine each pair of sentences to create your own sentence by using the given pattern.

1 **Reading** The most likely explanation for the Tunguska explosion was that it was a large methane gas explosion.

   Listening I, however, am certain that the event was caused by an asteroid exploding above the Earth as it entered the atmosphere.

   Combine _____
   _____
   _____
   _____

2 **Reading** Finally, no witnesses ever emerged to attest to the fact that they saw an asteroid streaking across the sky.

   Listening Many eyewitnesses reported a streak of bright light in the sky close to the Earth.

   Combine _____
   _____
   _____
   _____

3 **Reading** Known asteroid sites on the Earth leave large impact craters, but Tunguska has none.

   Listening Since the asteroid exploded before it struck the ground, there was no impact crater to be found.

   Combine _____
   _____
   _____
   _____

4 **Reading** The methane gas was then released, either by humans or naturally, causing it to explode when it was above the forest, thereby destroying many trees.

   Listening The area simply doesn't—and never did—have enough methane gas to have created this kind of explosion.

   Combine _____
   _____
   _____
   _____

Introduction	1 2
Body 1	3 4 5 6
Body 2	7 8 9
Body 3	10
Conclusion (Optional)	11

Read, listen, and answer the question following each step.

Read the following passage for 3 minutes. You may take notes while you read and use your notes to help you answer the question.

For centuries, man has pondered whether or not he is alone in the universe. One of the most likely places to find life is Mars. In fact, for decades, determining if life is or was ever there has been the goal of many scientific probes and observations. Now, it appears that there are signs that life in some basic form may actually exist on the planet.

One reason for this belief is the presence of methane gas on Mars. Methane is a naturally occurring gas produced by dead plant and animal matter and which is often found in coal mines and swampy regions on the Earth. Since methane exists only for a few hundred years before it dissipates, it needs to be replenished by living organisms even if it is something as small as bacteria. The presence of methane on Mars strongly suggests there is some form of living organism there replenishing the gas.

A recently found meteorite believed to have come from Mars shows some signs of having fossilized bacteria. The meteorite has magnetite crystals arranged in long chains. These minerals could only have been formed by bacteria. Researchers have compared the meteorite to a similar Martian one found in Antarctica in the 1990s. This meteorite too exhibits signs of bacteria.

For some time now, astronomers have been aware of evidence of the existence of hydrogen, a basic building block of life, on Mars although most of it is frozen ice at the two Martian poles. Moreover, recent space probes have found evidence of large quantities of water, which may be free-flowing, below the surface. Free-flowing water could support some forms of life, no matter how basic. It seems apparent, therefore, that the likelihood of life on Mars is rather high.

📕 Words & Phrases

ponder v to think about; to consider
probe n a search; an investigation
matter n material; substance
swampy adj having the characteristics of a swamp; marshy
dissipate v to dissolve; to waste away

replenish v to refill
exhibit v to show; to present
building block n an element; a unit
free-flowing adj moving without any obstacles
apparent adj obvious; clear

📝 Note Taking

Life Exists on Mars

📝 Note Taking

It's Not Certain that Life Exists on Mars

01-15

📖 Words & Phrases

obvious (adj) apparent

extraterrestrial (adj) alien; not from Earth

volcanic (adj) relating to volcanoes

indication (n) a sign; a suggestion

initial (adj) beginning; primary

stage (n) a period; a phase

specimen (n) an example; a sample

sampling (n) a sample; a specimen

clear-cut (adj) obvious; apparent

verify (v) to confirm as true

Writing Summarize the points made in the lecture, being sure to explain how they challenge specific claims made in the reading passage.

Self-Evaluation Check your response by answering the following questions.

	Yes	No
1 Are all the important points from the lecture presented accurately?	☐	☐
2 Is the information from the lecture appropriately related to the reading?	☐	☐
3 Is the response well organized?	☐	☐
4 Are all the sentences grammatically correct?	☐	☐
5 Are all the words spelled correctly?	☐	☐
6 Are all the punctuation marks used correctly?	☐	☐

Exercise 1 Read, listen, and answer the question following each step.

Reading Read the following passage and take notes.

One of the business world's latest marketing trends is the use of buzzers, people who are hired by companies to promote their products. Buzzers do this by using them—often in public places—and then telling others how much they love them. Unfortunately, this marketing method leaves much to be desired.

Marketing through buzzers is inherently dishonest since they receive money for promoting the companies' products. Moreover, most of them sign confidentiality agreements with their employers that forbid them to tell anyone they are buzzers. This means they are company employees and are not really giving their personal opinions. Some of them might not even like the product they are promoting, yet they are still announcing to families, friends, and total strangers that their product is the best one on the market.

Buzzers also make consumers less objective about the products they purchase. Nowadays, most people are skeptical of advertising. This is a primary reason why companies employ buzzers. If exposed to the constant hyping by buzzers, people might become less critical of products. This is even more true whenever the people in question are either related to or friends with a buzzer. They might easily ignore any possible defects of the products and get to believe they are of better quality than they really are.

Buzzers are therefore doing harm to society in general by causing distrust among members of society. People are more likely to want to trust buzzers since they appear to be promoting products on their own. However, once consumers know the truth about buzzers, they begin to be suspicious not only of buzzers but also of others in general. As trust in others decreases, society in general begins to fall apart.

📖 Words & Phrases

inherently adv innately; basically
confidentiality n privacy; secrecy
forbid v to prohibit; to ban
objective adj lacking in bias
skeptical adj cynical; disbelieving

hype v to promote; to publicize
critical adj disapproving; fault-finding
defect n a flaw; an imperfection
suspicious adj distrustful
fall apart v to collapse; to go to pieces

📝 Note Taking

Buzzers Have Negative Aspects

1 Dishonest
- Pretend to be consumers ➜ 1)_____ (may not even like the products)
- 2)_____ ➜ people don't know they are buzzers

2 3)_____
- Constant hyping by buzzers, esp. 4)_____ ➜ ignore defects & believe products are better than they really are

3 Cause harm to society
- Become suspicious of buzzers ➜ 5)_____ ➜ society falls apart

Listen to a lecture on the topic you just read about and take notes.

✏️ Note Taking

Buzzers Provide Valuable Services

01-16

1 Not everyone = a buzzer
- 1) ....
- Want buzzers who love their products

2 Know much about their products
- Potential customers → 2) ....
- Buzzers → 3) ....

3 Have positive influence on society
- Can help build trust → 4) ....
- Must provide good service otherwise 5) ....

📖 Words & Phrases

maintain [v] to state; to believe; to assert

financial compensation [phr] a monetary payment in return for doing something

in actuality [phr] in reality

deceitful [adj] dishonest

potential [adj] prospective; likely

impart [v] to provide; to tell

affect [v] to influence

word-of-mouth [phr] oral communication

societal [adj] relating to society

Comparing the Points Rewrite the main points from both notes as complete sentences.

Reading	Listening
Stance Buzzers have negative effects on consumers and society in general.	**Stance** Buzzers actually provide valuable services for potential customers.
Main point 1	Refutation 1
Main point 2	Refutation 2
Main point 3	Refutation 3

The following sentences are some important points from both the reading and the listening. Combine each pair of sentences to create your own sentence by using the given pattern.

1   **Reading**   Unfortunately, this marketing method leaves much to be desired.

    Listening   In actuality, many buzzers do like the products they're promoting, which makes them much more easily trusted than other forms of advertising.

    Combine   ....

                     ....

                     ....

                     ....

2   **Reading**   Marketing through buzzers is inherently dishonest since they receive money for promoting the companies' products.

    Listening   Testing has shown people can often tell when another person is being deceitful, so companies want buzzers who really love the products they're trying to sell.

    Combine   ....

                     ....

                     ....

                     ....

3   **Reading**   If exposed to the constant hyping by buzzers, people might become less critical of products.

    Listening   Unless potential customers receive the answers that they're looking for, they won't buy a product.

    Combine   ....

                     ....

                     ....

                     ....

4   **Reading**   Buzzers are therefore doing harm to society in general by causing distrust among members of society.

    Listening   For example, buzzers help build trust in society by telling others about good quality products.

    Combine   ....

                     ....

                     ....

                     ....

Organization Review the notes from the reading and the listening. Complete the following chart with complete sentences.

Introduction	1
Body 1	2 3 4 5
Body 2	6 7
Body 3	8 9 10
Conclusion (Optional)	11

Read the following passage for 3 minutes. You may take notes while you read and use your notes to help you answer the question.

Nowadays, an increasing number of people are leaving their jobs in corporations in order to start their own businesses. This trend is increasing rapidly. Now it is at the point where some companies are having trouble retaining their employees, particularly their best and brightest. This is not surprising as the negative aspects of working for a company have become more obvious.

Large companies have multiple levels of bureaucracy, which often makes it almost impossible for junior employees to have any contact with people in the upper echelons. Getting to the top of the corporate ladder might not be one's goal, but all employees are interested in having their ideas listened to and acted upon. This is often not possible in a corporation. Senior managers sometimes even take credit for the hard work their staff does. Starting one's own business is often the only way for an employee to make sure his ideas see the light of day.

In a constantly fluctuating economy, job security is a thing of the past. Corporations once believed to be secure have crumbled under the weight of financial miscalculations and scandals. Tens of thousands of people have been fired in the past few years. Having one's own business with oneself in charge gives a person a greater sense of financial security. These people are merely trying to protect themselves.

People depend upon insurance, pension plans, and retirement investments to protect themselves in times of need and for the future. But insurance costs are rising, pension funds are in trouble, and many retirement investments become worthless when a company goes bankrupt. Being a private business owner therefore guarantees future stability for its owner. All of these combine to make opening one's own business an appealing prospect.

▉ Words & Phrases

retain v to keep
aspect n a feature; a part
obvious adj clear; noticeable
bureaucracy n official procedures; formalities
echelon n a rank; a level
act upon phr to do; to implement
credit n recognition; praise

constantly adv continuously
fluctuate v to go up and down
secure adj safe
crumble v to fall apart
guarantee v to ensure; to assure
stability n constancy; strength
prospect n a possibility; an outlook

☑ Note Taking

Owning a Business = Good Idea

Now listen to a lecture on the topic you read about. You may take notes while you listen and use your notes to help you answer the question.

Note Taking

Owning a Business = Risky

01-17

Words & Phrases

ultimately adv eventually; in the end

bureaucratic adj relating to bureaucracy

nightmare n a bad situation

permit n authorization; certification

patent v to retain sole ownership over an invention or idea

chances are that phr it is likely that

debt n money owed

incur v to acquire

proverbial adj well-known; expected

take something into account phr to consider

set up v to arrange; to provide for

inventory n stock

fall apart v to go badly

Summarize the points made in the lecture, being sure to explain how they challenge specific claims made in the reading passage.

_____

_____

_____

_____

_____

_____

_____

_____

_____

_____

_____

_____

_____

_____

_____

_____

_____

_____

_____

Self-Evaluation Check your response by answering the following questions.

	Yes	No
1 Are all the important points from the lecture presented accurately?	☐	☐
2 Is the information from the lecture appropriately related to the reading?	☐	☐
3 Is the response well organized?	☐	☐
4 Are all the sentences grammatically correct?	☐	☐
5 Are all the words spelled correctly?	☐	☐
6 Are all the punctuation marks used correctly?	☐	☐

Exercise 1 Read, listen, and answer the question following each step.

Reading Read the following passage and take notes.

Most spiders build webs of some type. These webs are made from a sticky silk-like substance that spiders produce naturally. There are two main kinds of webs: orb webs and cobwebs. While both are able to capture and hold prey, it is the orb web that is much more efficient at doing so.

Orb webs are one-dimensional webs built on a flat plane. They consist of spirals of strands of web in an ever-increasing circular pattern that moves outward from a central point. The webs are difficult to see on account of the facts that they are one dimensional and that the strands are fine enough to be invisible even in bright sunlight, let alone at night. Thus, the majority of spiders build orb webs because insects fly or innocently walk into the webs, thereby becoming easy prey for them.

The flat shape and the one-dimensional aspect of the orb web are also more efficient uses of the spider's silk. This type of web enables the spider to use the least amount of web substance thanks to its relatively simple structure. This plain structure also permits the spider to build the web quickly. In fact, it takes only thirty to forty-five minutes to complete an orb web. Such efficiency is important because many species of spiders destroy and eat their webs around dawn and rebuild them with new silk each night.

Finally, the orb web allows spiders to know when their prey approaches and gets caught. Since the spider lies at the center of the web, it can feel the vibrations of insects from all directions once they get ensnared. The vibrations are practically a signal to the spider informing it that food is nearby. The spider can then easily locate its prey and approach it to kill and eat it.

📖 Words & Phrases

substance ⓝ a material
capture ⓥ to catch; to trap
orb ⓝ a sphere
efficient ⓐⓓⓙ resourceful; competent
plane ⓝ a flat surface
spiral ⓝ a continuous circling flat curve

strand ⓝ a thin strip
anchor ⓥ to attach
fine ⓐⓓⓙ very thin
aspect ⓝ a feature; a characteristic
ensnare ⓥ to entrap
vibration ⓝ a tremble; a tremor

📝 Note Taking

Orb Webs Are Ideal Webs for Spiders

1 Efficient in trapping insects
- One-dimensional & made of fine strands → [1) ....]
- Used by most spiders

2 [2) ....]
- Simple structure → saves web substance → [3) ....] → can build new webs every night

3 [4) ....]
- Spiders in center of web → [5) ....] → kill prey & eat it

✎ Note Taking

Cobwebs Are Ideal Webs for Spiders

1 1) _____ for prey to escape
   • 3-dimensional & cone-/triangle-shaped
   • Made of irregular strands of spider silk → dense structure

   01-18

2 Much stronger than orb webs
   • Orb webs: easily break → 2) _____
   • Cobwebs: don't break as easily → 3) _____

3 4) _____
   • Orb webs: spider in the center → makes it easy prey for birds
   • Cobwebs: spider hidden in dense folds → 5) _____

📖 Words & Phrases

dense [adj] thick
ensnared [adj] caught in a trap
integral [adj] crucial; important
can ill afford to-V [phr] scarcely to be able to-V
lest [conj] for fear that

from scratch [phr] from the beginning
repair [v] to fix; to mend
spot [v] to notice; to see
vulnerable [adj] susceptible; open to attack

Comparing the Points Rewrite the main points from both notes as complete sentences.

Reading	Listening
Stance Orb webs are more efficient webs than cobwebs.	**Stance** Cobwebs are more efficient types of webs than orb webs.
Main point 1	**Refutation 1**
Main point 2	**Refutation 2**
Main point 3	**Refutation 3**

The following sentences are some important points from both the reading and the listening. Combine each pair of sentences to create your own sentence by using the given pattern.

1 **Reading** While both are able to capture and hold prey, it is the orb web that is much more efficient at doing so.

Listening I, on the other hand, favor the cobweb as the spider's ideal kind of web for a number of different reasons.

Combine ....

....

....

....

2 **Reading** The majority of spiders build orb webs because insects fly or innocently walk into the webs, thereby becoming easy prey for them.

Listening Because cobwebs are made of irregular strands of spider silk and have a much denser structure, ensnared insects cannot escape as easily as they can from an orb web.

Combine ....

....

....

....

3 **Reading** This type of web enables the spider to use the least amount of web substance thanks to its relatively simple structure.

Listening Once an orb web breaks, a spider must start again from scratch to rebuild it.

Combine ....

....

....

....

4 **Reading** Since the spider lies at the center of the web, it can feel the vibrations of insects from all directions once they get ensnared.

Listening Because the spider must lie in the center of an orb web to feel the vibrations of captured prey, it is easily spotted by its natural enemies like birds.

Combine ....

....

....

....

Organization Review the notes from the reading and the listening. Complete the following chart with complete sentences.

Introduction	1
Body 1	2 3
Body 2	4 5 6 7
Body 3	8 9
Conclusion (Optional)	10

Read the following passage for 3 minutes. You may take notes while you read and use your notes to help you answer the question.

Humans and primates, the family of apes, gorillas, and chimpanzees, among others, share many common traits. While primates are deemed the most intelligent of animals, most researchers have believed they lack the capacity to produce language. However, a research project in the 1970s at the University of Georgia showed promise that chimpanzees have the ability to learn language, just like human children do.

The project used several chimpanzees as test subjects among which Lana, a female chimp was the study's focus. Since the primates lack the vocal constructions to make human speech patterns, the researchers created a language called Yerkish, using lexigrams made of symbols that represented sounds and words. 125 symbols were placed on a keyboard, and Lana was taught how to use the board to communicate with the researchers. She successfully expressed her thoughts by pressing different keys in succession. In some cases, she used up to seven at a time.

While Lana's ability to communicate was somewhat limited by using the keyboard, the researchers insisted the chimp was able to form the basis of language ability. She could form word combinations and could even distinguish between nouns and adjectives. For example, she used the term "finger bracelet" to describe a ring since she had no lexigram for that word. She had learned "finger" as a noun, but in that case, she managed to use it as an adjective.

When asked questions by the researchers, Lana could respond. The questions were put into the lexigram machine, and Lana seemed to understand what was being asked. She then would reply by using the keyboard to give seemingly logical answers. While the communication was limited, the researchers believed the Lana experiment proved that some primates have the ability to learn to communicate with language.

📖 Words & Phrases

primate n a monkey; any member of the ape family

trait n a characteristic

deem v to think; to believe

capacity n a capability; an ability

test subject n someone or something used in an experiment

vocal adj related to voice

in succession phr in a row

insist v to maintain; to claim

distinguish v to tell apart

seemingly adv apparently

📝 Note Taking

Chimps Can Learn Language

📝 **Note Taking**

Chimps Cannot Learn Language

01-19

💻 **Words & Phrases**

well-documented adj well-recorded

pheromone n a chemical substance released by animals

notion n an idea; a concept

breakthrough n an advance

skepticism n doubt

celebrated adj famous

be composed of phr to consist of

condition v to accustom; to control; to influence

expose v to show; to present

absorb v to soak

complex adj intricate; complicated

passive adj reactive

Writing ▶ Summarize the points made in the lecture, being sure to explain how they challenge specific claims made in the reading passage.

_____

_____

_____

_____

_____

_____

_____

_____

_____

_____

_____

_____

_____

_____

_____

_____

_____

_____

Self-Evaluation ▶ Check your response by answering the following questions.

	Yes	No
1 Are all the important points from the lecture presented accurately?	☐	☐
2 Is the information from the lecture appropriately related to the reading?	☐	☐
3 Is the response well organized?	☐	☐
4 Are all the sentences grammatically correct?	☐	☐
5 Are all the words spelled correctly?	☐	☐
6 Are all the punctuation marks used correctly?	☐	☐

Exercise 1 Read, listen, and answer the question following each step.

Reading Read the following passage and take notes.

Fish farming is the breeding and rearing of fish in captivity to produce food for human consumption. It is often done in large penned-in areas on the shores of lakes, rivers, and bays and in inlets connected to the ocean. The fish are raised from eggs and when large enough, sold to the public. Although this seems to be a good idea at first, fish farming has a number of safety issues, both to fish and consumers, which make it a dangerous activity.

The fish are kept closely confined in pens, an environment for which they are not naturally suited. This makes the instance of disease higher in captivity than it is in the wild. Due to the proximity between the fish, diseases also spread more rapidly than in natural settings. The chances of some disease going unnoticed and being passed on to the public when the fish are consumed are high.

Fish farmers add various chemicals to the water to prevent the spread of potential diseases. These chemical additives are also put in the fish's food in order to help the fish attain sizes larger than they would have reached in the wild. These chemicals, once absorbed into the bodies of the fish, can be dangerous to the people who are dining on them.

The fish feed mostly on other fish, which are killed and processed before being fed to the fish on the farms. However, the fish used as food are caught in the oceans and represent a large amount of food taken out of the wild. Since they are a potential source of protein for other sea creatures, the loss of this food source may have an adverse effect on ecosystems throughout the world's oceans.

Words & Phrases

breed v to raise; to rear
in captivity phr being kept enclosed
penned-in adj captive; contained in some kind of facility
inlet n a narrow strip of water which goes from a sea or lake into the land
confine v to keep in captivity

suited adj matched; suitable
proximity n nearness
unnoticed adj unseen
attain v to reach; to achieve
process v to prepare
adverse adj negative

Note Taking

Fish Farming Is Not Desirable

1 Likelihood of disease ↑
  • Fish kept close together in pens → 1) _____
  • 2) _____

2 3) _____
  • Make fish grow to larger-than-normal sizes
  • 4) _____ → can be harmful to people who eat them

3 Negative effect on ecosystems
  • 5) _____ → other fish lose food sources

Listen to a lecture on the topic you just read about and take notes.

Note Taking

Fish Farming Is Beneficial

01-20

1 Likelihood of disease ≠ high
- Living close together: 1) _____
- 2) _____

2 Chemicals are everywhere
- 3) _____ → not free from chemicals
- Farmed fish → 4) _____

3 Fish used for feed are not eaten by humans / other animals
- e.g. 5) _____ → used for fish feed

Words & Phrases

critic [n] an opponent

oppose [v] to be against

harvest [v] to reap; to collect

run rampant [phr] to spread quickly; to go out of control

school [n] a group of fish

identical [adj] the same

red flag [phr] a warning sign

absorb [v] to soak

enhance [v] to improve; to make stronger

consume [v] to eat

Comparing the Points

Rewrite the main points from both notes as complete sentences.

Reading	Listening
Stance Fish farming may appear good but is actually dangerous to fish and people.	**Stance** Fish farming is beneficial to many people around the world.
Main point 1	Refutation 1
Main point 2	Refutation 2
Main point 3	Refutation 3

The following sentences are some important points from both the reading and the listening. Combine each pair of sentences to create your own sentence by using the given pattern.

1   **Reading**   Fish farming has a number of safety issues, both to fish and consumers, which make it a dangerous activity.

       Listening   Fish farming is quite necessary because many fish raised on fish farms can no longer be harvested in the wild, and, fortunately, fish farming can provide fish that are safe to eat.

       Combine

                     ....

                     ....

                     ....

                     ....

2   **Reading**   Fish living closely together on fish farms makes the instance of disease higher in captivity than it is in the wild.

       Listening   Studies have shown the incidence of disease in the wild and on farms is identical.

       Combine

                     ....

                     ....

                     ....

                     ....

3   **Reading**   These chemicals, once absorbed into the bodies of the fish, can be dangerous to the people who are dining on them.

       Listening   Chemical usage on fish farms has raised some red flags as to the safety of the fish, but even ocean fish absorb large amounts of chemicals from pollution.

       Combine

                     ....

                     ....

                     ....

                     ....

4   **Reading**   However, the fish used as food are caught in the oceans and represent a large amount of food taken out of the wild.

       Listening   While some fish species are killed to produce the feed needed for fish on the farms, most of these fish are not even consumed by humans or many sea creatures.

       Combine

                     ....

                     ....

                     ....

                     ....

Organization Review the notes from the reading and the listening. Complete the following chart with complete sentences.

Introduction	1
Body 1	2 3
Body 2	4 5
Body 3	6 7 8 9
Conclusion (Optional)	10

Read the following passage for 3 minutes. You may take notes while you read and use your notes to help you answer the question.

Many ornithologists have noticed a disturbing trend in recent years. Namely, large numbers of species of birds are disappearing. In fact, over the past two centuries, over 100 species of birds have disappeared while another 1,200 are endangered. The evidence points toward humans as the reason why birds are slowly but surely being eradicated.

Humans are expanding the urban areas where they mostly live, so they are encroaching on birds'—and other creatures'—natural habitats. Almost half the world's population lives in urban centers of some sort, and green areas are low on the priority list in most places. Coupled with this urban sprawl are the increased amounts of pollution being produced in the cities. These factors are combining to take away the birds' habitats and to contaminate the places where they live.

As the Earth's population grows, there is an ever-increasing demand for food, so many lands are being cleared to make farmland to produce this food. Large tracts of forested areas are being cleared to grow crops on, and there is little thought given to the fate of the birds who nest in these forests. Approximately 50,000 to 170,000 square kilometers of forest are cut down yearly, which is putting many species of birds at risk.

Farmers often rely upon chemical insecticides to eliminate insect infestations. These chemicals are also killing many birds as well as other animals. This is one reason the insecticide DDT has been banned for almost forty years in the United States. It was simply killing too many birds, particularly the bald eagle. Unfortunately, in the rest of the world, DDT and other powerful chemicals are still being used on farms and are therefore killing large numbers of birds.

📖 Words & Phrases

ornithologist Ⓝ a person who studies birds
disturbing adj upsetting
eradicate Ⓥ to wipe out
urban adj metropolitan
encroach Ⓥ to intrude upon; to trespass

sprawl Ⓝ an irregularly spread group or mass
tract Ⓝ an area of land
fate Ⓝ the end result
nest Ⓥ to build a nest and to live in it
infestation Ⓝ an invasion

📝 Note Taking

Birds Are Becoming Endangered

📝 **Note Taking**

Birds Are Not in Any Danger

01-21

📖 **Words & Phrases**

endangered (adj) likely to become extinct soon

dire (adj) severe; terrible

decline (v) to decrease

adapt (v) to change; to alter

agriculture (n) farming

not by a long shot (phr) never; not by any means

dispute (v) to argue

genetically (adv) hereditarily

resist (v) to fight; to combat

utilize (v) to use

leap (v) to increase dramatically

Writing Summarize the points made in the lecture, being sure to explain how they challenge specific claims made in the reading passage.

_____

_____

_____

_____

_____

_____

_____

_____

_____

_____

_____

_____

_____

_____

_____

_____

_____

_____

Self-Evaluation Check your response by answering the following questions.

	Yes	No
1 Are all the important points from the lecture presented accurately?	☐	☐
2 Is the information from the lecture appropriately related to the reading?	☐	☐
3 Is the response well organized?	☐	☐
4 Are all the sentences grammatically correct?	☐	☐
5 Are all the words spelled correctly?	☐	☐
6 Are all the punctuation marks used correctly?	☐	☐

PART II

Writing for the Academic Discussion Task

....

In the academic discussion task, you will first be presented with a question by a professor that is written on a university online discussion board. You will then read two short responses by students in the class. These responses typically take opposite or different positions. Then, you must write your own response to the question posed by the professor. You will have 10 minutes to write an essay in response to the question. A typical essay is at least 100 words long.

Writing for an Academic Discussion Task

Overview

The second part of the Writing section of the TOEFL iBT is the TOEFL Writing for an Academic Discussion Task. This is a new task as of July 2023. You will see a question written by a university professor and then two responses by students. Your task is to write a response to the question. A typical response will be at least 100 words. You have ten minutes to write your response.

1 Yes/No

Sometimes the professor asks a question and then requests that the students provide a yes-no answer. The professor may also ask the students if they agree or disagree with a statement. You should determine whether your answer to the question is yes or no or if you agree or disagree with the statement and then support your position with appropriate reasons and examples.

2 Preference

For these questions, the professor provides the students with a choice and asks them which of the two they prefer. You should determine which choice you prefer and then support your position with appropriate reasons and examples.

3 Open-Ended

The professor states a question that has no right or wrong answer but merely asks the students what they think about a topic. You should state your opinion regarding the question and then support your position with appropriate reasons and examples.

Useful Tips

1 The questions asked in this section come from a variety of topics. Many of the topics concern the environment and economics. But there are also questions based on sociology, political science, and other subjects in the liberal arts.

2 You do not require any specialized background knowledge to answer the professor's question. Simply read the question and the two students' responses, and then you can formulate your own answer.

3 Be sure to comment on the responses by both students.

4 Be sure to provide your own opinion. One way to do this is to add extra information to a comment made by one of the students.

5 The minimum response is 100 words, but you should try to write more than that.

6 There is no right or wrong answer. Simply defend your choice with good arguments and examples.

7 Try to write at least one complex sentence—a sentence with a conjunction such as *because, however, although,* or *since*—and two compound sentences—a sentence with a conjunction such as *and, but, or,* or *so* in your response. This will improve the quality of your writing and give you a chance to have a higher score.

Key Strategies

1 Brainstorming

- Read the professor's questions carefully to make sure that you understand it.
- Read each student's response to make sure that you understand their arguments.
- Brainstorm some ideas on scratch paper before you begin writing.

2 Outlining & Organizing

- Organize your response in outline form.
- Develop your ideas into complete sentences.
- Be sure to include an introductory statement as well as a conclusion.

3 Completing the Essay

- Make sure that your introductory statement is clear.
- Be sure to refer to the argument that each student makes.
- Provide clear reasons and examples.
- Write a concluding sentence.
- There is no need to write multiple paragraphs. Your entire response can be a single paragraph.

4 Writing & Checking Your Essay

- Read the professor's question and two student responses and plan your essay in 2 minutes.
- Spend 5-6 minutes writing your essay.
- Take 2-3 minutes to read over your essay to make changes and to find mistakes.
- Make sure you use proper grammar, have correct spelling, and write logical sentences.

Your professor is teaching a class on urban development. Write a post responding to the professor's question.

In your response you should:

- express and support your opinion
- make a contribution to the discussion

An effective response will contain at least 100 words. You will have 10 minutes to write it.

Professor Hooper

Let's take some time to think about urban areas. These days, cities with populations of millions of people are common around the world. This has resulted in, essentially, the creation of concrete jungles. Some governments have been making an effort to create green spaces such as parks in urban areas. Do you agree with this policy? Why?

Jordan

I fully support every effort by local governments to create green zones within urban areas. Parks provide multiple benefits to local residents. For instance, they are places where people can escape from the hustle and bustle of life in the city and relax. They also help beautify areas thanks to the grass, trees, and ponds they feature. I wish cities would build as many parks as possible.

Natalie

In my opinion, cities should not be creating more parks nowadays. For one thing, many urban areas already have large numbers of parks, so more are not necessary. For another thing, the price of land in cities is expensive, and parks take up large amounts of space. So a city will have to spend tons of money just to acquire more land for a single park.

Sample Response

`Introductory sentence` Both Jordan and Natalie present good arguments, but I agree with Jordan and think city governments should create more green spaces wherever they can. `Reason 1` Like Jordan notes, parks are perfect places for people to relax while escaping their busy lives. While Natalie brings up a valid point that buying land in cities can be expensive, I do not consider that a waste of money. The reason is that the parks which are built will be available to all residents. Spending money that benefits large numbers of people is better than spending money on projects that benefit just a few individuals. `Reason 2` Another thing to consider is that the presence of parks can reduce the urban heat island effect. That can help decrease the temperatures in cities and cool them off. `Conclusion` Clearly, these green spaces can considerably help urban residents.

Exercise 1 Follow the directions in each step.

Brainstorming & Outlining

A Read the professor's comment and brainstorm some ideas. Then, use the outline to generate your ideas.

Professor
Nelson

These days, protecting the environment is a major issue for many people. Some people claim that factories can have the greatest effect on the environment by making their manufacturing processes cleaner. However, others believe that individuals can have a greater effect on the environment by their own personal actions. I would like you to consider the following question: Which do you think can have a greater impact on the environment? Why do you feel that way?

📖 **Words & Phrases**

issue n a concern; a problem

factory n a building where items are manufactured

process n a method; a way of doing something

personal adj relating to an individual

impact n an effect, often a major one

▪ **Outline for Brainstorming**

The More Important Factor on the Environment			
Factories		**Individuals**	
Reason 1	Reason 2	Reason 1	Reason 2

B Read the following comments by two students and complete the summary notes.

Jeff

Factories have a much greater influence on the environment than individuals do. After all, many of them operate twenty-four hours a day, and they spew large amounts of smoke and harmful chemicals. If factories make an effort to become cleaner, then they can reduce the amount of air, water, and ground pollution on the Earth by a tremendous amount.

🖥 Words & Phrases
operate v to run; to work
spew v to shoot out; to expel
harmful adj dangerous; capable of causing damage

reduce v to make less; to decrease
tremendous adj very great in number, quantity, or amount

✏ Summary Notes: Jeff

Factories

1 Have 1)_____ than individuals
  • Operate 2)_____ a day
  • Spew out 3)_____ + 4)_____

2 Can make effort to 5)_____
  • Reduce 6)_____

Stephanie

Individuals can have a powerful effect on the environment for a couple of reasons. For instance, they can act to help the environment by recycling and cleaning up waste, which can make the Earth cleaner. They can also lead boycotts of companies that are polluters, so they can force companies to produce less pollution and therefore help the environment improve.

🖥 Words & Phrases
powerful adj very strong or great
recycle v to save something so that it can be used again
boycott n to refuse to deal with a person, store, etc. to show disapproval regarding an action or belief

polluter n a person, business, etc. that makes the air, water, or land unclean
force v to make a person, business, etc. act in a certain way

✏ Summary Notes: Stephanie

Individuals

1 Can act to 1)_____
  • Recycle and 2)_____
  • Makes 3)_____

2 Can lead 4)_____
  • Force companies to 5)_____
  • Help 6)_____

⊙ Supporting Jeff's Opinion

Introduction	1
Body 1	2
	3
	4
Body 2	5
	6
Conclusion	7

⊙ Supporting Stephanie's Opinion

Introduction	1
Body 1	2
	3
Body 2	4
	5
Conclusion	6
	7

Follow the directions and write a response. You can refer to the outline and the summary notes.

Your professor is teaching a class on environmental science. Write a post responding to the professor's question.

In your response you should:

- express and support your personal opinion
- make a contribution to the discussion in your own words

An effective response will contain at least 100 words. You have ten minutes to write.

Professor
Jackson

In urban areas, people frequently drive personal vehicles to work, school, and other places despite public transportation being available. This is a serious problem because the vehicles consume large amounts of gas, create pollution, and cause traffic jams in cities. This causes numerous issues for city residents. In your opinion, what would be the best way to encourage more people to use public transportation?

📖 **Words & Phrases**

urban [adj] relating to a city
frequently [adv] often
vehicle [n] a means of carrying or transporting things

consume [v] to use
traffic jam [n] a situation in which many cars on the road are moving slowly

✖ **Outline for Brainstorming**

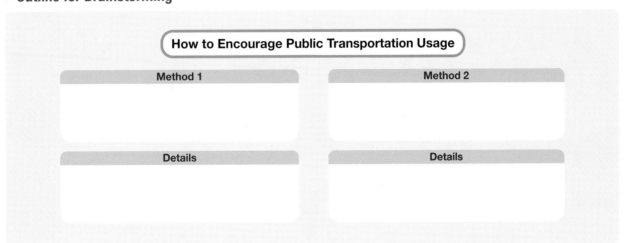

How to Encourage Public Transportation Usage

Method 1	Method 2
Details	Details

Lisa

I think that cities should make taking public transportation more appealing to local residents. For instance, they could reduce the price of taking the bus or the subway. I know people who want to take the bus, but they dislike how expensive the bus fare is. By lowering prices, cities can encourage people to use public transportation more often.

Theodore

Most people with cars use them without considering their effects on the environment. I therefore believe that governments need to restrict vehicular usage in some areas. City governments could ban driving in certain downtown areas. If only buses and other forms of public transportation are allowed in those places, people will have to stop driving their cars and use public transportation instead.

📖 Words & Phrases

appealing adj pleasing
resident n a person who lives in a certain area
reduce v to lower
expensive adj costly
fare n a fee for taking a bus, taxi, subway, etc.

consider v to think about
restrict v to put a limit on; to restrain
vehicular adj relating to a vehicle such as a car or bus
ban v to prohibit; not to allow
downtown adj relating to the inner part of a city

☑ Summary Notes

Lisa	Theodore

Self-Evaluation   Check your response by answering the following questions.

	Yes	No
1 Did you address the professor's question?	☐	☐
2 Did you refer to the comments by the two students?	☐	☐
3 Did you express your own opinion?	☐	☐
4 Did you provide examples to support your opinion?	☐	☐
5 Did you organize your response well?	☐	☐
6 Did you use correct grammar?	☐	☐
7 Did you use correct punctuation?	☐	☐
8 Did you spell all of the words correctly?	☐	☐

Exercise 1 Follow the directions in each step.

Brainstorming & Outlining

A Read the professor's comment and brainstorm some ideas. Then, use the outline to generate your ideas.

Professor Rendon

Technology is improving every year, and it has a tremendous effect on people's lives. Fields of study such as math and science are therefore more vital than ever. However, most high schools still insist on teaching subjects such as art and music. Do you believe high schools need to stress teaching math and science more and should cease teaching subjects such as art and music? Why?

📖 **Words & Phrases**

tremendous adj enormous; very great
vital adj important
insist v to demand or require something be done
stress v to focus on
cease v to stop

✖ **Outline for Brainstorming**

Teach Only Science and Math or Teach Other Subjects			
Teach Only Math and Science		**Teach Art and Music as Well**	
Reason 1	Reason 2	Reason 1	Reason 2

B Read the following comments by two students and complete the summary notes.

Daniel

Technology is such a huge part of our lives, but there are not enough people competent in the fields of math and science. Look at how many students here are majoring in math and various sciences. It is simply not enough. High school should start emphasizing math and science and should ignore art and music. That will ensure that we have enough people able to keep our technological society operational.

🖥 Words & Phrases

competent adj able; skilled

emphasize v to stress

ignore v not to pay attention to someone or something

ensure v to guarantee

operational adj working; running properly

✍ Summary Notes: Daniel

Teach Only Math and Science

1 Technology huge in 1) ....
  • Not enough 2) ....
  • Not many college student 3) ....

2 High schools ➜ emphasize 4) .... + 5) .... art and music
  • Can keep 6) ....

Emily

Art and music are important fields, and it is crucial that high school students be introduced to them. I remember taking those classes in high school. Even though I cannot create good art, nor can I sing or play a musical instrument, I benefitted from those classes. If we want students to get balanced educations, we must demand that high schools continue teaching all subjects, not just math and science.

🖥 Words & Phrases

crucial adj important

benefit v to gain; to obtain something positive

balanced adj well-proportioned or regulated

education n the learning a person gets

demand v to say that one wants something, often in a strong way

✍ Summary Notes: Emily

Teach Art and Music as Well

1 Crucial to 1) ....
  • Took 2) ....
  • Cannot do 3) ....
  • Still 4) ....

2 Need to have students with 5) ....
  • Should demand 6) ....

⊙ Supporting Daniel's Opinion

Introduction	1
Body 1	2 3
Body 2	4
Conclusion	5

⊙ Supporting Emily's Opinion

Introduction	1 2
Body 1	3 4
Body 2	5
Conclusion	6

Exercise 2 Follow the directions and write a response. You can refer to the outline and the summary notes.

Your professor is teaching a class on sociology. Write a post responding to the professor's question.

In your response you should:

- express and support your opinion
- make a contribution to the discussion

An effective response will contain at least 100 words. You will have 10 minutes to write it.

Professor
Martin

Families no longer live in the same place for decades like people once did in the past. Instead, families move with great frequency nowadays. As a result, children often change schools, which can be problematic for them because they have to make new friends and get used to new learning environments. How do you believe that schools can help these students adjust to their new environments?

📖 **Words & Phrases**

no longer phr not anymore
decade n a period of ten years
frequency n the number of times something happens in a
set period of time

problematic adj difficult; hard
adjust v to settle an issue; to get used to something

✖ **Outline for Brainstorming**

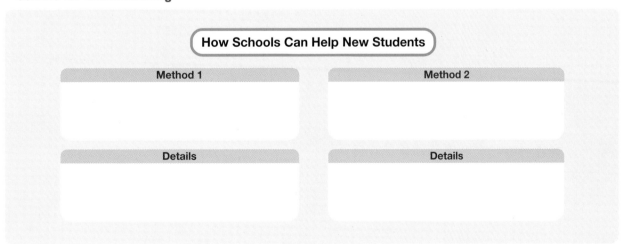

How Schools Can Help New Students

Method 1	Method 2
Details	**Details**

Carla

I have some personal experience with this since my family moved regularly, so I attended seven different schools. It was never a pleasant experience for me. In my opinion, schools should assign a student to act like a buddy or mentor to a newcomer. The student would help the newcomer find his or her way around the school and could introduce the newcomer to other students.

Russell

The best thing schools could do to assist new students is to have an orientation program. At the beginning of the semester, new students would be given a tour of the campus and get the opportunity to meet their instructors. They would be informed about what kinds of classes and extracurricular activities are available. The school could also encourage new students to be active and to attempt to make friends.

📖 Words & Phrases

pleasant (adj) nice; pleasing

assign (v) to appoint; to instruct a person to do a certain activity

buddy (n) a friend

mentor (n) a person with experience who teaches someone how to do something

newcomer (n) a person who is new to a certain place

orientation (n) the act of being acquainted with a place

semester (n) one of the two halves of a school year

instructor (n) a teacher

extracurricular activity (n) something extra a student does at school that is not related to classes

encourage (v) to urge; to try to persuade

✏ Summary Notes

Carla	Russell

Self-Evaluation — Check your response by answering the following questions.

	Yes	No
1 Did you address the professor's question?	☐	☐
2 Did you refer to the comments by the two students?	☐	☐
3 Did you express your own opinion?	☐	☐
4 Did you provide examples to support your opinion?	☐	☐
5 Did you organize your response well?	☐	☐
6 Did you use correct grammar?	☐	☐
7 Did you use correct punctuation?	☐	☐
8 Did you spell all of the words correctly?	☐	☐

Exercise 1 Follow the directions in each step.

Brainstorming & Outlining

A Read the professor's comment and brainstorm some ideas. Then, use the outline to generate your ideas.

Professor
Donaldson

I would like for everyone to consider happiness. The factors that create happiness tend to vary from person to person. However, for a large number of individuals, their career has a major effect on their happiness. For others, their family plays a crucial role. In your opinion, is a career or a family more important in determining a person's happiness? Why?

📖 **Words & Phrases**

factor Ⓝ someone or something that contributes to a result
vary Ⓥ to change
career Ⓝ the profession a person is trained in and works in
crucial adj important
role Ⓝ a function

✖ **Outline for Brainstorming**

The More Important Factor for Happiness			
Career		**Family**	
Reason 1	Reason 2	Reason 1	Reason 2

B Read the following comments by two students and complete the summary notes.

Eric

For me, a person's career is much more important in determining that individual's level of happiness. Many people spend more than half of their waking hours at their jobs and think about their jobs when they are not working. If they are displeased with their careers, it shows in their actions. Likewise, people who are unhappy with their careers often have miserable lives and suffer from depression.

📖 **Words & Phrases**

waking hours (n) the time when a person is not sleeping but is awake
displeased (adj) unhappy

likewise (adv) similarly
miserable (adj) very unhappy or sad
suffer (v) to endure

📝 **Summary Notes: Eric**

Career
1 People spend ¹⁾ _____
• Think about jobs ²⁾ _____
• Displeased w/careers = ³⁾ _____
2 People ⁴⁾ _____
• Have ⁵⁾ _____
• Suffer from ⁶⁾ _____

Rachel

Family is definitely more important than a career in making people happy. When people have happy lives with their families, their jobs are not particularly important even if they do not make much money or have an incompetent or annoying supervisor. My parents do not think too much about their jobs, but they focus on their family, and that makes them happy.

📖 **Words & Phrases**

definitely (adv) for sure
particularly (adv) very; really
incompetent (adj) lacking the ability or skill to do something

annoying (adj) bothersome
supervisor (n) a boss; a manager

📝 **Summary Notes: Rachel**

Family
1 People have happy lives ¹⁾ _____
• Jobs not ²⁾ _____
• Don't ³⁾ _____ + ⁴⁾ _____ = okay
2 Parents don't think ⁵⁾ _____
• Focus on ⁶⁾ _____
• Makes them ⁷⁾ _____

Review the outline and the summary notes on the previous pages and then complete each chart.

⊙ Supporting Eric's Opinion

Introduction	1	
	2	
	3	
Body 1	4	
	5	
	6	
Body 2	7	
	8	
Conclusion	9	

⊙ Supporting Rachel's Opinion

Introduction	1	
Body 1	2	
	3	
Body 2	4	
	5	
Conclusion	6	
	7	

Exercise 2 Follow the directions and write a response. You can refer to the outline and the summary notes.

Your professor is teaching a class on sociology. Write a post responding to the professor's question.

In your response you should:

- express and support your opinion
- make a contribution to the discussion

An effective response will contain at least 100 words. You will have 10 minutes to write it.

Professor
Cleveland

These days, thanks to the power of the Internet and social media in particular, people know more about celebrities than ever before. In fact, celebrities are vastly more influential today than at any time in history. But is the influence of celebrities on society positive or negative? What do you think? Why?

📔 **Words & Phrases**

social media 🄽 a form of online communication in which users make various types of posts

in particular phr specifically

celebrity 🄽 a famous or well-known person

vastly adv greatly

influential adj having the power to cause an effect in a certain way

✘ **Outline for Brainstorming**

Celebrities Have a Positive or Negative Influence

Positive Influence	Negative Influence
Details	**Details**

Andrea

There is no denying that celebrities are very important nowadays. Overall, I would say their influence on society has more positive features than negative ones. For instance, many celebrities support various causes and promote them on social media. One of my favorite celebrities encourages people to eat healthy food and to exercise. Others have come out in favor of studying hard, having good family values, and other positive behaviors.

Peter

One of the worst things about social media is how people are influenced by celebrities, most of whom are terrible people engaged in awful activities. Reality television shows promote celebrities and show how they have poor values and are people of low character. What is worse is that many people see celebrities as individuals worth emulating. That could not be further from the truth.

📖 Words & Phrases

deny v to refuse to admit; to say that something is not true

feature n a special attraction; a prominent part or character

cause n a cause that a person may support

in favor of phr in support of

value n a principle or quality that is desired

terrible adj very bad

awful adj very bad

promote v to present through publicity

character n the primary nature of a person

emulate v to imitate; to act the same as another person

☑ Summary Notes

Andrea	Peter

_____

_____

_____

_____

_____

_____

_____

_____

_____

_____

_____

_____

_____

_____

_____

_____

_____

Self-Evaluation   Check your response by answering the following questions.

	Yes	No
1 Did you address the professor's question?	☐	☐
2 Did you refer to the comments by the two students?	☐	☐
3 Did you express your own opinion?	☐	☐
4 Did you provide examples to support your opinion?	☐	☐
5 Did you organize your response well?	☐	☐
6 Did you use correct grammar?	☐	☐
7 Did you use correct punctuation?	☐	☐
8 Did you spell all of the words correctly?	☐	☐

Exercise 1 Follow the directions in each step.

Brainstorming & Outlining

A Read the professor's comment and brainstorm some ideas. Then, use the outline to generate your ideas.

Professor Cromartie

In our next class, we shall discuss the impact of humans on other species. As you are aware, human actions have caused some animals to become endangered and others to go extinct. Many times, large infrastructure projects such as interstates cause harm to animals. Here is a thought: Infrastructure projects that may hurt endangered species should be canceled. Do you agree or disagree? Why?

📕 **Words & Phrases**

impact (n) an effect
endangered (adj) being in danger of disappearing
go extinct (phr) to disappear; to die out; to vanish
infrastructure (n) all of the public works, such as roads and bridges, in a place
interstate (n) a major expressway that goes through multiple states or provinces

✖ **Outline for Brainstorming**

Cancel Large Infrastructure Projects or Not			
Agree		**Disagree**	
Reason 1	Reason 2	Reason 1	Reason 2

B Read the following comments by two students and complete the summary notes.

Irene

Humans should be stewards of the environment and protect animals since they cannot protect themselves in many cases. When an infrastructure project threatens to hurt an endangered species, the project should be canceled immediately. We need to stress our commitment to the members of the animal kingdom by putting them ahead of our needs if necessary.

📖 **Words & Phrases**

steward n a person whose job it is to look after and protect something

hurt v to damage; to cause harm to

immediately adv at once

commitment n an agreement to do something in the future

✍ **Summary Notes: Irene**

Agree

1 Humans = [1]) _____
   • Protect animals since [2]) _____
   • Species threatened ➡ [3]) _____

2 Stress commitment to [4]) _____
   • Put them [5]) _____

Chad

I could not disagree more with the notion that infrastructure projects should be canceled due to some animals. I am not saying that we should ignore animals though. Humans can improvise and act to help themselves and animals. For instance, interstates that bisect animal migration routes can have animals bridges built over them and tunnels beneath them. In places where they have been built, animals are known to use them.

📖 **Words & Phrases**

disagree v not to agree with or think the same way as someone or something

improvise v to make without planning

bisect v to cross, often at a 90-degree angle

migration n the act of moving from one place to another, typically with the seasons

tunnel n an underground path

✍ **Summary Notes: Chad**

Disagree

1 Should not [1]) _____
   • Don't [2]) _____
   • Can [3]) _____

2 Some interstates [4]) _____
   • Build [5]) _____ + [6]) _____ beneath them
   • Animals known to [7]) _____

Organization Review the outline and the summary notes on the previous pages and then complete each chart.

⊙ Supporting Irene's Opinion

Introduction	1
Body 1	2 3
Body 2	4
Conclusion	5

⊙ Supporting Chad's Opinion

Introduction	1
Body 1	2 3 4
Body 2	5 6
Conclusion	7

Exercise 2 Follow the directions and write a response. You can refer to the outline and the summary notes.

Your professor is teaching a class on environmental science. Write a post responding to the professor's question.

In your response you should:

- express and support your opinion
- make a contribution to the discussion

An effective response will contain at least 100 words. You will have 10 minutes to write it.

Professor Hopewell

In the past few years, great improvements have been made in the quality of electric vehicles so that they are now mass-produced around the world. Considering the amount of pollution produced by vehicles powered by gasoline, I would like for you to consider this question: Should governments mandate that all new cars manufactured be electric vehicles? What is your opinion? Why?

📖 Words & Phrases

improvement n the act of making something better
quality n the character of something; the feature of something

mass-produce v to use machinery to produce something in great quantities
power v to supply with energy to operate
mandate v officially to require something; to order

✖ Outline for Brainstorming

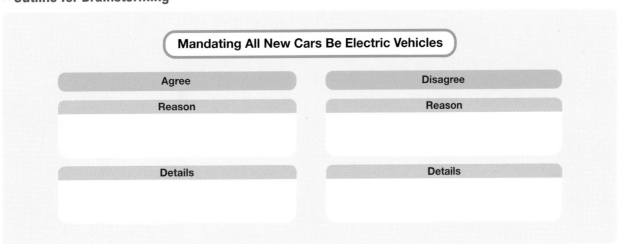

Mandating All New Cars Be Electric Vehicles

Agree	Disagree
Reason	Reason
Details	Details

Wilson

Gasoline-powered cars and trucks are huge polluters, and I cannot stand how the environment has been damaged by them. For that primary reason, I would support a law that only permits electric vehicles to be manufactured. Think of how quickly the air would become breathable again if gas were no longer burned to run cars. It would be an enormous improvement over the current situation.

Amanda

I am a huge supporter of electric vehicles and think they will be vital to the future, but I do not believe governments should order all new cars made to be electric vehicles. First, electric vehicles are tremendously expensive, so many people could not afford to purchase a personal vehicle in this situation. In addition, I disapprove of the idea of the government telling people what they can and cannot do.

📕 Words & Phrases

polluter n a person, company, etc. that creates pollution

primary adj main

permit v to allow

breathable adj suitable for breathing; fresh, as in air

enormous adj great; very large; huge

supporter n one that promotes or defends someone or something

order v to demand; to require

tremendously adv greatly; highly

afford v to have enough money to pay for a good or service

disapprove v to reject; to turn down

☑ Summary Notes

Wilson	Amanda

_____

_____

_____

_____

_____

_____

_____

_____

_____

_____

_____

_____

_____

_____

_____

_____

_____

_____

_____

_____

_____

📝 Self-Evaluation   Check your response by answering the following questions.

	Yes	No
1 Did you address the professor's question?	☐	☐
2 Did you refer to the comments by the two students?	☐	☐
3 Did you express your own opinion?	☐	☐
4 Did you provide examples to support your opinion?	☐	☐
5 Did you organize your response well?	☐	☐
6 Did you use correct grammar?	☐	☐
7 Did you use correct punctuation?	☐	☐
8 Did you spell all of the words correctly?	☐	☐

Exercise 1 Follow the directions in each step.

▶ **Brainstorming & Outlining**

A Read the professor's comment and brainstorm some ideas. Then, use the outline to generate your ideas.

Professor
Robinson

Nearly seventy million American households own at least one dog while approximately forty-five million have one or more cats. Pets are an integral part of many Americans' lives. Nevertheless, small children can often be hurt and even killed by family pets, particularly large, aggressive dogs. What are your thoughts on letting children have pets? Should they be allowed to do that by their parents? Why do you think so?

📖 **Words & Phrases**

household (n) all of the people who live in the same house
integral (adj) important
nevertheless (adv) still; however
aggressive (adj) tending to be hostile or to attack others
allow (v) to let something happen

✖ **Outline for Brainstorming**

Children Owning Pets			
Should Be Allowed		**Should Not Be Allowed**	
Reason 1	Reason 2	Reason 1	Reason 2

B Read the following comments by two students and complete the summary notes.

Linda

I have had pets my entire life and see no problem with children having them. We had large dogs such as German shepherds that never threatened my brothers or me. My parents taught us how to behave around the dogs and not to tease or hit them. Our dogs were well behaved and never bit anyone. Children can learn so much from pets that the benefits outweigh the potential dangers.

Words & Phrases

entire adj complete; whole
threaten v to express intent or willingness to do harm; to menace

behave v to act in a certain manner
tease v to annoy or disturb by being provoking
outweigh v to be greater in importance or value

Summary Notes: Linda

Should Be Allowed

1 Have had [1) _____] → German shepherds
  • Never [2) _____]

2 Parents taught how to [3) _____]
  • Don't [4) _____] them
  • Dogs [5) _____]
  • Never [6) _____]

Fred

I once visited my friend's home. He had a dog that his family neglected and kept on a chain. Unfortunately, the dog got loose and bit me. I still have a scar from that bite. The dog was big whereas I was small and had no ability to defend myself. I think children should be kept away from pets until they are big enough to protect themselves from vicious animals.

Words & Phrases

neglect v to give or pay little attention to; to ignore
get loose phr to escape, often from being tied up
scar n a mark on the skin that remains after a wound or injury has healed

defend v to protect
vicious adj fierce; willing to be violent

Summary Notes: Fred

Should Not Be Allowed

1 Visited [1) _____] → had [2) _____]
  • Dog got loose and [3) _____]
  • Still have [4) _____]

2 Keep children [5) _____]
  • Must be [6) _____] to protect themselves

Review the outline and the summary notes on the previous pages and then complete each chart.

⊙ Supporting Linda's Opinion

Introduction	1
Body 1	2
	3
	4
	5
Body 2	6
Conclusion	7

⊙ Supporting Fred's Opinion

Introduction	1
Body 1	2
	3
Body 2	4
	5
Conclusion	6
	7

Exercise 2 Follow the directions and write a response. You can refer to the outline and the summary notes.

Your professor is teaching a class on child studies. Write a post responding to the professor's question.

In your response you should:

- express and support your opinion
- make a contribution to the discussion

An effective response will contain at least 100 words. You will have 10 minutes to write it.

Professor Durham

Many parents have begun expressing displeasure with the school system for a variety of reasons, so they are taking their children out of both public and private schools and are homeschooling them instead. In recent years, the number of homeschoolers has increase by millions. What are your thoughts on homeschooling? Do you believe it offers more advantages or disadvantages? Why?

📖 **Words & Phrases**

express v to state out loud
displeasure n unhappiness
public school n a school run by the government

private school n a school run by a nongovernmental organization
homeschooling n the act of teaching school subjects to one's child at home

✖ **Outline for Brainstorming**

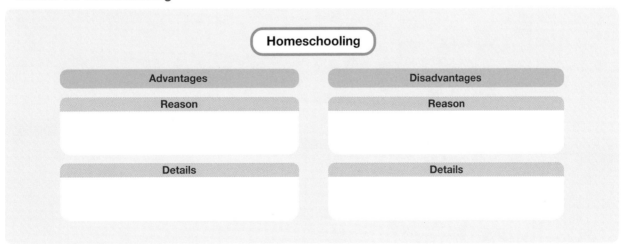

Kevin

While I was not homeschooled, several of my friends were. I am highly impressed with the quality of education they received. They know much more than most people their ages, and they spent much less time studying than regular students did. Additionally, they were still able to participate on sports teams and to do extracurricular activities while their social skills are remarkable.

Molly

I really dislike the homeschooling movement because it separates kids from their peers. A lot of homeschooled children stay at home all day and are taught lessons by their parents, most of whom are not teachers. This cannot be a good way to educate children. Homeschooled children are losing opportunities to meet others their age and to have social interactions with them.

📖 Words & Phrases

impress (v) to admire or be interested in
regular (adj) normal; typical
participate (v) to take part in; to join
skill (n) an ability
remarkable (adj) uncommon; extraordinary

separate (v) to divide
peer (n) one who is equal to another
lesson (n) a piece of instruction
educate (v) to teach
interaction (n) mutual action or influence

☑ Summary Notes

Kevin	Molly

📝 Self-Evaluation Check your response by answering the following questions.

	Yes	No
1 Did you address the professor's question?	☐	☐
2 Did you refer to the comments by the two students?	☐	☐
3 Did you express your own opinion?	☐	☐
4 Did you provide examples to support your opinion?	☐	☐
5 Did you organize your response well?	☐	☐
6 Did you use correct grammar?	☐	☐
7 Did you use correct punctuation?	☐	☐
8 Did you spell all of the words correctly?	☐	☐

Exercise 1 Follow the directions in each step.

Brainstorming & Outlining

A Read the professor's comment and brainstorm some ideas. Then, use the outline to generate your ideas.

Professor
Redding

In our next class, we are going to consider the shopping behavior of people in different situations. So please share your thoughts about this with me. These days, people shopping for food can choose between large chain supermarkets and small grocery stores situated near their homes. Which of these two types of stores do you prefer to buy food at? Why?

📖 **Words & Phrases**

behavior n the way a person acts

share v to use, experience, or partake in something with others

chain n a group of businesses that have the same function

grocery store n a store that sells food and household supplies

situated adj located

✖ **Outline for Brainstorming**

Preferred Shopping Location			
Large Chain Supermarkets		**Small Local Grocery Stores**	
Reason 1	Reason 2	Reason 1	Reason 2

B Read the following comments by two students and complete the summary notes.

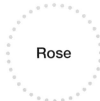

Rose

When it comes to shopping, I prefer the convenience of large chain supermarkets. They typically offer various choices of foods. For instance, I can buy numerous brands of pasta sauce and obtain a wide variety of fruits and vegetables from around the world throughout the year. The sheer number of options I have means that I only have to shop at one store for everything I need.

📕 Words & Phrases

convenience 🄝 something that provides comfort or ease
offer 🅥 to provide
brand 🄝 the name of a good provided by a single company

obtain 🅥 to get; to purchase; to acquire
sheer adj utter

☑ Summary Notes: Rose

> **Large Chain Supermarkets**
>
> **1** Various [1)] ....
> - Numerous [2)] ....
> - Wide variety of [3)] ....
> - From around world and [4)] ....
>
> **2** Only need to [5)] .... for everything

Anthony

Small local grocery stores are so much better than large chain supermarkets. My local grocer sells fresh fruits, vegetables, and meat, all of which are locally sourced, which is ideal for the environment. Sure, the prices might be a bit higher than at other places, but I love the personal touch I get, and the store is just a three-minute walk away from my home.

📕 Words & Phrases

local adj relating to a particular place
grocer 🄝 a person who sells food and household supplies
sourced adj relating to a specific place

ideal adj perfect
personal touch phr a special quality, often done for a specific individual

☑ Summary Notes: Anthony

> **Small Local Grocery Stores**
>
> **1** Local grocer has fresh [1)] ....
> - All [2)] ....
> - Ideal for [3)] ....
>
> **2** Get [4)] ....
> - Store just [5)] .... from home

Review the outline and the summary notes on the previous pages and then complete each chart.

⊙ Supporting Rose's Opinion

Introduction	1
Body 1	2
	3
Body 2	4
	5
Conclusion	6
	7

⊙ Supporting Anthony's Opinion

Introduction	1
Body 1	2
	3
	4
Body 2	5
	6
Conclusion	7

Exercise 2 Follow the directions and write a response. You can refer to the outline and the summary notes.

Your professor is teaching a class on economics. Write a post responding to the professor's question.

In your response you should:

- express and support your personal opinion
- make a contribution to the discussion in your own words

An effective response will contain at least 100 words. You have ten minutes to write.

Professor
Holmes

Everywhere you look, there are signs advertising all kinds of goods. People are encouraged to purchase as many items as they can no matter whether or not they are necessary. Our society has become one based on consumerism. This leads to an important question: Do you think that people consume too much? Why?

📖 **Words & Phrases**

advertise v to promote in an attempt to sell a good or service
no matter phr without regard to
necessary adj needed

be based on phr to have a foundation on
consumerism n the theory that purchasing more goods benefits the economy

✖ **Outline for Brainstorming**

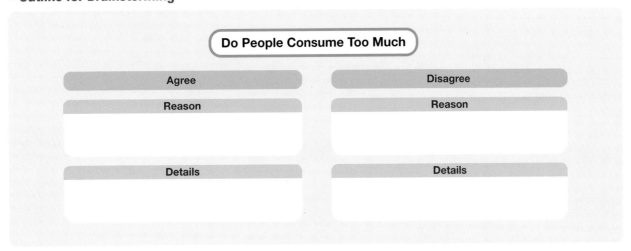

Claude

When I look around my dorm room, I see numerous items I purchased but do not need. Similarly, when I visit my friends' rooms, I notice they have done the same thing as me. Overconsumption is a problem vast numbers of people have to deal with. The astronomical number of ads, commercials, celebrity endorsements, and other inducements to make purchases are too much for most people, myself included, to resist.

Rebecca

While it is true that people are encouraged to consume, I do not accept as true that most people overconsume. For instance, my wardrobe does not contain too many clothes, nor do my friends' wardrobes. I also prefer to borrow books from the library than to purchase them. In fact, I make a conscious effort to limit the number of purchases I make.

📖 Words & Phrases

overconsumption [n] the act of purchasing too much

deal with [phr] to handle

astronomical [adj] very high in number, quantity, or amount

endorsement [n] the act of recommending or promoting someone or something

inducement [n] a motive that causes one to act in a certain way

accept [v] to approve or admit

wardrobe [n] the clothes a person owns

contain [v] to have

borrow [v] to take something with the intention of returning it after a short time

conscious [adj] done or acting with awareness

✍ Summary Notes

Claude	Rebecca

Self-Evaluation Check your response by answering the following questions.

	Yes	No
1 Did you address the professor's question?	☐	☐
2 Did you refer to the comments by the two students?	☐	☐
3 Did you express your own opinion?	☐	☐
4 Did you provide examples to support your opinion?	☐	☐
5 Did you organize your response well?	☐	☐
6 Did you use correct grammar?	☐	☐
7 Did you use correct punctuation?	☐	☐
8 Did you spell all of the words correctly?	☐	☐

Exercise 1 Follow the directions in each step.

Brainstorming & Outlining

A Read the professor's comment and brainstorm some ideas. Then, use the outline to generate your ideas.

Professor Reynolds

Prior to making purchases, particularly ones that require people to spend large sums of money, they often seek the opinions of others. For certain individuals, this means that they ask their friends for advice regarding purchases. For others, they prefer to read online reviews of certain products. Which of these two methods do you prefer? Why?

📖 **Words & Phrases**

sum ⓝ an amount of money
seek ⓥ to look for; to ask for
advice ⓝ a recommendation on an action or a decision
regarding (prep) concerning; with regard to
review ⓝ an evaluation of a product

✖ **Outline for Brainstorming**

Getting Opinions before Making Large Purchases			
Asking Friends for Advice		**Reading Online Reviews**	
Reason 1	Reason 2	Reason 1	Reason 2

B Read the following comments by two students and complete the summary notes.

Orlando

On the rare occasions when I make large purchases, I always ask one or two of my friends whose opinions I value. First of all, they know me and my preferences, so they can provide insight as to whether I should make a purchase. They also have my best interests in mind, so I know I can trust them when they tell me what to buy and avoid.

📖 **Words & Phrases**

value Ⓥ to consider something important

preference Ⓝ the fact of liking one thing more than another

insight Ⓝ an understand of what something is like

trust Ⓥ to believe

avoid Ⓥ to prevent something bad from happening

📝 **Summary Notes:** Orlando

Asking Friends for Advice

1 Ask 1) ....

  • Value their 2) ....

  • Know 3) ....

  • Can provide 4) .... regarding 5) ....

2 Have 6) .... in mind

  • Can trust when they say to 7) ....

Sally

I always make sure to peruse online reviews of products I am contemplating purchasing. People who post reviews typically have a considerable amount of knowledge about the products, so they can provide excellent evaluations of them. Online reviews also frequently compare and contrast two or more products. As a result, I sometimes change my mind and make different purchases than what I had intended after reading online reviews.

📖 **Words & Phrases**

peruse Ⓥ to examine; to read over

contemplate Ⓥ to consider; to give serious thought to

post Ⓥ to publish online, often on an Internet forum

evaluation Ⓝ a critical review

intend Ⓥ to plan; to have in mind

📝 **Summary Notes:** Sally

Reading Online Reviews

1 Reviewers have 1) ....

  • Provide 2) ....

2 May 3) .... 2+ products

  • Make me 4) ....

  • Make 5) .... than had intended

Review the outline and the summary notes on the previous pages and then complete each chart.

⊙ Supporting Orlando's Opinion

Introduction	1	
Body 1	2	
	3	
	4	
Body 2	5	
	6	
Conclusion	7	

⊙ Supporting Sally's Opinion

Introduction	1	
Body 1	2	
	3	
Body 2	4	
	5	
Conclusion	6	

Exercise 2 Follow the directions and write a response. You can refer to the outline and the summary notes.

Your professor is teaching a class on sociology. Write a post responding to the professor's question.

In your response you should:

- express and support your personal opinion
- make a contribution to the discussion in your own words

An effective response will contain at least 100 words. You have ten minutes to write.

Professor
Sullivan

I want you to consider an important aspect of your personal behavior. When you are absent from school and are residing at your homes, how do you prefer to consume your meals? Do you prefer to eat meals cooked at home by yourself or a family member? Or do you prefer dining out at restaurants? Why?

📖 **Words & Phrases**

aspect ⓝ an appearance
absent adj away from
reside ⓥ to live at

consume ⓥ to eat
dine out ⓥ to eat at a restaurant

✖ **Outline for Brainstorming**

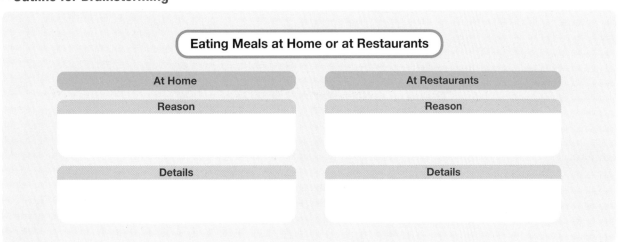

Mary

My mother is a fabulous cook, and my dad can grill all kinds of foods, so the choice is simple for me. I would much rather stay at home and eat dinner with my family than go out to a restaurant. For one thing, restaurants are expensive and often provide poor service. For another thing, I love sitting at home, having dinner, and chatting with my parents and sister.

Douglas

I prefer to dine at restaurants than to cook dinner at home. When I am home, I am always occupied doing something, so I lack the hour or two necessary to prepare a meal. For me, it is more convenient to visit a restaurant and to order dinner. I know some restaurants which serve wholesome, filling food for low prices, so I am a regular at them.

📖 Words & Phrases

fabulous adj wonderful; amazing
grill v to cook food on bars over heat
rather v to prefer
service n the act of serving
chat v to talk in a casual manner

occupied adj busy
lack v not to have something
serve v to provide a person with food
wholesome adj good for a person's health or wellbeing
filling adj making a person feel full

📝 Summary Notes

Mary	Douglas

_____

_____

_____

_____

_____

_____

_____

_____

_____

_____

_____

_____

_____

_____

_____

_____

Self-Evaluation Check your response by answering the following questions.

	Yes	No
1 Did you address the professor's question?	☐	☐
2 Did you refer to the comments by the two students?	☐	☐
3 Did you express your own opinion?	☐	☐
4 Did you provide examples to support your opinion?	☐	☐
5 Did you organize your response well?	☐	☐
6 Did you use correct grammar?	☐	☐
7 Did you use correct punctuation?	☐	☐
8 Did you spell all of the words correctly?	☐	☐

Exercise 1 Follow the directions in each step.

Brainstorming & Outlining

A Read the professor's comment and brainstorm some ideas. Then, use the outline to generate your ideas.

Professor Carlton

Numerous city roads are in poor condition and need repairs. Yet city governments often claim they lack the money to pay for repairs. Would you be in favor of raising local taxes to pay for road repairs? Or do you believe that all local vehicle owners should pay a yearly fee that will be used to improve the roads? Why do you prefer this choice?

📕 **Words & Phrases**

numerous (adj) many; great in number or amount
claim (v) to declare; to say that something is true
raise (v) to increase
tax (n) money that must be paid to a government
fee (n) an amount of money paid for a service

✖ **Outline for Brainstorming**

Who Pays for Road Repairs			
Taxpayers		**Vehicle Owners**	
Reason 1	Reason 2	Reason 1	Reason 2

B Read the following comments by two students and complete the summary notes.

Kaye

Given the two choices, I would opt for the former one. There is nothing wrong with raising local taxes so long as taxpayers know how the money will be spent. Improving infrastructure such as roads is a worthy cause and something the government should do. If sales taxes are raised by one percent, that should provide enough funding for road repairs.

📕 **Words & Phrases**

opt (v) to choose
former (n) the first of two things that are listed
taxpayer (n) a person who pays taxes to the government

worthy (adj) having value
funding (n) money that is available for a specific use

✏️ **Summary Notes: Kaye**

Taxpayers
1 Okay to 1) ....
• Taxpayers know how 2) ....
• Improving 3) .... = 4) .... government should do
2 Raise sales taxes by 5) ....
• Can provide enough for 6) ....

Scott

It seems profoundly unfair to me that everyone who lives in a city should have to pay for something they do not use. Vehicle owners are the ones who use the roads, so they should cover the cost of repairs. I never drive or even take the bus. I walk everywhere I go, so I do not want to pay for something of no use to me.

📕 **Words & Phrases**

profoundly (adv) exceedingly; very
unfair (adj) being unjust or deceptive
owner (n) a person who has property, a possession, etc.

cover (v) to pay for
drive (v) to operate a motor vehicle

✏️ **Summary Notes: Scott**

Vehicle Owners
1 1) .... to make people pay for something they 2) ....
• Vehicle owners 3) ....
• Should pay 4) ....
2 Never drives or 5) ....
• 6) .... everywhere
• Doesn't want to pay for something 7) ....

Review the outline and the summary notes on the previous pages and then complete each chart.

⊙ Supporting Kaye's Opinion

Introduction	1
Body 1	2
	3
Body 2	4
	5
Conclusion	6

⊙ Supporting Scott's Opinion

Introduction	1
Body 1	2
	3
Body 2	4
	5
Conclusion	6
	7

Your professor is teaching a class on urban development. Write a post responding to the professor's question.

In your response you should:

- express and support your personal opinion
- make a contribution to the discussion in your own words

An effective response will contain at least 100 words. You have ten minutes to write.

Professor Reyes

Let's think about public libraries and their collections. Many libraries are still purchasing printed books despite a lack of space. They must often dispose of old books in their collections to make room for new ones. If they were to acquire e-books, however, there would be no space considerations. Do you believe that libraries should focus on buying e-books instead of printed books? Why?

📘 Words & Phrases

collection n an accumulation of similar items; all the books in a library

despite prep in spite of

dispose v to throw away

space n room; an area

consideration n a matter that a person must think about

✖ Outline for Brainstorming

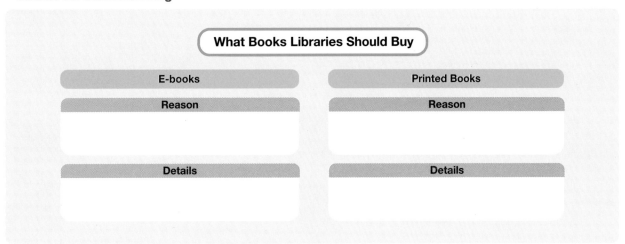

What Books Libraries Should Buy

E-books	Printed Books
Reason	Reason
Details	Details

Donald

I adore public libraries yet abhor how they dispose of books in their collections when they run out of room. Many of the books they are discarding are out of print and hard for people to find. Libraries should try to build up their collections as much as possible, and the best way to do this, thanks to modern technology, is to acquire e-books that they can lend to patrons.

Wendy

I harbor a strong distrust of e-books and only like to read printed books. The reason is that e-books can be updated without the owner's consent and may even be deleted from the owner's collection at times. Printed books never change, so libraries should get them. They can always put books people seldom read in storage and take them out upon request if space is a problem.

📖 Words & Phrases

adore v to love

abhor v to hate

discard v to throw away

out of print adj no longer available from a publisher

patron n a person who uses a facility such as a library

harbor v to hold in one's mind or thoughts

distrust n the absence of trust or belief

consent n approval

seldom adv rarely; occasionally

storage n a place where unneeded items are kept

☑ Summary Notes

Donald	Wendy

_____

_____

_____

_____

_____

_____

_____

_____

_____

_____

_____

_____

_____

_____

Self-Evaluation Check your response by answering the following questions.

	Yes	No
1 Did you address the professor's question?	☐	☐
2 Did you refer to the comments by the two students?	☐	☐
3 Did you express your own opinion?	☐	☐
4 Did you provide examples to support your opinion?	☐	☐
5 Did you organize your response well?	☐	☐
6 Did you use correct grammar?	☐	☐
7 Did you use correct punctuation?	☐	☐
8 Did you spell all of the words correctly?	☐	☐

Exercise 1 Follow the directions in each step.

Brainstorming & Outlining

A Read the professor's comment and brainstorm some ideas. Then, use the outline to generate your ideas.

Professor
Robinson

The economy is cyclical, so sometimes there are periods of expansion while other times there are recessions or even depressions when the economy declines. During poor economic times, people often turn to the government to take action to help citizens. Here is a question for the discussion board: What is the best action the government can take during a poor economy?

📕 **Words & Phrases**

cyclical adj relating to moving in a cycle
expansion n the act of becoming bigger
recession n a period of declining economic production lasting at least a few months
depression n an extended period of declining economic production lasting two or more years
turn to phr to look to

✖ **Outline for Brainstorming**

Government Actions during a Poor Economy	
Provide Loans to Companies	**Provide Extended Unemployment Benefits**
Reason 1	Reason 2	Reason 1	Reason 2

B Read the following comments by two students and complete the summary notes.

Allen

There are many actions the government can take, but the best would be to provide loans to companies suffering financially. The one condition for receiving a loan would be that the company could not fire any of its employees. The company could instead use the loaned money to pay its employees' salaries. This would result in fewer people losing their jobs, which would be helpful during tough economic times.

 Words & Phrases

loan n money a person borrows that must be paid back with interest
financially adv with respect to money

condition n a stipulation; something necessary for an agreement to be fulfilled
fire v to dismiss a person from a job
salary n money a person earns, often monthly, for doing a job

☑ Summary Notes: Allen

Provide Loans to Companies

1 Provide loans to companies 1) ....

   • Can't fire employees if 2) ....

2 Use 3) .... to pay salaries

   • Fewer people 4) ....

   • Helpful in tough 5) ....

Robyn

When the economy is in bad shape, people often lose their jobs. They also commonly have trouble finding replacement positions. When people get laid off, they can usually collect unemployment benefits for approximately six months. But during a recession or depression, that is not enough time to find new work. The government should therefore extend unemployment benefits for up to a year, which would help people immeasurably.

☐ Words & Phrases

shape n a condition
replacement adj substitute; being used in place of another thing

get laid off phr to lose one's job
extend v to make longer
immeasurably adv vastly; greatly

☑ Summary Notes: Robyn

Provide Extended Unemployment Benefits

1 People lose jobs → trouble finding 1) ....

   • Collect unemployment benefits for 2) ....

   • Not enough in 3) ....

2 4) .... for one year

   • Help people 5) ....

Review the outline and the summary notes on the previous pages and then complete each chart.

⊙ Supporting New Ideas: Decreasing Taxes

Introduction	1
	2
Body 1	3
	4
Body 2	5
	6
	7
	8
Conclusion	9

⊙ Supporting New Ideas: Doing Nothing

Introduction	1
	2
Body 1	3
	4
	5
Body 2	6
	7
Conclusion	8
	9

Exercise 2 Follow the directions and write a response. You can refer to the outline and the summary notes.

Your professor is teaching a class on economics. Write a post responding to the professor's question.

In your response you should:

- express and support your opinion
- make a contribution to the discussion

An effective response will contain at least 100 words. You will have 10 minutes to write it.

Professor
Kennedy

After graduating, most students will enter the workforce as they initiate their careers. A large percentage of students opt to work for large corporations whereas a smaller number of them become entrepreneurs and start their own businesses. When you conclude your studies, what would you rather do? Would you prefer to be employed at a large corporation or to go into business for yourself? Why?

📖 **Words & Phrases**

initiate v to start
opt v to choose; to decide
whereas conj while; however

entrepreneur n a businessperson
conclude v to end; to finish

✖ **Outline for Brainstorming**

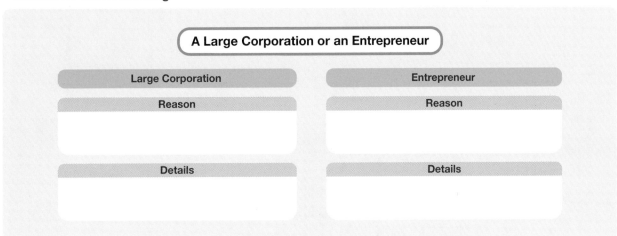

Wanda

For me, the choice is a simple one. I would choose to find a position at a large corporation. For one thing, large corporations are mostly financially stable, so I would probably be guaranteed a job so long as I worked hard and competently. For another thing, large corporations offer employees the opportunity to be promoted. This would let me improve both my rank and my salary.

Stuart

I am planning to become an entrepreneur after college. Being a business owner would give me freedom I could never have if working for someone else. In addition, if I come up with something original or become a pioneer in my industry, there is a chance I could have phenomenal success and maybe even become a billionaire. I just need to work hard and be a bit fortunate.

📖 Words & Phrases

position n a job
stable adj steady; constant
guarantee v to provide security to
competently adv capably
be promoted phr to be given a higher ranking or better job

come up with phr to think of; to create
pioneer n a person who helps start a new activity
phenomenal adj remarkable; extraordinary
billionaire n a person with at least one billion dollars
fortunate adj lucky

☑ Summary Notes

Wanda	Stuart

		Yes	No
Self-Evaluation Check your response by answering the following questions.			
1	Did you address the professor's question?	☐	☐
2	Did you refer to the comments by the two students?	☐	☐
3	Did you express your own opinion?	☐	☐
4	Did you provide examples to support your opinion?	☐	☐
5	Did you organize your response well?	☐	☐
6	Did you use correct grammar?	☐	☐
7	Did you use correct punctuation?	☐	☐
8	Did you spell all of the words correctly?	☐	☐

Exercise 1 Follow the directions in each step.

Brainstorming & Outlining

A Read the professor's comment and brainstorm some ideas. Then, use the outline to generate your ideas.

Professor
Davis

One way to help preserve precious natural resources is to recycle glass, plastic, paper, and metal items. By recycling these materials, we can also reduce waste and pollution. However, some people claim that recycling is pointless and offers few benefits. Here is a question for you: Should people be obligated to recycle? Why do you think so?

📖 **Words & Phrases**

precious adj valuable
waste n the act of using something improperly
pointless adj senseless; having no use or meaning
offer v to provide
obligate v to require; to force

✖ **Outline for Brainstorming**

Being Obligated to Recycle			
Agree		**Disagree**	
Reason 1	Reason 2	Reason 1	Reason 2

B Read the following comments by two students and complete the summary notes.

Henry

I wholeheartedly agree that everyone should be required to recycle. Think of how many plastic bottles most people use in a week. If they throw those bottles out, garbage dumps will become full too quickly. By recycling them, we can decrease the amount of trash created and also get additional usage out of the materials they are made of. The same is true of other recyclable items.

📖 **Words & Phrases**

wholeheartedly adv enthusiastically; totally

garbage dump n a landfill; a place where garbage is taken and deposited

trash n garbage

usage n the act of using something

recyclable adj able to be recycled

📝 **Summary Notes: Henry**

Agree
1 Lots of plastic bottles used 1) ....
• Fill up 2) .... if throw out
2 Recycle 3) ....
• 4) .... trash created
• Get 5) .... of materials
• Same for other 6) ....

I do not believe in forcing anyone to recycle even though I believe recycling is advantageous to the environment. I am against the government making people do certain activities even if they are for the common good. As a general rule, the majority of people will do the right thing without being forced to do it. If a small minority do not recycle, that is acceptable to me.

Geena

📖 **Words & Phrases**

force v to make a person do something

advantageous adj beneficial; helpful

the common good phr the advantage of everyone; the public good

as a general rule phr for the most part; generally speaking

minority n the smaller of two groups

📝 **Summary Notes: Geena**

Disagree
1 Don't believe in 1) ....
• Against 2) .... making people do activities
• Shouldn't do even if for 3) ....
2 Majority of people will 4) ....
• 5) .... might not recycle → is okay

Review the outline and the summary notes on the previous pages and then complete each chart.

⊙ Supporting Henry's Opinion

Introduction	1
	2
Body 1	3
	4
Body 2	5
	6
Conclusion	7

⊙ Supporting Geena's Opinion

Introduction	1
Body 1	2
	3
Body 2	4
	5
Conclusion	6

Exercise 2 Follow the directions and write a response. You can refer to the outline and the summary notes.

Your professor is teaching a class on environmental science. Write a post responding to the professor's question.

In your response you should:

- express and support your opinion
- make a contribution to the discussion

An effective response will contain at least 100 words. You will have 10 minutes to write it.

Professor
Montague

When humans develop new areas, wild animals lose their habitats. This is causing some animals to become endangered species while others go extinct and disappear forever. Most people recognize the need to protect animals to help them maintain healthy numbers. In your opinion, what is the best way for humans to ensure that various species of animals do not go extinct? Why?

📖 **Words & Phrases**

develop v to use for commercial or residential purposes
wild animal n an animal that lives in nature and is not tame
habitat n a place where an animal lives

forever adv for all time
maintain v to keep

✖ **Outline for Brainstorming**

Ensuring Animals Do Not Go Extinct

Feeding Wild Animals	Restricting Land Development
Reason	Reason
Details	Details

Lee Anne

In my opinion, countries around the world should establish large wildlife preserves in various areas. These would be places where humans are not allowed to develop the land and where animals can live safely in their natural habitats. If enough nations make these wildlife preserves, then animals will be able to live stress-free lives, which will enable them to reproduce in greater numbers.

Anthony

In recent history, many animals have gone extinct or become endangered because of humans. Hunting has caused animals such as the passenger pigeon, which once numbered in the billions, no longer to exist. Governments need to pass laws restricting or even banning the hunting of certain animals. Hunting bans would help certain species of animals, such as mountain lions and wolves, to increase their populations.

📖 Words & Phrases

wildlife preserve [n] a place where animals are protected
natural [adj] relating to nature
nation [n] a country
stress-free [adj] having no stress
reproduce [v] to create offspring

endangered [adj] having reduced numbers
hunting [n] the act of trying to kill animals for sport or food
no longer [phr] not anymore
restrict [v] to restrain; to limit
ban [v] to prohibit; not to allow a certain activity

☑ Summary Notes

Lee Anne	Anthony

Self-Evaluation Check your response by answering the following questions.

	Yes	No
1 Did you address the professor's question?	☐	☐
2 Did you refer to the comments by the two students?	☐	☐
3 Did you express your own opinion?	☐	☐
4 Did you provide examples to support your opinion?	☐	☐
5 Did you organize your response well?	☐	☐
6 Did you use correct grammar?	☐	☐
7 Did you use correct punctuation?	☐	☐
8 Did you spell all of the words correctly?	☐	☐

Actual
Test

Actual Test 01

Writing Section Directions

02-01

In this section, you will be able to demonstrate your ability to use writing to communicate in an academic environment. There will be two writing tasks.

In the first task, you will read a passage about an academic topic; you will have 3 minutes to read it. Then you will listen to a lecture about the same topic. After that, you will have **20 minutes** to combine/summarize what you have listened to and read.

For the second task, you will read an online discussion. A professor has posted a question about a topic, and some classmates have responded with their ideas. You will then write a response that contributes to the discussion. You will have **10 minutes** to write your response.

Your responses will be scored on your ability to write correctly, clearly, and coherently, as well as on your ability to respond to the questions as fully as possible.

Now, listen to the directions for the first writing task.

Writing Based on Reading and Listening
Directions

02-02

For this task, you will have three minutes to read a passage about an academic topic. A clock at the top of the screen will show how much time you have to read. You may take notes while you read. You will be able to see the reading passage again when it is time for you to write. You may use your notes to help you answer the question.

You will then have **20 minutes** to write a response to a question that asks you about the relationship between the lecture you have heard and the reading passage. Try to answer the question as completely as possible using information from the reading passage and the lecture. The question does **not** ask you to express your personal opinion.

Typically, an effective response will be 150 to 225 words. Your response will be judged on the quality of your writing and on the completeness and accuracy of the content.

Now you will see the reading passage for 3 minutes. Remember that it will be available to you again while you are writing. Immediately after the reading time ends, the lecture will begin, so keep your headset on until the lecture has ended.

Task **1**

While there may be a few sound historical reasons for preserving aging buildings, this should not prevent the majority from being torn down so as to make way for new construction. The practice of conserving older buildings should be halted immediately. Old buildings need to make way for new ones.

Buildings considered to be of historical importance are typically protected and even refurbished with government funds. While this practice may be necessary for truly historical important places, such as the birthplace of a president, many old buildings simply do not meet the current criteria established by the government to be called important. They only incur unnecessary government expenditures on maintaining them. Instead, government funds should be redirected toward more worthy causes, including fighting crime and improving schools and hospitals.

Many older buildings are not aesthetically pleasing to look at and in fact serve no practical purpose. The majority of people prefer buildings constructed with modern architectural designs and desire places where they can engage in the activities they want. Older buildings should be torn down to make way for modern ones like shopping centers and places of entertainment. These will satisfy the public's needs much better than old buildings ever will.

Over the years, building codes and standards have changed dramatically. Older buildings simply do not meet these standards. Their water pipes are made from hazardous lead; their electrical systems are old and outdated; they use cancer-causing asbestos as their insulating material. Replacing and upgrading all of these old buildings is both extremely expensive and time consuming. It would actually be safer and financially sounder to remove them.

02-03

Directions You have 20 minutes to plan and write your response. Your response will be judged on the basis of the quality of your writing and on how well your response presents the points in the lecture and their relationship to the reading passage. Typically, an effective response will be 150 to 225 words.

Question Summarize the points made in the lecture, being sure to explain how they cast doubt on specific points made in the reading passage.

Copy   Cut   Paste   Word Count   0

While there may be a few sound historical reasons for preserving aging buildings, this should not prevent the majority from being torn down so as to make way for new construction. The practice of conserving older buildings should be halted immediately. Old buildings need to make way for new ones.

Buildings considered to be of historical importance are typically protected and even refurbished with government funds. While this practice may be necessary for truly historical important places, such as the birthplace of a president, many old buildings simply do not meet the current criteria established by the government to be called important. They only incur unnecessary government expenditures on maintaining them. Instead, government funds should be redirected toward more worthy causes, including fighting crime and improving schools and hospitals.

Many older buildings are not aesthetically pleasing to look at and in fact serve no practical purpose. The majority of people prefer buildings constructed with modern architectural designs and desire places where they can engage in the activities they want. Older buildings should be torn down to make way for modern ones like shopping centers and places of entertainment. These will satisfy the public's needs much better than old buildings ever will.

Over the years, building codes and standards have changed dramatically. Older buildings simply do not meet these standards. Their water pipes are made from hazardous lead; their electrical systems are old and outdated; they use cancer-causing asbestos as their insulating material. Replacing and upgrading all of these old buildings is both extremely expensive and time consuming. It would actually be safer and financially sounder to remove them.

Writing for an Academic Discussion
Directions

For this task, you will read an online discussion. A professor has posted a question about a topic, and some classmates have responded with their ideas.

Write a response that contributes to the discussion. You will have **10 minutes** to write your response. It is important to use your own words in the response.

Typically, an effective essay will contain a minimum of 100 words.

Click on **Continue** to go on.

Task 2

Your professor is teaching a class on business. Write a post responding to the professor's question.

In your response you should:

- express and support your opinion
- make a contribution to the discussion

An effective response will contain at least 100 words. You will have 10 minutes to write it.

Professor Wilkins

Next week, we are going to talk about small businesses. Small businesses are vital to the country because they employ millions of people. Many times, when people go into business, they have a partner or two. So here is a question for you to consider: Do you think it is a good idea for people to go into business with members of their own family? Why?

Melissa

I fully support family members going into business together. They typically know one another well, so they are familiar with how each person will work. In addition, family members are more willing to work hard in order to make their company succeed. My father and uncle are in business together, and they have a great working relationship.

Chris

I do not believe it is a good idea for family members to go into business together. For one thing, when there are problems, they can affect other family members, especially when the issues are financial in nature. Another thing to consider is that some family members may not have the knowledge or expertise necessary to run a business, so they may hinder rather than help the business.

Copy　Cut　Paste　　　　　　　　　　　Word Count 0

Actual Test 02

02-04

Writing Section Directions

In this section, you will be able to demonstrate your ability to use writing to communicate in an academic environment. There will be two writing tasks.

In the first task, you will read a passage about an academic topic; you will have 3 minutes to read it. Then you will listen to a lecture about the same topic. After that, you will have **20 minutes** to combine/summarize what you have listened to and read.

For the second task, you will read an online discussion. A professor has posted a question about a topic, and some classmates have responded with their ideas. You will then write a response that contributes to the discussion. You will have **10 minutes** to write your response.

Your responses will be scored on your ability to write correctly, clearly, and coherently, as well as on your ability to respond to the questions as fully as possible.

Now, listen to the directions for the first writing task.

Writing Based on Reading and Listening
Directions

02-05

For this task, you will have three minutes to read a passage about an academic topic. A clock at the top of the screen will show how much time you have to read. You may take notes while you read. You **will** be able to see the reading passage again when it is time for you to write. You may use your notes to help you answer the question.

You will then have **20 minutes** to write a response to a question that asks you about the relationship between the lecture you have heard and the reading passage. Try to answer the question as completely as possible using information from the reading passage and the lecture. The question does **not** ask you to express your personal opinion.

Typically, an effective response will be 150 to 225 words. Your response will be judged on the quality of your writing and on the completeness and accuracy of the content.

Now you will see the reading passage for 3 minutes. Remember that it will be available to you again while you are writing. Immediately after the reading time ends, the lecture will begin, so keep your headset on until the lecture has ended.

Task **1**

While print media has long dominated news sources, it is quickly being crowded out by online media. In fact, the day may come in the near future when the last newspaper will be published.

The news found on the Internet is both fast and up to date. When a newsworthy event happens anywhere around the world, it can almost instantly be found on a majority of news servers. For example, once a sporting event finishes, within a few minutes, a complete recap and an analysis of the game is typically available on the Internet. With print media, a person has to wait until the next day—or even two days if the event happened after the paper has already gone to press—to learn about the news.

Online news is diversified, which means people can read whatever they want from wherever they want. For instance, a person who enjoys entertainment can find hundreds of sites covering that. People can even get alerts sent to them by email when something noteworthy happens to their favorite celebrity or when there is some news about a show they might like. With print media, a person has to wade through all of the other news in order to find what he or she is interested in.

Online media can also provide current, instantaneous news from around the world, not just regional or national coverage. People can read about news from anywhere which is not sanitized like much of print media is. Print media, and even television news, typically concentrate on local and national stories, and their content is heavily edited. It is often hard to know the truth when reading print media.

02-06

Directions You have 20 minutes to plan and write your response. Your response will be judged on the basis of the quality of your writing and on how well your response presents the points in the lecture and their relationship to the reading passage. Typically, an effective response will be 150 to 225 words.

Question Summarize the points made in the lecture, being sure to explain how they cast doubt on specific points made in the reading passage.

Copy   Cut   Paste   Word Count 0

While print media has long dominated news sources, it is quickly being crowded out by online media. In fact, the day may come in the near future when the last newspaper will be published.

The news found on the Internet is both fast and up to date. When a newsworthy event happens anywhere around the world, it can almost instantly be found on a majority of news servers. For example, once a sporting event finishes, within a few minutes, a complete recap and an analysis of the game is typically available on the Internet. With print media, a person has to wait until the next day—or even two days if the event happened after the paper has already gone to press—to learn about the news.

Online news is diversified, which means people can read whatever they want from wherever they want. For instance, a person who enjoys entertainment can find hundreds of sites covering that. People can even get alerts sent to them by email when something noteworthy happens to their favorite celebrity or when there is some news about a show they might like. With print media, a person has to wade through all of the other news in order to find what he or she is interested in.

Online media can also provide current, instantaneous news from around the world, not just regional or national coverage. People can read about news from anywhere which is not sanitized like much of print media is. Print media, and even television news, typically concentrate on local and national stories, and their content is heavily edited. It is often hard to know the truth when reading print media.

Writing for an Academic Discussion
Directions

For this task, you will read an online discussion. A professor has posted a question about a topic, and some classmates have responded with their ideas.

Write a response that contributes to the discussion. You will have **10 minutes** to write your response. It is important to use your own words in the response.

Typically, an effective essay will contain a minimum of 100 words.

Click on **Continue** to go on.

Task 2

Your professor is teaching a class on sociology. Write a post responding to the professor's question.

In your response you should:

- express and support your opinion
- make a contribution to the discussion

An effective response will contain at least 100 words. You will have 10 minutes to write it.

Professor Collins

Now that the school year is coming to an end, many people, particularly students and their families, are making plans to take trips. When people travel, some prefer to have all of their activities planned out ahead of time. However, others prefer not to have any plans when they travel. Which kind of traveler are you, and why do you prefer that method of travel?

Gregory

I cannot understand why anyone would travel, especially to a foreign country, without having any plans. I am the type of person who wants to know precisely what I am going to be doing each day of my trip. That lets me prepare ahead of time and enables me to know what to bring on my trip. I do this whenever I travel and always have wonderful trips.

Carmen

I do not travel often, but when I do, I like to make each day a surprise. I therefore do not make any plans other than reserving a hotel room. Sometimes I just remain at my hotel and relax, but other times, I may hear about an interesting place from another traveler, so I go there. This method lets me enjoy my time away from home.

| Copy | Cut | Paste | Word Count | 0 |

How to
Master Skills for the
TOEFL® iBT
WRITING

Answers, Scripts, and Translations

Advanced

DARAKWON

How to
Master Skills for the

TOEFL® iBT
WRITING Advanced

| Answers, Scripts,
and Translations

DARAKWON

Unit 01 Anthropology

Exercise 1 .... p.14

Reading

해석

오늘날 미국 남서부의 일부 주가 위치한 지역에, 때때로 푸에블로 인디언이라고 불리기도 하는, 아나사지 인디언들이 살았다. 아나사지인들의 역사는 선사 시대로 거슬러 올라간다. 이들은 약 1150년까지 수백 년 동안의 황금기를 경험하기도 했다. 하지만 아나사지인들은 그 후 2세기만에 갑자기 사라졌다. 많은 인류학자들은 그들의 소멸이 전쟁 때문이라고 생각한다.

고고학자들은 과거 아나사지 정착지의 유적을 철저히 조사해 왔다. 그들이 알아낸 한 가지 특징은 불에 탄 장소가 많다는 것이다. 심지어 아나사지인들이 의식을 거행하던 일부 장소들도 불에 탔다. 이는 그러한 화재가 전쟁을 일으킨 부족의 침입 때문에 발생했다는 점을 강력히 시사한다. 많은 미 인디언 부족들은 전쟁에서 무찌른 부족의 주거지를 불태우곤 했다. 아나사지인들의 거주지가 불에 탔다는 사실은 그들 역시 분명 정복을 당했을 것이라는 점을 보여 준다.

고고학자들은 또한 동일한 유적지에서 아나사지족 사람들이 소장했던 다수의 개인 물품들을 발굴했다. 도자기, 보석, 기타 개인 물품을 포함하여, 이들 중 다수는 소유주에게 귀중한 물건이었을 것이다. 대부분의 경우 소유주가 그 물건들을 버리지는 않았을 것이다. 하지만 많은 사람들은 갑작스런 전쟁의 발발로 소유주가 살해당했거나 혹은 다가오는 적들로부터 달아나느라 그들에게 소장품을 챙길 시간이 없었을 것으로 생각한다.

또한 아나사지족과 관련된 지리적 특성도 존재한다. 그들의 주거지는, 주로 현재의 애리조나와 뉴멕시코에 해당되는데, 미국 남서부 지역치고는 특이하게도 풍부한 수원을 가진 지역에 위치해 있었다. 당연히 그처럼 풍요로운 지역을 탐낸 다른 부족들이 아나사지인을 상대로 전쟁을 일으켜 이들을 몰아내려고 했을 것이고, 그러한 시도는 성공했던 것으로 보인다.

Note Taking

1) Invading Indian tribes
2) conquered by others
3) pottery, jewelry, & personal effects
4) suddenly killed / driven away by enemies
5) Settled in area with abundant water sources

Listening

Script 🎧 01-02

M Professor: That concludes my lecture on the golden age of the Anasazi. Strangely enough, relatively soon after that age ended, the Anasazi disappeared as a culture. The question, of course, is . . . Why did they disappear? Many of my colleagues suggest war was the reason. However, I, and some other anthropologists, subscribe to a, uh, a different theory. We believe that it was due to a water shortage that the Anasazi disappeared.

First, there is the curious feature of the burned areas around Anasazi settlements. Remember that some of these burned areas include their ritual sites. Well, some of us believe that it was the Anasazi themselves who burned their own sites. No, seriously. We think they were holding ceremonies in which they burned their own sites in a plea to their gods to help them find new sites with access to water.

Another point of interest at many digs is the large number of scattered articles. Normally, archaeologists don't find this many objects of importance at a dig site. However, the evidence again points to a, er, water shortage. The Anasazi, thirsting for water, simply had no need for extra personal belongings, so they left them in their settlements when they departed in search of new homes.

Finally, let me again call your attention to the fact that the Anasazi had just enjoyed a golden age in which their population increased to almost, uh, let me think . . . ah, yes, ten times its original number. Ten times. When the rains began to fall less frequently, what was once a land with lots of water suddenly became barren and dry. What few water supplies remained simply could not satisfy such a large population. This, in turn, led to the rapid decline and eventual disappearance of the Anasazi Indians.

해석

M Professor: 이것으로 아나사지인들의 황금기에 대한 강의는 마치도록 하죠. 이상하게도 그러한 시기가 끝나고 얼마 되지 않아서 아나사지 문화는 사라졌어요. 물론 궁금한 점은… 왜 사라졌을까요? 많은 동료 학자들은 전쟁이 원인이었다고 주장합니다. 하지만 저를 비롯한 몇몇 인류학자들은, 어, 다른 이론을 지지하죠. 우리는 아나사지인들이 사라진 것이 물 부족 때문이었다고 생각합니다.

첫째, 아나사지인들의 주거지 주변에 불에 탄 곳이 있다는 점은 흥미로운 부분입니다. 이들 화재 지역의 일부에는 의식을 치루었던 곳이 포함된다는 점을 기억하세요. 음, 우리 중 일부는 바로 아나사지인들 스스로가 자신들의 장소를 불태웠다고 믿습니다. 아니에요, 농담이 아닙니다. 우리는 그들이 새로운 수원을 찾게 해 달라고 신에게 간청하면서 자신들의 장소를 태우는 의식을 치루었다고 생각해요.

많은 발굴 현장에서 관심을 끄는 또 다른 요인은 다수의 유물들이 흩어져 있다는 점입니다. 보통은 고고학자들이 한 발굴 현장에서 중요한 유물들을 이처럼 많이 발견하지는 못해요. 하지만 이러한 증거는 또 다시, 어, 물 부족을 가리킵니다. 물을 갈망하던 아나사지인들은 여분의 개인 소지품들을 필요로 하지 않았기 때문에 새로운 주거지를 찾아 떠나면서 이들을 살던 곳에 두고 갔던 것입니다.

마지막으로 아나사지족이 황금기를 누렸던 때는 인구가 처음 인구의 거의, 어, 그러니까… 아, 그래요, 10배 정도 증가한 때였다는 사실을 다시 한번 알려드리죠. 10배입니다. 비가 오는 횟수가 줄어들기 시작하면서 한때 수량이 풍부했던 땅이 갑자기 건조하고 메마른 곳으로 바뀌었습니다. 남아 있는 물이 거의 없어지자 그처럼 많은 인구를 감당할 수가 없었을 거예요. 이로 인해 아나사지 인디언들은 급격히 쇠퇴하기 시작해서 결국 소멸하게 되었습니다.

1) Part of ceremonies 2 beg gods 4 new places with water
2) Left for new places with water
3) 2 many people 2 support w/o water
4) 10 times
5) Rain stopped falling

Comparing the Points

Reading	Listening
Stance The Anasazi disappeared because they were defeated in wars with other tribes.	**Stance** The Anasazi disappeared because of a lack of water.
Main point 1 Many of their settlements were burned by invaders.	**Refutation 1** They burned their own settlements in ceremonies to their gods.
Main point 2 They left their personal items since they were killed or driven away by enemies.	**Refutation 2** They left their personal belongings behind while searching for new lands with enough water.
Main point 3 They lived on land with abundant water sources that were desired by other tribes.	**Refutation 3** They had too large of a population to support without enough water.

Synthesizing

1   The reading passage states that many archaeologists believe the Anasazi disappeared all of a sudden because of war; however, the professor insists that a water shortage actually caused them to disappear.

2   Although the author of the reading claims that the Anasazi must have been defeated in war because their settlements were burned, the professor counters that argument by asserting that these sites were burned by the Anasazi themselves in rituals to their gods during which they prayed for help in finding new sources of water.

3   While the reading mentions that the Anasazi either died when the invaders attacked or they fled their enemies without taking their possessions, the professor believes that the Anasazi left all of their unnecessary belongings behind when they abandoned their homes to find new places with water.

4   In contrast to the reading, which claims that other tribes were naturally jealous of the Anasazi's water-rich lands and thus attacked and defeated them, the professor states that the Anasazi's increased population could not survive on the small amount of water that remained.

Organization

1   The reading claims that the Anasazi Indians disappeared suddenly because they were defeated in war.

2   The professor, meanwhile, states that a lack of water caused them to vanish.

3   First, the reading declares that conquering Indian tribes, as was their tradition, burned the Anasazi settlements.

4   The professor, however, claims that these settlements were burned by the Anasazi themselves.

5   He thinks they were holding ceremonies to appease their gods and to beg for water, and they burned their own sites as part of the rituals.

6   Second, the professor claims that the large numbers of personal items archaeologists have found in Anasazi sites were left there intentionally since they did not need them in their search for water.

7   The reading, on the other hand, makes the argument that the Anasazi left them either when they were defeated in war or fleeing invaders.

8   Finally, although the reading mentions that invaders, eager to settle on the Anasazi's water-rich lands, took the lands from the Anasazi in war, the professor states that the Anasazi's large population increase proved fatal to them when the rain stopped falling.

9   According to him, their population rose ten times during the golden age, but it decreased rapidly as they suffered severely from a lack of water supplies.

10   In conclusion, the professor believes that a lack of water caused the Anasazi's downfall while the reading attributes it to war.

Exercise 2 .... p.18

Reading

해석

네안데르탈인은 약 13만년에서 5만년 전에 살았던 고대 인류였다. 그들은 주로 현재의 유럽과 서아시아에 해당하는 지역에 거주했다. 인류학자들이 네안데르탈인의 모든 것에 대해 알지는 못하지만 많은 학자들은 네안데르탈인이 실제로 언어를 구사했다는 결론에 도달했다.

다수의 화석 잔해를 조사함으로써 인류학자들은 네안데르탈인의 뇌가 컸다는 점을 알게 되었다. 실제로 네안데르탈인의 뇌 용량은 현대 인류 보다 10% 정도 더 컸다. 인류학자들은 그처럼 커다란 뇌를 지닌 네안데르탈인들이 틀림없이 언어를 통해 커뮤니케이션을 했을 것이라고 생각한다.

약 20년 전에 네안데르탈인의 설골이 발견되었다. 설골은 후두와 혀 사이의 근육을 연결하는 뼈이다. 이 뼈는 매우 다양한 방식으로 혀를 움직일 수 있게 만들기 때문에 언어 구사의 가능성이 더 높아진다. 이는 네안데르탈인이 말을 할 수 있었고 이러한 능력을 활용했을 가능성이 높다는 점을 입증해 준다.

또한 연구자들은 네안데르탈인의 복부에 다양한 근육이 발달해 있었다는 점을 알아냈다. 이러한 근육은 호흡을 조절하는 기능뿐만 아니라 말을 하기 위해 필요한 소리를 내는 것에도 도움이 되었다. 인간도 가지고 있는 이러한 근육 덕분에 또 다시 네안데르탈인은 언어로 의사소통을 했을 가능성이 높다. 따라서 네안데르탈인이 말을 할 수 있었고 실제로 언어를 사용해서 서로 의사소통을 했다는 점은 명백하다.

Neanderthals Could Speak

1 Large brains
- Had cranial capacity 10% bigger than modern humans
- Large brain ➡ ability to speak
2 Hyoid bone between larynx & tongue
- Allows one to move one's tongue in many diff. directions ➡ more likelihood of speech communication
3 Various muscles in stomach area
- Control breathing
- Help create sounds of speech

Listening

Script 🎧 01-03

W Professor: Now, there are many controversies in the field of anthropology. And one of the biggest is over Neanderthals. Some anthropologists allege that Neanderthals actually had the ability to speak. Ludicrous, I say. I believe they couldn't be more wrong in their analysis. Please let me give you the reasons I feel that way.

A lot has been made about the fact that Neanderthals had large brains. In fact, they had brains which were somewhat larger than ours. But remember . . . The size of the brain isn't the most important aspect. Its complexity is more important. And, simply put, Neanderthals did not have the complex brains necessary to enable them to, uh, speak.

Here's something else. Your book mentions the finding of the hyoid bone in some Neanderthal remains. Okay, yes, the hyoid bone does permit the tongue to have a much wider range of movement. However, that alone does not guarantee that they would've been able to speak. Why do I say this? Well, several species of monkeys also have that exact same bone, yet they aren't able to speak at all.

Finally, again, I will concede that Neanderthals had highly developed stomach muscles. That much is true. But . . . On the other hand, these muscles do not just affect one's speech production. Basically, they are integral to a person's, uh, Neanderthal's, ability to control his or her breathing. Remember that the Neanderthals lived in harsh climates and had harder lives than we do today. They could've used these muscles to enable them

to travel long distances quickly or even to climb mountains more easily. We shouldn't assume they used those muscles to speak.

W Professor: 자, 인류학 분야에는 많은 논쟁거리가 있습니다. 가장 큰 논란 중 하나가 네안데르탈인에 관한 것이에요. 일부 인류학자들은 실제로 네안데르탈인에게 말을 할 수 있는 능력이 있었다고 주장합니다. 터무니없는 주장이죠. 저는 그들의 분석이 크게 잘못되었다고 생각해요. 그렇게 생각하는 이유를 말씀해 드리죠.

네안데르탈인의 뇌가 컸다는 사실에 대한 많은 증거들이 있습니다. 실제로 우리보다 뇌가 약간 더 컸어요. 하지만 기억하셔야 하는데… 뇌의 크기가 가장 중요한 측면은 아니에요. 복잡성이 더 중요합니다. 간단히 말해서 네안데르탈인은, 어, 말을 하는데 필요한 복잡한 뇌를 가지고 있지 않았습니다.

또 다른 점을 알려 드리죠. 여러분의 교재에는 일부 네안데르탈인의 유해에서 설골이 발견되었다고 나와 있어요. 그래요, 네, 설골로 인해 혀가 움직일 수 있는 범위가 훨씬 더 커질 수 있습니다. 하지만 그것만으로는 그들이 말을 할 수 있었다는 점이 보장되지는 않아요. 제가 왜 이러한 점을 말할까요? 음, 몇몇 종의 원숭이들 또한 동일한 뼈를 가지고 있지만 그들은 전혀 말을 하지 못합니다.

마지막으로 네안데르탈인이 매우 발달된 복부 근육을 가지고 있었다는 점은 저도 인정하죠. 그건 사실이니까요. 하지만… 그러나 이 근육이 발성에만 영향을 미치지는 않습니다. 기본적으로 이들 근육은 사람의, 어, 네안데르탈인의 호흡을 조절하는 능력에 필수적이에요. 네안데르탈인이 가혹한 기후에서 살았고 오늘날 우리보다 힘든 삶을 살았다는 점을 기억하세요. 그들은 이 근육을 이용해 먼 거리를 빠르게 이동하거나 더 쉽게 산을 오를 수도 있었을 거예요. 그들이 이 근육을 사용해서 말을 했다고 가정해서는 안 됩니다.

Neanderthals Couldn't Speak

1 Size of brain ≠ important
- Complexity more important than size
- Lacked brains complex enough to speak
2 Hyoid bone ≠ ability to speak
- Monkeys have hyoid bone ➡ cannot speak
- Stomach muscles for other uses
- Could have used them for travel / climbing

Writing

Sample Response

The author of the reading passage argues that Neanderthals had the capability to speak. Meanwhile, the professor insists that they actually were not able to speak.

To begin with, while the reading passage states that Neanderthals had brains which were ten percent larger than those of modern-day humans, the professor counters by insisting that size is not the most important aspect. She instead believes that complexity is more important. She also states that Neanderthals lacked brains complex enough to speak.

In addition, the professor acknowledges that Neanderthals had hyoid bones. According to the reading, this bone, which enables the tongue to move greatly, facilitated speaking for Neanderthals. However, the professor points out that monkeys also have hyoid bones, yet they cannot speak.

As a final point, both the reading and the lecture mention that Neanderthals had developed muscles in their stomach. To argue against the reading's assertion that these muscles helped Neanderthals to speak, the professor argues that these muscles could have been used for other purposes. Instead, she states that perhaps the muscles helped them travel farther or climb mountains easier.

To conclude, the professor firmly believes that Neanderthals could not speak, and she counters the points made by the reading, whose author thinks Neanderthals had the ability to speak.

해석

읽기 지문의 저자는 네안데르탈인에게 말을 할 수 있는 능력이 있었다고 주장한다. 반면에 교수는 그들이 실제로 말을 하지 못했을 것이라고 주장한다.

우선 읽기 지문은 네안데르탈인의 뇌가 현대 인류의 뇌보다 10% 더 컸다고 주장하지만, 교수는 뇌의 크기가 가장 중요한 요소는 아니라고 말함으로써 이를 반박한다. 그 대신에 복잡성이 더 중요하다고 생각한다. 그녀는 또한 네안데르탈인에게 말을 할 수 있을 정도의 복잡한 뇌가 없었다고 주장한다.

또한 교수는 네안데르탈인에게 설골이 있었다는 점은 인정한다. 읽기 지문에 따르면 혀를 보다 잘 움직일 수 있게 만드는 이 뼈 때문에 네안데르탈인은 말을 할 수 있었을 것이다. 하지만 교수는 원숭이들도 설골을 가지고 있지만 이들이 말을 하지는 못한다고 주장한다.

마지막으로 읽기 지문과 교수 모두 네안데르탈인의 복부 근육이 발달했다는 점을 언급한다. 이 근육이 네안데르탈인의 언어 구사에 도움을 주었다는 읽기 지문의 주장을 반박하기 위해 교수는 이 근육이 다른 목적으로 사용되었을 수도 있다고 주장한다. 그녀는 이 근육이 아마도 빠르게 이동하거나 더 쉽게 산을 오르는데 도움을 주었을 것이라고 주장한다.

결론적으로 교수는 네안데르탈인이 말을 할 수 없었을 것으로 확신하면서 네안데르탈인에게 말을 할 수 있는 능력이 있었다는 읽기 지문의 논점을 반박한다.

Unit 02 Biology I

Exercise 1 .... p.21

Reading

해석

도도새는 인도양의 모리셔스 섬에 자생하는 몸집이 크고 날지 못하는 새였다. 모리셔스 섬은 16세기 후반 네덜란드 정착민에 의해 식민지가 되었는데, 그 후 백 년이 지나기도 전에 마지막 도도새가 자취를 감추었다. 도도새가 자취를 감춘

이유에 대해 여러 가지 추측이 존재하지만 전문가들은 그 이유를 인간의 활동 때문이라고 생각한다.

네덜란드인들이 도착하기 전까지 모리셔스 섬에는 사람이 살지 않았기 때문에 도도새는 사람을 두려워하지 않았고 그 결과 쉽게 사냥을 당했다. 네덜란드인들은 또한 개, 고양이, 돼지, 그리고 다양한 가축과 같은 동물들을 데려왔는데, 이 동물들이 도도새를 사냥하거나 이들의 알과 둥지를 파괴하는 일이 잦았다. 날지 못했던 도도새는 숲이 우거진 땅에 둥지를 짓고 둥지 안에 알을 낳았다. 따라서 알과 새끼 도도새들에게는 포식자들을 막아 줄 아무런 보호 장치가 없었다.

네덜란드인들이 모리셔스 섬을 식민지로 삼았을 때 그들은 빠른 속도로 땅을 농지로 바꾸기 시작했다. 도도새의 자연 서식지인 숲을 밀어 버렸다. 곧 도도새가 둥지를 짓고 알을 낳을 수 있는 장소가 줄어들었다. 또한 도도새는 그 섬에 자생하는 열대 과일을 먹었는데, 네덜란드인들이 나무를 베어 버리자 도도새의 먹이 공급원 중 상당 부분이 파괴되었다.

또한 어떤 사람들은 외부인이 들여온 질병으로 도도새가 모두 자취를 감추었다고 추측한다. 일부 질병은 사람에게서 동물로 전파될 수 있고, 보다 일반적으로는 동물에게서 사람으로 전파될 수 있다. 이로써 도도새가 사실상 하룻밤 사이에 사라진 것이 설명될 수 있다. 새로운 종의 도입은 종종 자생종에게 재앙이 된다. 예를 들어 유럽인 정착민들이 미국에 도착했을 때 많은 미 원주민들은 새로운 질병에 대한 면역력을 가지고 있지 못해서 사망했다. 똑같은 일이 도도새에게 쉽게 일어날 수 있었을 것이다.

📝 Note Taking

1) Hunted the dodos
2) did not fear humans
3) Changed the land for farming
4) destroyed dodos' natural habitat
5) Passed disease on to dodos

Listening

Script 🎧 01-04

M Professor: One of history's great mysteries is the sudden extinction of the dodo bird. It was last spotted in the late seventeenth century on the island of Mauritius, the only place it ever existed. The cause of its extinction isn't precisely known, but it's certain that humans didn't cause it.

Now, the dodo couldn't fly, nor was it very fast. It developed this way for ages because, well, it had no enemies on the island . . . At least not until humans arrived. Yet despite the ease with which they could catch it, the Dutch settlers were disgusted by it. Actually, the Dutch name for the dodo was *walgvogel*, meaning "disgusting bird." Since the meat was tough and bad tasting, people didn't hunt the dodo or try to kill it at all.

Some experts claim that the clearing of trees helped kill off the dodos, which built their nests in forested areas. While the Dutch deforested some areas for farmland, large parts of the island remained intact. Even when the last dodo was spotted in 1662, much land was free from deforestation. Additionally, many other species of birds have survived on the island since humans arrived.

Besides, the dodo, which couldn't fly, didn't make its nests in trees. It made them on the ground. So it's obvious that tree clearing wasn't a reason for the loss of this bird.

Strangely, it may have been nature itself, not humans, which eliminated the dodos. There is evidence that they were already in decline when humans arrived. Massive cyclones struck the island many times in the past, and their high winds may have been responsible for destroying the dodos' nests and eggs while they lay unprotected on the open ground. Perhaps the birds encountered by the Dutch were the last remnants of a once populous species that was already on its way to dying out.

해석

M Professor: 역사상 놀라운 미스터리 중의 하나가 도도새의 갑작스런 멸종입니다. 마지막으로 목격된 곳이 17세기 말의 모리셔스 섬이었는데, 이곳은 도도새의 유일한 서식지였죠. 멸종 원인이 정확히 밝혀지지는 않았지만 인간이 원인이 아니었다는 점은 확실합니다.

자, 도도새는 날지도 못했고 움직임도 그다지 빠르지 않았어요. 오랜 세월 동안 이런 식으로 진화한 것은, 음, 그 섬에 천적이 없기 때문이었는데… 적어도 인간이 도착하기까지는 말이죠. 하지만 네덜란드 정착민들은 도도새를 쉽게 잡을 수 있었음에도 불구하고 그 새를 혐오했어요. 실제로 도도새의 네덜란드 이름은 발그보겔로, "혐오스러운 새"라는 뜻이죠. 고기가 질기고 맛도 없었기 때문에 사람들은 결코 도도새를 사냥하거나 죽이려고 하지 않았어요.

일부 전문가들은 벌목이 도도새의 멸종에 일조했다고 주장하는데, 도도새들은 숲이 우거진 곳에 둥지를 지었습니다. 네덜란드인들이 일부 지역을 개간하기는 했지만 섬의 많은 부분이 손상되지 않은 채로 남아 있었어요. 심지어 마지막 도도새가 목격된 1662년에도 많은 땅이 삼림 파괴를 당하지 않은 상태였죠. 또한 많은 다른 종의 새들은 인간이 도착한 뒤에도 섬에서 생존했어요. 게다가 도도새는 날지 못했기 때문에 나무에 둥지를 짓지 않았습니다. 땅 위에 지었죠. 따라서 벌목이 이 새의 멸종 이유는 아니라는 점이 명백합니다.

이상하겠지만 도도새를 멸종시킨 것은 인간이 아니라 바로 자연일 수도 있어요. 인간이 도착했을 때 이미 도도새의 수가 줄고 있었다는 증거가 존재합니다. 과거에 대규모 싸이클론이 그 섬을 여러 차례 강타해서 거센 바람이 무방비 상태로 땅 위에 노출되어 있던 도도새의 둥지와 알을 파괴했을 수도 있어요. 어쩌면 네덜란드인들이 마주쳤던 새들은, 한때 번성했지만 이미 멸종의 기로에 있던 종의 마지막 일부였을 것입니다.

Note Taking

1) disgusting bird
2) Tough & bad-tasting meat
3) Did not deforest the entire island for farming
4) Dodos did not nest in trees
5) Massive cyclones hit the island

Comparing the Points

Reading	Listening
Stance The actions of humans account for the extinction of the dodo.	**Stance** Humans were not the reason why the dodo became extinct.

Main point 1 Both the Dutch and their animals hunted the dodo.

Main point 2 The Dutch deforested the island, destroying the dodo's nesting grounds and fruit trees used for food.

Main point 3 Diseases brought by the Dutch may have killed many dodos.

Refutation 1 Humans did not hunt dodos because they disliked the taste of the meat.

Refutation 2 The Dutch did not deforest the whole island for farming, and dodos nested on the ground, not in trees.

Refutation 3 Repeated powerful cyclones probably destroyed many dodo nests and eggs.

Synthesizing

1 While the reading attributes the disappearance of the dodo to actions taken by humans, the professor claims humans were not the reason why the dodo disappeared.

2 According to the reading passage, however, the professor makes it clear that the Dutch did not hunt the dodo because they did not enjoy the taste of its meat.

3 A fact mentioned in the reading is that the deforestation policies of the Dutch destroyed the dodos' natural habitats, yet the professor believes this is unimportant because the flightless dodo never made its nests in trees.

4 In opposition to the reading, which claims that a disease introduced by the Dutch killed the dodo population, the professor thinks that repeated powerful cyclones were to blame for destroying both the dodos' nests and their eggs.

Organization

1 The reading states that humans were responsible for the dodo's extinction.

2 The professor, however, disagrees and claims it was not humans who killed the dodo bird.

3 The first point the reading mentions is that the flightless dodo was unafraid of humans, so they could easily hunt it.

4 It also maintains that many animals brought by the Dutch hunted dodos and their eggs.

5 On the contrary, the professor asserts that the Dutch did not hunt the dodo because they despised the taste of its meat.

6 The next point brought up is that deforestation by the Dutch destroyed the dodos' natural habitats.

7 However, the professor first claims that deforestation did not cover the entire island nor did it kill many other bird species.

8 He next declares that dodos did not nest in trees, so their disappearance should not have bothered the dodo.

9 Finally, in contrast to the reading's argument that a disease brought by the Dutch may have killed the dodos, the professor says the dodo population may have already been declining.

10 He then blames the extinction of the dodo on massive cyclones that destroyed their nests and eggs.

11 All in all, while the reading brings up several reasons to blame humans for the dodo's extinction, the professor provides refutations and his own theory about the dodo's extinction.

Exercise 2 ··· p.25

Reading

해석

1859년 출간된 이후 많은 비판을 받았던 찰스 다윈의 진화론은 시조새라고 알려진 선사 시대 조류의 화석에 근거하여 1985년 영국의 과학자 프레드 호일에게 또 한 번 공격을 받았다. 호일의 비판 중 상당 부분은, 최초의 온전한 시조새 골격인 런던 표본과 온전한 머리를 가지고 있어서 런던 표본보다 더 나은 표본으로 여겨지는 베를린 표본에 집중되었다.

런던 표본은 1861년 독일에서 처음 발견되었고, 이후 영국의 생물학자 리처드 오웬의 지시로 영국의 자연사 박물관이 이를 구입했다. 호일은 다윈의 이론이 발표되고 단 2년 후에 이 표본이 발견된 점이 이상하다고 주장하면서 그 표본이 가짜라고 주장했다. 그는 오웬 자신이 철저한 진화론자였기 때문에 다윈의 이론을 뒷받침하려고 그가 표본을 위조했다고 비난했다.

호일은 또한 런던 표본과 베를린 표본 모두, 특히 그 당시 알려진 다른 시조새 화석들과 비교해 볼 때, 너무 완벽해서 진짜일 수가 없다고 주장했다. 예를 들어 두 표본은 깃털이 존재했다는 세부적인 증거를 보여 주는데, 다른 화석에는 그러한 깃털이 없었다. 사실 그는 화석화된 깃털이 실제로는 얇은 시멘트층에 깃털을 찍어 만든 자국이며, 이것이 위조된 주요 부분이라고 생각했다.

호일의 마지막 논점은 화석이 발견된 석회암층에 관한 것이다. 그 화석들은 완벽하게 두 부분으로 쪼개진 석회암 덩어리에서 발견되었다. 화석의 반은 완벽하게 보존되어 있었지만 나머지 반은 그렇지 않았다. 게다가 화석의 두 반쪽이 부분이 일치하지 않았다. 호일은 화석의 완벽한 반쪽이 가짜라고 결론지었다.

📝 **Note Taking**

Archaeopteryx Fossils = Fakes

1 The London Specimen
- Discovered 2 years after publication of Darwin's theories ➡ fraudulent
- Richard Owen = evolutionist ➡ forged it

2 Too perfect to be true
- Other fossils ➡ no feathers
- The London & Berlin Specimens ➡ detailed feathers = impressions made in cement

3 Limestone fossil split exactly in 2
- One side is perfect; the other is not
- 2 halves don't match

Listening

Script 🎧 01-05

W Professor: One of the more interesting controversies surrounding Charles Darwin concerns the fossils of the prehistoric Archaeopteryx found in Germany in the nineteenth century. While several papers were written in the 1980s by British scientist Fred Hoyle and others claiming these fossils were faked to support Darwin's theory of evolution, it's clear to me that these were not forgeries at all.

First, the motives Hoyle gave for the forgery focus on Richard Owen, the scientist who prepared the fossils back in London. Hoyle claimed that Owen faked the fossils to support Darwin and his ideas. However, Owen was not an advocate of Darwin's model of evolution and therefore had no reason . . . none whatsoever . . . to support Darwin. Owen himself wrote a paper on the fossils that were found, and if the fossils had really been faked, he would've been risking both his career and credibility.

Hoyle's claim that the feathers of the fossil specimens were made by impressions in cement is totally inaccurate. Hoyle was an astronomer, not a paleontologist, and he knew nothing about how fossils are created. In fact, the German limestone the fossils were found in is very smooth and has yielded many nearly perfect fossils. This is true even for fossils showing the shapes of bird feathers. The existence of other fossilized feathers confirms that these specimens are real.

Another argument Hoyle put forward was that the fossil in two sections was a fake because only one half of it had the bulk of the fossil. But this can happen if a dead animal falls onto a hardened surface and then gets covered in a layer of limestone. And the reason the two halves don't match is that one half was polished in order to make the details of the feathers clearer. Hoyle, however, was unaware of this fact.

해석

W Professor: 찰스 다윈을 둘러싼 가장 흥미로운 논쟁 가운데 하나는 19세기 독일에서 발견된 선사 시대의 시조새 화석과 관련된 것이에요. 1980년대 영국의 과학자 프레드 호일과 다른 이들은 이들 화석이 다윈의 진화론을 지지하기 위해 위조된 것이라는 몇 편의 논문을 작성했지만, 제게는 이들이 결코 위조된 것이 아니라는 점이 분명해 보입니다.

먼저 호일이 위조를 주장했던 동기는 런던에 돌아와 화석을 준비했던 과학자인 리처드 오웬에게 있었어요. 호일은 오웬이 다윈과 그의 이론을 지지하기 위해 화석을 위조했다고 주장했죠. 하지만 오웬은 다윈의 진화론 모델을 지지하지 않았기 때문에 다윈을 지지할 아무런… 그 어떤 이유도… 가지고 있지 않았습니다. 발견된 화석들에 관한 논문은 오웬 자신이 작성했는데, 만약 화석이 정말로 위조된 것이었다면 그의 경력과 신뢰도 모두가 위험에 처했을 것입니다.

화석 표본의 깃털이 시멘트에 찍힌 자국이라는 호일의 주장은 전혀 맞지가 않습니다. 호일은 천문학자였지 고생물학자가 아니었기 때문에 화석이 어떻게 만들어지는지 전혀 모르고 있었어요. 실제로 화석이 발견된 독일의 석회암은 매우 매끄러워서 거의 완벽한 형태의 화석들을 많이 만들어 내죠. 새의 깃털 모양을 보여 주는 화석들의 경우도 마찬가지에요. 화석화된 다른 깃털도 존재한다는 점에서 그러한 표본이 진짜라는 점을 확인할 수 있죠.

호일이 내세운 또 다른 주장은 두 부분으로 쪼개진 화석의 한쪽 면에만 대부분의 화석이 남아 있기 때문에 화석이 위조품이라는 것입니다. 하지만 죽은 동물이 딱딱한 표면 위에 떨어진 후 석회암층으로 덮이게 되면 이런 일이 발생할 수 있어요. 그리고 두 부분이 일치하지 않는 이유는 깃털의 미세한 부분이 더 선명하게 보이도록 한쪽을 연마했기 때문이에요. 하지만 호일은 이러한 사실을 모르고 있었습니다.

📝 Note Taking

Archaeopteryx Fossils ≠ Fakes

1 Was not forged
   • Richard Owen ≠ supporter of Darwin's theory
   • Wrote paper on fossils → would have destroyed his own career
2 Feathers ≠ impressions in cement
   • Hoyle = astronomer → did not know about fossils
   • German limestone → yielded near-perfect fossils
3 Fossil in 2 sections explained
   • Dead animal onto hardened surface & covered in limestone → bulk of fossil on 1 half
   • 1 half polished → halves don't match

Writing

Sample Response

The reading cites Fred Hoyle, who asserts the London and Berlin Specimens of Archaeopteryx were fakes, but the professor provides evidence to show they are actually legitimate fossils.

According to the reading, Fred Hoyle claimed the London Specimen was forged by Richard Owen to provide convenient evidence for evolution. The professor, meanwhile, says Richard Owen was not a supporter of Darwin's theories. He would have been risking his career had he been promoting fakes.

The reading also claims the fossilized feathers found were impressions made in concrete and could not be real because they are too detailed. In contrast, the professor asserts that Hoyle, an astronomer, knew nothing about the way fossils are created. She also declares that the German limestone is so smooth that it has yielded fossils showing almost perfect representations of feathers.

Finally, to respond to the reading's claim that the fossils were perfectly preserved on only one half of two sections of the limestone slabs and the two halves did not match, the professor says it is possible if dead animals fall onto a hardened surface and then get covered in a layer of Filimestone. In addition, one side was polished to make the details of the feathers clearer, which explains why the two sides do not match.

In short, the professor firmly believes the fossils are real while the reading passage author disagrees with that assertion.

해석

읽기 지문은 시조새의 런던 표본과 베를린 표본이 위조품이라고 주장하는 프레드 호일의 말을 인용하지만, 교수는 그 표본들이 실제로 진짜 화석이라는 증거를 제시한다.

읽기 지문에 따르면 프레드 호일은 진화에 대한 적합한 증거를 제시할 목적으로 런던 표본이 리처드 오웬에 의해 위조되었다고 주장한다. 하지만 교수는 리처드 오웬이 다윈 이론의 지지자가 아니었다고 말한다. 만약 그가 위조 화석을 홍보했다면 그의 경력이 위태로웠을 것이다.

또한 읽기 지문은 화석에 있는 깃털이 콘크리트에 찍힌 흔적이며 너무 세밀하기 때문에 진짜일 수 없다고 주장한다. 반면에 교수는 호일이 천문학자로서 화석이 어떻게 만들어지는지를 전혀 몰랐다고 주장한다. 그녀는 또한 독일의 석회암은 매우 매끄럽기 때문에 거의 완벽한 깃털 형태를 보여 주는 화석들이 많이 나왔다고 주장한다.

마지막으로, 화석이 석회암판의 두 쪽 중 오직 한 쪽에만 완벽하게 보존되어 있고 양쪽이 일치하지 않는다는 읽기 지문의 주장에 대해, 교수는 죽은 동물이 단단한 표면 위에 떨어진 후 석회암층으로 덮이면 그렇게 될 수 있다고 말한다. 또한 깃털의 미세한 부분이 더 명확하게 보일 수 있도록 한 쪽을 연마했는데, 이로써 두 면이 일치하지 않는 이유가 설명된다.

간단히 말해서 교수는 화석이 진짜라고 굳게 믿는 반면 읽기 지문의 저자는 그러한 주장에 동의하지 않는다.

Unit 03 Environmental Science I

Exercise 1 .... p.28

Reading

해석

국립 공원 관리청은 1972년부터 자연 화재라고 불리는 산불에 대한 정책을 수립했다. 번개에 의해 발생하는 산불과 같은 일부 산불은 숲이 생태계의 균형을 유지하는데 필요하므로 그대로 타게 놔두어야 한다고 여겨졌다. 하지만 1988년에 발생한 옐로스톤 국립 공원의 대규모 산불로 이러한 정책은 중단되었는데, 그 이유는 이 산불을 초기에 놔두었다가 곧 걷잡을 수 없이 산불이 번져 공원의 대부분의 지역이 파괴되었기 때문이다. 산불의 결과로 많은 사람들은 공원이 심각하고 회복 불가능한 피해를 입었다고 생각했다.

1988년의 산불로 미국에서 가장 오래 되고 가장 많은 사랑을 받는 국립 공원인 옐로스톤 국립 공원의 많은 부분이 파괴되었다. 방대한 초목 지역이 파괴되었고, 넓은 텅 빈 공간과 새까맣게 잿더미로 변한 수많은 나무들이 관광객을 맞이했다. 강과 개울은 재로 인해 물길이 막혔고 공원의 생태계는 복구가 불가능할 정도로 바뀌었다.

또한 엄청난 수의 동물들이 걷잡을 수 없이 번진 산불로 목숨을 잃었다. 일부 경우 하루 10마일의 속도로 부는 강풍에 의해 산불이 확산되었다. 많은 작은 동물들이 화염 속에서 죽었다. 급속하게 번지는 산불 속에서 야생 동물들이 도망칠 기회는 거의 없었다. 심지어 오늘날에도 이러한 작은 숲 속 생물들 중에서 다시 공원으로 돌아온 생물은 거의 없다.

산불이 일어난 직후 몇 년 동안 관광객의 수가 엄청나게 감소했다. 휴가 기간에 나무도 없이 까맣게 변해 버린 공원을 보고 싶어하는 사람은 없었다. 이전에 옐로스톤은 경이로운 풍경과 간헐천인 올드 페이스풀과 같은 독특한 지형으로 명성이 자자했다. 하지만 지금은 미국의 진경으로서의 명성이, 공원과 마찬가지로, 영구히 손상된 것으로 보인다.

📝 Note Taking

1) Destroyed by the fire of 1988
2) Rivers & streams filled with ash
3) Animals killed by the fires
4) couldn't escape the fast-moving flames
5) An enormous decrease in visitors

Listening

Script 🎧 01-06

W Professor: The great fire of 1988 in Yellowstone National Park led to a change in the natural burn policy so that there's a more, um, more active firefighting stance nowadays. However, I feel this was merely a reaction to the idea that this policy had ruined one of America's great wonders. On the contrary though, Yellowstone was not destroyed permanently, and there are numerous signs that the park is recovering while still receiving a great many visitors.

When a forest burns, much of the dead material goes into the soil. This makes the soil much richer than in the past and allows for new vegetation to spring up. The loss of trees also enables more sunlight to penetrate, thereby allowing more vegetation to grow. All of this is happening in Yellowstone right now, which is accelerating the recovery process.

This new vegetation has attracted more of nature's small creatures to replace those that died in the fires. Some species that were previously never even a part of the park's ecosystem have found their way to Yellowstone. Rabbits . . . yes, rabbits, once very rare in the park, are coming in droves to feast on the new undergrowth vegetation.

In the years after the fires, the number of visitors to Yellowstone did decline. That is true. However, this was not only because of the fires but was also due to an economic crisis the United States was enduring at that time. The late 1980s and early 1990s were hard times for a lot of people, so they couldn't afford to take vacations. If you look at the numbers, you'll see that Yellowstone was not the only place that saw a decline in tourism. Fortunately, by the mid-1990s, once the crisis had passed, the numbers of tourists had risen again.

해석

W Professor: 1988년 옐로스톤 국립 공원에서 발생한 대형 화재로 자연 화재 정책이 바뀌어서 지금은 더욱, 어, 더욱 적극적인 소방 대책이 존재합니다. 하지만 저는 이것이, 그러한 정책으로 미국의 가장 큰 볼 거리 중 하나가 파괴되었다는 생각에 대한 하나의 반응에 지나지 않는다고 생각해요. 그와 반대로 옐로스톤은 영구히 파괴된 것이 아니며, 공원이 회복되고 있다는 수많은 징후들이 존재하고 여전히 많은 관광객들이 이곳을 찾고 있습니다.

산불이 발생하면 죽은 물질의 상당 부분은 토양으로 되돌아갑니다. 이로 인해 토양은 예전보다 훨씬 더 비옥해져서 새로운 초목이 자라날 수 있어요. 또한 나무가 사라짐으로써 이전보다 더 많은 햇빛이 들어오게 되는데, 그 결과 더 많은 초목이 자라게 되죠. 이러한 모든 현상들이 바로 지금 옐로스톤에서 일어나고 있으며, 이로써 회복 과정이 가속화되고 있습니다.

새로운 초목으로 인해 산불에 타 죽은 동물들을 대신할 수 있는 자연의 작은 동물들이 유입되고 있습니다. 이전에는 공원 생태계에 존재하지도 않았던 몇몇 종들도 옐로스톤에 들어와 있어요. 토끼… 네, 토끼들도, 한때는 공원에서 매우 보기가 힘들었지만, 새로운 덤불을 찾아 무리를 지어 공원으로 들어오고 있죠.

산불이 일어난 이후 몇 년 동안 옐로스톤의 관광객 수는 감소했습니다. 그건 사실이에요. 하지만 그것은 산불 때문만이 아니라 당시 미국이 겪고 있었던 경제 위기 때문이기도 했습니다. 1980년대 후반과 1990년대 초반은 많은 이들에게 힘든 시기였기 때문에 휴가를 즐길 여유가 없었어요. 수치를 보면 옐로스톤에서만 관광객 수가 감소한 것이 아니라는 점을 알게 될 것입니다. 다행히도 1990년대 중반에 위기가 지나자 관광객 수는 다시 증가했어요.

📝 Note Taking

1) helps new vegetation grow faster
2) more sunlight to penetrate forest
3) Many small creatures coming back to the park
4) Once rare creatures like rabbits
5) national economic situation

Comparing the Points

Reading	Listening
Stance The fire of 1988 destroyed much of Yellowstone and permanently altered it for the worse.	**Stance** Although the fire did severely hurt Yellowstone, the park is starting to recover.
Main point 1 Many trees were burned, and rivers and streams were filled with ash.	**Refutation 1** Burned vegetation and more sunlight from a lack of trees are helping new plant life grow.
Main point 2 Numerous small animals died in the fires, and new ones have not returned.	**Refutation 2** Many new animals like rabbits are moving into the park in large numbers.
Main point 3 The number of visitors to the park has decreased greatly.	**Refutation 3** Now that the economy is better, more tourists are visiting Yellowstone.

Synthesizing

1 In opposition to the author of the reading passage, who believes the fire greatly and permanently damaged Yellowstone National Park, the professor is convinced that the park is beginning to heal itself while also attracting more tourists.

2 The reading passage declares that the waterways and forests were ruined, thereby destroying the park's ecosystem; however, the professor mentions the richer soil and the higher amounts of sunlight are helping the park recover more quickly.

3 Although the reading passage's author states that few small animals are coming back to live in Yellowstone, the professor indicates that some new species of animals are moving into the park.

4 While the reading contends that the number of tourists to Yellowstone greatly decreased right after the fire, the professor comments that after the American economy improved, more tourists began returning to the park.

Organization

1 The reading passage describes the reasons why Yellowstone National Park has been permanently ruined by the fire of 1988, but the professor counters by suggesting some reasons as to why the park is recovering.

2 The reading first mentions the extreme problems caused to the forests, rivers, and streams in the park.

3 The author believes the park cannot recover from all of this damage.

4 However, the professor says that the burned material and the increased amounts of sunlight will help new vegetation grow more quickly.

5 In response to the reading passage's assertion that the animals killed or driven away by the fire have not been replaced, the professor claims that new species of animals are now moving into the park to eat the growing vegetation.

6 For example, rabbits were rare in the park in the past, but they are now coming in large numbers to dwell in the park.

7 The reading passage then describes how tourism to the park declined greatly after the fire.

8 The professor agrees with that claim but blames the decline on the poor economic situation in the country in the late 1980s and the early 1990s.

9 She then declares that more and more tourists are starting to return to the park nowadays.

10 While the author of the reading passage believes that the park will never return to the way it used to be, the professor is convinced of Yellowstone's recovery.

Reading

해석

미국에는, 특히 서부 지역 주들과 알래스카에, 국토의 많은 부분을 차지하는 광활한 국립 공원들이 있다. 현재 국립 공원들은 공원, 방문객의 연령, 그리고 체류 기간에 따라 방문객들에게 입장료를 달리 부과하고 있다. 하지만 이러한 입장료는 폐지되어야 하며 모든 방문객이 무료로 국립 공원에 입장할 수 있어야 한다.

기억해야 할 가장 중요한 점은 이들이 국립 공원이라는 점으로, 이는 국립 공원이 실제로 국가의 시민을 의미하는 국가에 귀속되어 있다는 점을 의미한다. 어떤 장소의 주인에게 입장료를 부과한다는 것은 말이 되지 않는다. 어찌되었든 자신의 집에 들어갈 때마다 입장료를 낼 필요는 없다. 국립 공원의 경우에도 그럴 필요가 없는 것이다.

또한 국립 공원에 대한 입장료를 부과하면 국립 공원을 방문해서 그곳의 자연적인 아름다움을 즐기려는 의욕이 저하될 수 있다. 특히 며칠씩 국립 공원에 머물고자 하는 대규모 단체의 경우 엄청난 요금을 지불해야 하기 때문에 더욱 그러하다. 높은 비용 때문에 많은 이들이 휴가를 다른 곳에서 보내고 있으며, 그 결과 국립 공원에서 즐거운 시간을 보낼 수 있는 기회를 잃고 있다.

방문객을 일일이 확인하고 입장료를 징수하는 것 역시 시간이 많이 소요되는 과정이다. 이들 공원의 입구에는 이미 긴 줄이 늘어서 있는데, 이는 특히 여름 여행 기간에 심하다. 사람들은 이러한 줄에 대해 불만을 토로하며 몇몇 사람들은 공원에 입장하기까지 한 시간 또는 심지어 그 이상을 기다려야 할 수도 있다. 그리고 공원 인력이 요금 징수에 이용되어 다른 곳에서는 일을 할 수가 없기 때문에 공원 전체의 서비스 품질이 떨어지게 된다.

Note Taking

No Admission Fees 4 National Parks

1 Parks belong to all the citizens
   • Shouldn't have 2 pay to enter a place you own

2 Fees discourage people from visiting
   • Large groups ➡ must pay lots of money
   • High costs ➡ people go to other places

3 Takes time to collect money
   • Collect fees at park entrance ➡ makes for long wait to enter the park
   • Park personnel must collect fees ➡ lowers service in other parts of parks

Listening

Script 🎧 01-07

M Professor: The American national parks system is one of the greatest things about the country. I've visited large numbers of them, and one thing has always struck me . . . People often complain about having to pay entrance fees. I must disagree with them. Paying admission fees to national parks is something that simply must continue.

National parks rely upon these fees to ensure that their facilities are up to date and also to pay the salaries of many park employees. If there were no admission fees, then federal and state taxes would have to be raised to cover the parks' budgets. And I'm sure none of you is willing to pay higher taxes. So let the people who use the parks pay for their maintaining. That's fair.

As strange as it may seem, I have found that charging admission fees actually encourages people to visit many of our smaller and not particularly famous national parks. For example, Yellowstone, our most famous park, gets tens of thousands of visitors a year despite its high admission fees. Now, imagine how overcrowded the park would be if it didn't charge so much. Not a pleasant thought, is it? Instead, many people head to other smaller parks, which charge minimal fees that are more affordable to most families.

I also firmly believe that charging entrance fees improves the quality of the service of the parks and increases their safety. When people pay their fees, they have to go through various checkpoints set up around the parks. This enables park rangers to inspect these people and their cars. So if they find anyone or anything suspicious or potentially dangerous, rangers can stop them before they enter the park, where they could pose a threat to the visitors and the park itself.

해석

M Professor: 미국의 국립 공원 시스템은 미국에서 가장 훌륭한 것 중 하나입니다. 저도 여러 곳을 방문했는데 항상 저를 놀라게 만드는 한 가지는… 사람들이 입장료를 내야하는 것에 종종 불만을 제기한다는 것이에요. 저는 그들과 의견이 다릅니다. 국립 공원의 입장료는 계속 유지되어야 하죠.

국립 공원은 이러한 요금을 이용해서 시설을 최신식으로 유지하고 또한 많은 공원 종사자들에게 급여를 지급합니다. 입장료가 없다면 공원 예산을 감당하기 위해 연방세 및 주세를 인상해야 할 거에요. 그리고 분명 여러분 가운데 누구도 기꺼이 세금을 더 내려고 하지는 않을 것입니다. 그러니 공원을 이용하는 사람들이 공원 유지를 위해 돈을 내도록 해야 해요. 그것이 공정합니다.

이상하게 보일 수도 있지만 저는 입장료 징수가 실제로는 사람들로 하여금 작고 특별히 유명하지 않은 국립 공원을 찾도록 만든다는 점을 알게 되었어요. 예를 들어 미국에서 가장 유명한 국립 공원인 옐로스톤에는 높은 입장료에도 불구하고 연간 수만 명의 관광객이 유입되고 있습니다. 자, 그처럼 높은 입장료를 부과하지 않으면 그 공원이 얼마나 더 붐빌지 상상해 보세요. 유쾌한 일은 아닐 거예요, 그렇죠? 그 대신 사람들은 대다수 가정에 보다 부담이 덜한 최소한의 요금을 부과하는 보다 작은 규모의 공원을 찾게 됩니다.

저는 또한 입장료를 부과함으로써 서비스 품질이 올라가고 안전성이 향상될 것으로 굳게 믿습니다. 사람과 자동차는 입장료를 낼 때 공원 주변에 세워진 여러 개의 검문소를 거쳐야 해요. 이로 인해 공원 경비원이 이들 사람과 자동차를 검문할 수 있습니다. 그래서 만약 수상하거나 잠재적으로 위험하다고 판단되는 사람이나 물건을 발견하면 그들이 공원에 들어가서 방문객들과 공원 자체에 위협을 가하기 전에 경비원들이 이들을 제지할 수 있죠.

Admission Fees 4 National Parks

1 Important to maintaining parks
 • Use fees to upgrade facilities & pay salaries
 • No fees = higher taxes
2 High fees ➜ people visit smaller parks
 • Yellowstone Park ➜ high fees
 • Smaller parks ➜ smaller fees ➜ many people visit them
3 Improve park safety
 • Rangers ➜ collect fees & look for suspicious people ➜ keep the park safe

Writing

Sample Response

The author of the reading passage feels that admission fees to the country's national parks should be abolished. On the contrary, the professor is convinced that everyone should pay admission to get into them.

The first point the reading passage's author makes is that since national parks technically belong to all of the county's citizens, they should not have to pay to enter something they already own. However, the professor mentions how important the fees are to paying to improve facilities and to cover employees' salaries. Without these fees, he says, taxes would have to be raised.

Second, while the reading passage states that many admission fees are too high, especially for large groups staying for many days, the professor believes that these high fees keep attendance at popular parks down and get people to visit smaller, lesser-known parks. Because these parks charge less, they are more appealing to many families.

Finally, the author of the reading passage dislikes the fact that collecting admission fees makes lines to get into the park very long. However, the professor feels that these checkpoints are good because they let park rangers observe visitors and make sure no suspicious individuals or vehicles enter the park to cause problems.

The professor clearly supports admission fees while the writer of the reading passage does not.

해석

읽기 지문의 저자는 미국의 국립 공원에 부과되는 입장료를 폐지해야 한다고 주장한다. 그에 반해 교수는 국립 공원에 들어가기 위해서는 누구나 입장료를 내야 한다고 믿는다.

읽기 지문의 저자가 제기하는 첫 번째 논점은 국립 공원이 원칙적으로 미국 시민의 재산이기 때문에 시민이 자신의 소유지에 들어가기 위해 돈을 낼 필요는 없다는 것이다. 하지만 교수는 시설 개선 및 공원 직원들의 급여 지급에 입장료가 매우 중요한 역할을 한다고 언급한다. 그의 말에 따르면 이러한 요금이 없다면 세금이 인상되어야 할 것이다.

둘째, 읽기 지문은 많은 경우, 특히 여러 명이 여러 날 머무는 경우에 입장료가 너무 높다고 주장하는 반면에 교수는 그러한 높은 요금 덕분에 인기 있는 공원을 찾는 사람들의 수가 억제되며 사람들이 규모가 더 작고 덜 알려진 공원을 찾는다고 생각한다. 이러한 공원들은 보다 적은 입장료를 부과하기 때문에 보다 많은 가족들에게 더 매력적으로 보인다.

마지막으로, 읽기 지문의 저자는 입장료 징수로 인해 공원 안으로 들어오는 줄이 매우 길어진다는 점을 반기지 않는다. 하지만 교수는 이러한 검문소 덕분에 공원 경비원들이 방문객을 검문해서 수상한 사람 및 차량이 문제를 일으킬 수 없도록 만들기 때문에 검문소가 바람직하다고 생각한다.

교수는 분명하게 입장료를 지지하고 있지만 읽기 지문의 저자는 그렇지 않다.

Unit 04 Health

Exercise 1 .... p.35

Reading

해석

지난 60년 동안 미국 내 공공 식수에 불소가 첨가되었다. 이러한 조치로 미국인들의 치아 건강과 뼈 구조가 개선되어서 미국인들의 건강이 크게 향상되었다. 이 화학 물질 덕분에 식수가 정화되어 마시기에 더 안전해졌다.

식수에 불소를 첨가하는 주된 이유는 충치 발생을 예방하기 위해서이다. 이러한 효과는 불소가 사람들의 치아 표면에 있는 에나멜과 결합함으로써 나타나는데, 이로써 치아가 건강하게 유지될 수 있다. 수십 년에 걸쳐 여러 지역에서 이루어진 연구에 따르면 불소 덕분에 충치 발생률이 평균 12.5% 이하로 감소했고 충치로 인한 치아 손실은 2.25개 이하로 줄어들었다. 질병 통제 예방 센터는 또한 식수를 불소로 처리할 경우 충치 발생률을 30% 가까이 줄일 수 있다고 주장한다.

또한 불소 처리된 식수는 그렇지 않은 식수보다 훨씬 더 깨끗하다. 그 이유는 불소가 정화제로 작용하기 때문이다. 불소는 박테리아 및 기타 유기물들을 공격해서 이들을 기본적으로 식수에서 제거시킨다. 이러한 이유 하나만으로 세계 보건 기구(WHO)는 깨끗한 식수를 항상 쉽게 얻지는 못하는 수많은 개발도상국들에게 식수원의 불소 함량을 늘리도록 권고해 왔다.

심지어 일부 과학자들은 불소 처리된 식수를 매일 마시면 사람의 뼈 구조가 개선된다는 많은 증거가 존재한다고 주장한다. 연구에 따르면 이러한 사람들의 골밀도가 증가했으며, 나이든 여성이 불소 처리된 물을 마시는 경우 이들이 골다공증에 걸리는 경우도 줄어들었다. 마지막으로 불소 처리된 물을 마시지 않은 사람들에 비해 단순 낙상에 의한 골절이 발생하는 경우도 더 적다.

Note Taking

1) Can prevent tooth decay
2) Purifies drinking water
3) kills bacteria & other organisms
4) Improves bone structure
5) reduces osteoporosis in women

Listening

Script 🎧 01-08

W Professor: Many people have described the benefits of drinking water treated with fluoride. However, this issue is not as cut and dry as people have let you believe. Oh, no. It's actually rather controversial. In fact, many people, myself included, believe that fluoride's effects can be somewhat detrimental to people.

The main argument in favor of fluoride has been its tooth-care properties. Countless studies show how much our teeth are being protected by the inserting of fluoride in drinking water. What these studies forget to mention, however, is that practically every brand of toothpaste already has fluoride in it. This means it's totally unnecessary to put fluoride in drinking water. As a matter of fact, many European countries have abandoned adding fluoride to their drinking water. Some, like Sweden and the Netherlands, haven't done so for over, uh, thirty years, yet they have exhibited no decline in dental health.

While fluoride does purify water, it can still lead to harmful side effects if taken in large amounts since it's a toxic chemical. It has also been noted for discoloring water pipes and even, get this . . . dissolving lead, another toxic chemical element, out of the pipes. So it must be carefully monitored if introduced to the water supply. Actually, there are other safer methods of water purification, such as filtration, the adding of chlorine, and using ultraviolet light.

Another point is that high levels of fluoride may cause cancer in some people. In several cases, it has been deemed responsible for a rare form of bone cancer called osteosarcomas, which usually only appears in young boys. Fluoride may also cause skeletal fluorosis, a condition caused by excessive fluoride exposure in which fluoride is deposited directly into the bones. This may cause stiffness, pain, and a brittle bone structure prone to fractures.

해석

W Professor: 많은 사람들이 불소 처리된 물을 마시는 것의 이점을 설명합니다. 하지만 이 문제는 사람들이 생각하는 것처럼 단순명료하지가 않아요. 오, 절대 그렇지 않죠. 사실 논쟁의 여지가 있어요. 실제로 제 자신을 포함하여 많은 사람들은 불소가 사람들에게 어느 정도 해로운 효과를 나타낼 수도 있다고 생각합니다.

불소를 지지하는 주된 이유는 치아 관리와 관련된 불소의 특성 때문이에요. 수많은 연구들이 식수에 불소를 넣음으로써 우리의 치아가 얼마나 많이 보호되는지 보여 줍니다. 하지만 이러한 연구들이 간과하는 것은 사실상 모든 치약에 이미 불소가 들어 있다는 점이에요. 이 말은 식수에 불소를 넣을 필요가 전혀 없다는 뜻이죠. 실제로 유럽의 여러 국가들은 더 이상 식수에 불소를 첨가하지 않습니다. 스웨덴이나 네덜란드 같은 일부 국가들은, 어, 30년 이상 첨가하지 않고 있지만 치아 건강이 나빠졌다는 점은 보고되지 않았어요.

불소는 물을 정화시키지만 유독성 화학 물질이기 때문에 다량 섭취할 경우 해로운 부작용이 나타날 수도 있습니다. 또한 불소는 수도관을 변색시키고, 심지어… 수도관에서 또 다른 유독성 화학 물질인 납을 용해시킨다고 알려져 있어요. 그래서 식수원에 첨가할 경우 세심하게 감시해야 합니다. 실제로 여과, 염소 첨가, 그리고 자외선 이용과 같은 보다 기타 안전한 정수 방법들도 존재하고요.

또 다른 점은 높은 수치의 불소가 일부 사람들에게 암을 유발할 수도 있다는 것이에요. 일부 경우, 주로 나이 어린 남자 아이들에게서만 발병하는, 골육종이라는 희귀성 골암을 유발하는 것으로 생각됩니다. 불소는, 또한, 과다한 불소에 노출됨으로써 불소가 뼈 속에 직접 쌓여 생기는, 불소침착증을 유발할 수도 있습니다. 그 결과 몸이 뻣뻣해지고, 통증이 생기며, 그리고 뼈가 약해져 쉽게 골절이 일어날 수 있어요.

✍ Note Taking

1) Toothpaste has fluoride in it
2) dissolves lead out of them
3) filtration, chlorine, & ultraviolet light
4) Can cause serious diseases
5) stiffness, pain, & brittle bones

Comparing the Points

Reading	Listening
Stance The use of fluoride in drinking water has improved people's dental health and bone structure.	**Stance** Fluoride in drinking water can have some harmful effects on people.
Main point 1 Studies show that fluoride helps prevent tooth decay and the loss of teeth.	**Refutation 1** Dental health can be ensured without adding fluoride to drinking water.
Main point 2 Fluoride in drinking water purifies the water and kills harmful bacteria and microorganisms.	**Refutation 2** There are better and safer methods to purify the water supply.
Main point 3 Fluoride improves people's bone structures and keeps the bones healthier and stronger.	**Refutation 3** Too much fluoride can cause cancer and damage people's bones.

Synthesizing

1 Whereas the reading believes adding fluoride to drinking water has given Americans better dental health and better bone structure, the professor thinks fluoride can have harmful effects on people.

2 Despite the reading passage's author asserting that fluoride in water can prevent tooth decay, the professor mentions that some European countries have maintained public dental health without adding fluoride to their water for more than three decades.

3 Although the writer of the reading passage thinks water with fluoride is purer than water without it, the professor claims too much fluoride intake can cause damage to people since the chemical is toxic.

4 Contrasting the reading passage's argument that fluoride strengthens people's bone structures when they drink it daily, the professor declares that fluoride can cause serious bone problems such as skeletal fluorosis.

Organization

1 The reading passage asserts that adding fluoride to drinking water is highly beneficial, yet the professor feels that the addition of fluoride can actually cause damage to people's health.

2 While the reading states that studies show fluoride helps to cut down considerably on tooth decay and the loss of teeth, the professor believes these studies forget that people also use toothpaste with fluoride in it.

3 She cites some European examples, where fluoride has not been added to the water for thirty years but people's dental health is not suffering.

4 The reading next mentions that treating water with fluoride helps to purify it.

5 The professor agrees but also says that fluoride can have some dangerous side effects if taken too much, and it even dissolves lead out of water pipes.

6 According to the professor, there are safer ways to purify water, including filtration, chlorine treatment, and ultraviolet light.

7 Finally, the reading passage claims that people drinking fluoride have stronger bones, suffer from osteoporosis less, and break fewer bones.

8 However, the professor counters by stating that fluoride can cause some rare types of cancer in people.

9 She also adds that it may make some people's bones stiff, painful, and weak.

10 The lecture and the reading passage have virtually opposite opinions of the benefit of adding fluoride to drinking water supplies.

Exercise 2 ···································· p.39

Reading

해석

현재 인터넷에서 화제가 되고 있는 것 중 하나는 기본적으로 사이버 공간에 존재하는 온라인 약국이다. 소비자들은 온라인에 접속해서 필요한 약을 고르고 집으로 바로 오도록 주문을 한다. 온라인 약국은 자주 찾는 실제 약국보다 값이 저렴한 경우가 많다. 하지만 안타깝게도 온라인 약국과 관련된 수많은 문제들이 존재하며, 공공의 이익 차원에서 이들을 없애는 것이 최선일 것이다.

한 가지 중요한 쟁점은 온라인으로 판매되는 많은 의약품들이 미 식품 의약국(FDA)의 제품 안전 기준을 충족하지 못한다는 것이다. 특히 우려되는 것은 약으로 간주되지는 않지만 질병 치료에 사용되는 한방 치료제 및 기타 실험을 거치지 않은 제품들이다. 동식물성 원료로 만든 많은 조제약들이 적절한 실험 및 FDA의 승인을 거치지 않고 판매되고 있는데, 이들은 아무것도 모르는 소비자에게 실제로 피해를 입힐 수 있다.

소비자들은 온라인 약국에서 직접 약을 구매함으로써 구매 과정의 중요한 부분을 피해가고 있다. 의사의 상담을 받지 않는다는 것이다. 많은 구매자들이 자신의 의학적인 상태에 대한 중요한 정보를 얻지 못하는데, 그 이유는 그들이 먼저 진료를 받지 않아서 복용해야 할 의약품에 대한 조언을 얻지 못하기 때문이다. 일부 경우 복용하는 약이 불쾌한 부작용을 유발하거나 심지어 치명적인 결과를 가져오기도 하며, 약이 올바르더라도 부적당한 양을 복용함으로써 득보다는 실이 더 클 수도 있다.

소비자들은 보통 온라인 약국에서 파는 많은 약품과 한약재의 원산지가 어디인지 모른다. 예를 들어 그중 일부는 미국과 승인 기준이 다른 외국에서 제조되었다. 간단히 말해서 많은 곳들이 합법적인 약으로 위장한 기준 이하의 제품을 판매한다. 소비자들은 라벨 및 주의 사항이 영어로 적혀 있다고 하더라도 그러한 약들을 믿어서는 안 된다. 사람의 목숨이 달린 문제라는 점을 고려하면 온라인 약국의 의약품 판매는 금지되어야 한다.

📝 Note Taking

Online Pharmacies Should Be Banned

1 Sell unsafe medical products
  - Don't meet FDA standards
  - Untested herbal remedies ➔ may harm people using them

2 Consumers bypass doctors
  - No consultations from doctors ➔ lack of important information
  - Taking wrong medicine / wrong amounts ➔ can cause damage / death

3 Sell drugs of unclear origins
  - Drugs made in foreign countries ➔ don't meet American standards
  - Offer inferior products masquerading as legitimate drugs

Listening

Script 🎧 01-09

M Professor: Online pharmacies may replace corner drugstores in the future, which would be of benefit to, well, all of us. Sadly, current FDA restrictions prevent many Americans from gaining access to the medicines they require. Fortunately, online pharmacies offer these drugs and provide patients with more treatment options at lower prices. Those calling for their abolition are wrong. Online pharmacies are crucial to numerous people.

While some drugs sold online aren't FDA approved, this shouldn't deter consumers from buying them. Many of the herbal remedies online pharmacies offer have been used for hundreds of years, especially in Asian countries, and they have strong safety records. Other medicines may come from foreign countries, but they aren't harming the people who use them in their own countries. Take, um, the "morning after" birth control pill as an example. It has been used safely for many years in France and other European countries, yet it was only fairly recently allowed in the U.S.

Nowadays, just getting in to see a doctor seems to take forever, and then there are the expenditures of time and money to get tests done and to await the results. Thanks to the Internet, customers now know more about available medicines than ever before and are therefore competent enough to take them without having to consult a doctor. The Internet, after all, is filled with information about all kinds of drugs. Much of it has even been written by doctors and pharmaceutical companies themselves.

Another issue to consider is money. Healthcare costs in America are rising every year, and pharmaceutical companies are making billions. Online pharmacies typically sell their drugs at lower prices than hospital pharmacies and corner drugstores. Consumers shouldn't be blamed for seeking cheaper alternatives and refusing to, you know, line the pockets of already wealthy companies and stores.

해석

M Professor: 미래에는 온라인 약국이 동네 약국을 대체할 수도 있는데, 이는 음, 우리 모두에게 도움이 될 수 있을 거예요. 안타깝게도 현재의 FDA 규제 때문에 많은 미국인들이 필요한 의약품을 구입하지 못하고 있습니다. 다행히 온라인 약국들이 그러한 약품을 제공하고 있으며 환자들에게 보다 저렴한 가격으로 더 다양한 치료법을 제시하고 있어요. 온라인 약국의 폐지를 요구하는 사람들은 틀렸습니다. 많은 사람들에게 온라인 약국은 필수적인 존재입니다.

온라인에서 판매되는 일부 약들이 FDA의 승인을 받지 않았다고 해서 소비자들이 이를 구입하지 못하도록 해서는 안 됩니다. 온라인 약국에서 판매되는 한약재 중 다수는 수백 년에 걸쳐, 특히 아시아 국가에서 사용되어 왔고 안전성도 확인되었어요. 외국에서 온 의약품도 있을 수 있는데, 이들이 자국 사용자들에게 피해를 끼치지는 않고 있습니다. 음, "사후 피임약"을 예로 들어 보죠. 이는 프랑스 및 기타 유럽 국가에서 수년 동안 안전하게 사용되었지만 미국에서는 아주 최근에야 승인을 받았습니다.

요즘에는 의사의 진료를 받는데 엄청난 시간이 걸리며 그 후 검사를 받고 결과를 기다리기까지 시간과 비용이 듭니다. 인터넷 덕분에 소비자들은 과거 어느 때보다 구입 가능한 약품에 대해 더 많이 알고 있으며, 그 결과 의사와의 상담 없이도 약을 충분히 잘 구입할 수 있어요. 어찌되었든 인터넷에는 온갖 종류의 약에 대한 정보가 가득하니까요. 심지어 그중 상당 부분은 의사나 제약 회사들이 직접 작성한 것입니다.

고려해야 할 또 다른 문제는 비용이에요. 미국에서 보건 의료비는 해마다 증가하고 있고 제약 회사는 엄청난 수익을 거두고 있죠. 온라인 약국들은 대개 병원 약국이나 동네 약국보다 저렴한 가격으로 약을 판매합니다. 소비자들이 보다 저렴한 대안을 찾아, 아시다시피, 이미 배가 부른 회사 및 약국들의 주머니를 채워 주지 않으려 한다는 이유로 비난을 받아서는 안 됩니다.

📝 Note Taking

Online Pharmacies Are Beneficial

1 Proved safe in other countries
  - Herbal remedies ➔ used for centuries in Asia
  - Don't harm people using them in other countries

14

2 Save time & money
- Can learn about many medicines on the Internet ➜ no need to consult doctors
- Can get much information written by doctors & pharmaceutical companies

3 Rising costs of health care
- Can get drugs cheaply online ➜ don't need to pay extra money to wealthy companies

Writing

The reading passage is strongly against the existence of online pharmacies. The professor, however, feels that online pharmacies benefit society very much.

The author of the reading claims that many online pharmacies sell medicines that have not been approved by the FDA. According to the reading, this is especially true for various herbal remedies, which may wind up harming consumers. However, the professor claims that many of the medicines sold online have been proven safe in other countries for a long time. He thinks that since people in other countries are using them without being harmed, then the medicines should be good enough for Americans as well.

The next point made by the reading is that many customers bypass doctors by going straight to online pharmacies. The professor, meanwhile, complains about the complications involved in seeing a doctor. So he favors people getting their information about medicines over the Internet, especially since doctors and pharmaceutical companies post much of the information.

Finally, in contrast to the complaints that many customers are purchasing inferior medicines from foreign countries that they cannot trust, the professor mentions the rising cost of health care in America. He thinks it is fine for people to seek cheaper alternatives over the Internet.

So while the reading passage author wants to ban online pharmacies, the professor supports them.

해석

읽기 지문은 온라인 약국의 존재를 강력히 반대한다. 하지만 교수는 온라인 약국이 사회에 대단히 유익하다고 생각한다.

읽기 지문의 저자는 많은 온라인 약국들이 FDA의 승인을 받지 않은 약을 판매한다고 주장한다. 지문에 따르면 이는 특히 다양한 한약재의 경우에 사실인데, 이로 인해 결국 소비자들이 피해를 입을 수 있다. 하지만 교수는 온라인으로 판매되는 많은 약들이 외국에서 오랫동안 안전한 것으로 입증되어 온 것이라고 주장한다. 그는 외국 국민들이 아무런 부작용을 겪지 않고 약들을 사용하고 있기 때문에 그러한 약이 미국인들에게도 충분히 효과가 있을 것이라고 생각한다.

읽기 지문이 제시한 그 다음 논점은 많은 소비자들이 의사의 상담을 받지 않

고 온라인 약국으로 직행한다는 것이다. 반면에 교수는 진료와 관련된 복잡한 과정에 불만을 제기한다. 따라서 그는 사람들이 인터넷으로 약에 관한 정보를 얻는 것을 환영하는데, 그 이유는 특히 의사와 제약 회사가 상당한 양의 정보를 게시하기 때문이다.

마지막으로, 많은 소비자들이 신뢰할 수 없는 국가에서 수입한 기준 이하의 약품을 구매한다는 지적에 대응하여 교수는 미국 내 보건 의료비의 상승을 언급한다. 그는 사람들이 인터넷에서 보다 저렴한 대안을 찾는 것은 좋은 일이라고 생각한다.

따라서 읽기 지문의 저자는 온라인 약국의 폐지를 원하는 반면에 교수는 이들을 지지한다.

Unit 05 History

Exercise 1 .... p.42

Reading

해석

중세 시대의 가장 위대한 탐험가 중 한 사람은 베니스 사람인 마르코 폴로였다. 그의 저술에 따르면 그는 13세기 말에 중국으로 가서 그곳에서 17년 동안 머물렀다. 하지만 마르코 폴로의 이야기에는 항상 논란이 뒤따랐으며, 그는 그 당시부터 현재에 이르기까지 의심의 대상이 되어왔다. 의심하는 사람의 생각이 맞는 것처럼 보인다. 실제로 마르코 폴로는 중국으로 모험을 떠난 적도 없고, 그가 했다고 알려진 일 중 어떤 것도 실제로 이루어진 것은 없을 가능성이 높다.

그의 여행 기록이라고 추정되는 몇 가지 원본 기록들이 존재한다. 이 기록들은 이탈리아어, 라틴어, 그리고 고대 프랑스어로 쓰여져 있다. 하지만 기록마다 세부적인 내용이 달라서 그의 여행의 진실성에 의문이 생긴다. 비평가이자 영국의 역사가인 피터 잭슨은 폴로의 저술이 로맨스 소설 작가가 극동 지역에서 시간을 보냈던 여러 여행가들의 이야기를 이용해 쓴 글이라고 생각한다.

또 다른 비판은, 마르코 폴로가 중국에 있었다고 알려진 시기에 사실로 판명된, 중국에 관한 여러 기본적인 사실들을 그가 언급하지 않았다는 것이다. 그는 중국 여인들의 전족에 관한 관습이나 차를 마시는 관습에 대해 결코 언급한 적이 없다. 또한 세계에서 가장 인상적인 구조물 중 하나인 만리장성에 관해서도 기술하지 않았다. 그리고 마르코 폴로는, 중국에서 17년을 보냈다는 자신의 주장에도 불구하고, 중국어를 말하거나 읽거나 쓰지 못했다.

가장 확실한 사실 가운데 하나는 중국 역사 기록 어디에서도 마르코 폴로의 이름이 등장하지 않는다는 것이다. 자신이 통치자였던 쿠빌라이 칸의 절친한 친구이자 대사였으며 궁궐을 자주 드나들었다는 그의 주장을 고려할 때, 그러한 점은 믿기 어려울 정도로 놀라운 일이다. 그는 또한 몽골 공주를 페르시아로 데려오는 일에 자신이 일조했다고 썼지만, 이 역시 동시대의 어떠한 역사책에서도 등장하지 않는 내용이다.

Note Taking

1) Existence of several original accounts of his trip
2) foot binding / tea drinking
3) Couldn't communicate in Chinese
4) Absent from Chinese history books
5) Claimed to have been close to Kublai Khan

Listening

Script 🎧 01-10

W Professor: The controversy surrounding the authenticity of Marco Polo's story about his life in China is based on simple misunderstandings and misinterpretations of facts. Polo indeed traveled to China and then wrote an accurate account of his journey, which became one of the most important books in history.

After returning to Europe, Polo spent some time as a prisoner of war. The first account of his travels was written by a fellow prisoner, a romance writer, who told his tale in Old French. This accounts for the stories of a romance novelist writing fables. Years later, Polo wrote his own story in Italian. This was translated into Latin and later retranslated in Italian once the original manuscript was lost. This explains the many small discrepancies between the texts, a major source of the controversy.

Many critics note that Polo failed to record various common Chinese things, like tea drinking and the Great Wall. However, Polo spent most of his time in the north, where tea wasn't often consumed. It's also possible he never saw the Great Wall since he entered China from the west yet the wall mostly faces north. And keep in mind that the Great Wall wasn't the finished version that exists today. It was actually smaller and included many sections that had eroded or disappeared and were later built after Polo's departure.

Polo never learned Chinese because he didn't need to. Kublai Khan provided Persian translators since he was fluent in that language. He often even used Persian names to describe Chinese places. As for his absence from any Chinese books, this may be related to the fact that he used a different form of his name in Chinese or Mongolian or simply that he wasn't important enough to merit the honor of being mentioned.

해석

W Professor: 마르코 폴로의 중국 생활에 관한 이야기의 신빙성에 관한 논쟁은 단순히 사실들에 대한 오해와 오역에서 비롯되었어요. 마르코 폴로는 실제로 중국으로 여행을 한 후 여행에 대한 정확한 기록을 남겼으며, 이는 역사상 가장 중요한 기록 중의 하나가 되었습니다.

유럽으로 돌아온 후 그는 얼마 동안 전쟁 포로로 지냈습니다. 그의 여행에 관한 첫 번째 기록은 로맨스 소설 작가였던 동료 포로가 쓴 것으로, 그는 그 이야기를 고대 프랑스어로 썼어요. 이는 로맨스 소설 작가가 이야기를 지어냈다는 것을 설명해 주죠. 몇 년이 지나 폴로는 이탈리아어로 자신의 이야기를 직접 썼습니다. 이것이 라틴어로 번역되었는데, 원본 원고가 사라지자 이는 이탈리아어로 재번역되었어요. 이로써 기록 사이에 사소한 부분이 일치하지 않게 되었고, 이것이 논란을 일으킨 주요 원인이 되었습니다.

많은 비평가들은 그가 차 마시는 관습이나 만리장성과 같은 다양하고 일상적인 중국의 특징들을 기록하지 못했다는 점을 지적합니다. 하지만 폴로는 주로 중국 북부에서 시간을 보냈고, 그곳 사람들은 차를 자주 마시지 않았어요. 또한 만리장성은 주로 북쪽을 향하고 있는데, 그는 서쪽으로 중국에 들어갔기 때문에 만

리장성을 전혀 보지 못했을 가능성도 있습니다. 그리고 만리장성이 오늘날 존재하는 것처럼 완공된 상태가 아니었다는 점을 기억하세요. 실제로 크기도 더 작았고, 침식되거나 소실되었다가 폴로가 떠난 뒤에 만들어진 부분들이 많았습니다.

폴로는 그럴 필요가 없었기 때문에 중국어를 배우지 않았어요. 그가 페르시아어에 능통했기 때문에 쿠빌라이 칸이 그에게 페르시아어 통역사를 붙여 주었죠. 그는 종종 페르시아 명칭을 사용해서 중국의 장소를 설명하기도 했습니다. 그가 중국 역사책에서 언급되지 않은 이유에 대해서는 그가 중국이나 몽골로 된 다른 이름을 사용했다는 점과, 혹은 그가 언급될 가치가 있을 만큼 중요한 인물이 아니었다는 사실로 설명될 수 있을 거예요.

📝 Note Taking

1) written in Italian by Marco Polo
2) Stayed in northern China
3) didn't see the Great Wall
4) No need 2 learn Chinese
5) used different name / wasn't that important

Comparing the Points

Reading	Listening
Stance Marco Polo did not go to China, and his story is unreliable.	**Stance** Marco Polo really did go on the trip to China as he said that he had.
Main point 1 All of the original accounts of his story give different versions.	**Refutation 1** A romance novelist wrote the first account of his story in French, and Marco Polo later wrote his own account in Italian, which was translated into Latin.
Main point 2 He never mentioned common Chinese things such as foot binding, tea, or the Great Wall.	**Refutation 2** He did not see things commonly associated with the Chinese since he was in the wrong part of the country.
Main point 3 His name is not written in any contemporary Chinese history books.	**Refutation 3** He spoke Persian and used a different form of his name, so he is absent from Chinese history books.

Synthesizing

1 Although the reading passage's author thinks Marco Polo never went to China or did any of the things he claimed that he did, the professor firmly believes Marco Polo went to China and accurately told his story.

2 To respond to the assertion that Marco Polo's story was just a compilation of tales taken from people who had been to Asia, the professor claims that the first person to write about Polo's journey really was a romance novelist writing in French.

3 While the author of the reading states that Polo never mentioned any common activities the Chinese were known to have engaged in, the professor excuses this by stating that Polo was in northern China, where most people did not drink tea.

4 The reading notes that Marco Polo's name was never recorded by any contemporary Chinese; however, the professor counters by arguing that he might have used a different name or was not considered very important by the Chinese and was therefore omitted from their books.

Organization

1 While the reading asserts that Marco Polo never went to China, the professor provides evidence contrary to this assertion and believes Marco Polo really did go to China.

2 In response to the accusation that the original accounts of Polo's tale written in different languages all have different versions of the story, the professor mentions that the first writing of Marco Polo's adventures came from a romance novelist, not Polo himself.

3 The professor says that Polo later wrote his own account, which was translated and retranslated into other languages. This naturally caused various mistakes.

4 The reading also points out that Polo never mentioned China-related things, such as foot binding, tea drinking, and the Great Wall.

5 However, the professor says that in Polo's location in China, they did not drink tea and that he might never have even seen the Great Wall.

6 Finally, according to the reading, Polo could neither communicate in Chinese, nor was he mentioned in any contemporary Chinese histories.

7 The professor mentions that Polo did not need to learn Chinese since he spoke Persian and used translators.

8 She also claims that Polo may have used a different form of his name or not have been important enough to have been mentioned in any Chinese history texts.

9 In short, the reading is skeptical of Marco Polo's claims; however, the professor fully believes the stories that Polo told.

Exercise 2 ·························· p.46

Reading

해석

1492년 콜럼버스의 역사적인 항해에 앞서 바이킹이 아메리카 대륙을 방문했다는 것은 확실하다. 하지만 중국인들이 그보다 먼저 아메리카 대륙에 도달했다는 주장도 일리가 있다. 1405년과 1433년 사이에 중국의 해군 제독 정화가 일곱 번의 원정을 통해 전 세계의 대양을 가로질렀다. 한 번의 항해에서 그는 분명 북아메리카의 동해안과 서해안에 다다랐다.

증거는 확실하다. 바하마 제도 해안에서 떨어진 곳에 도로 모양으로 생긴 수중 구조물인 비미니 로드가 있다. 영국의 역사가 개빈 멘지스는 이것이 정화 함대가 1421년 바하마 제도에 도착했을 때 만든 부두 또는 도로였다고 믿는다. 구조물 자체 또한 확실한 중국 양식을 지니고 있으며 돌들이 의도적으로 배치된 것처럼 보인다.

두 번째 증거는 캘리포니아 팔로스 버디스 연안의 태평양 해역에서 발견된

20여개의 닻이다. 이 닻들은 중국산이다. 돌로 만들어졌고 가운데 구멍이 뚫려 있어서 특이한 닻 형태를 나타낸다. 수천 년 동안 중국인들은 로프로 묶어 배의 닻으로 사용할 수 있도록 그처럼 크고 가운데에 구멍이 있는 돌을 사용했다. 이러한 닻은 중국 함대, 아마도 정화의 함대가 아메리카에 도달했음을 입증해 준다.

이러한 초기 중국 원정대의 또 다른 흔적은 로드 아일랜드 뉴포트에 있는 뉴포트 타워이다. 이는 중국식 등대의 형태로 지어졌고, 중국의 수도인 베이징과 같은 위도에 위치해 있다. 또한 부순 조개 껍질이 벽돌용 회반죽으로 사용되었는데, 이는 중국 등대를 만들 때 흔히 사용되던 방식이었다. 역사가들에게 등대가 세워진 날짜는 알려져 있지 않지만 탄소 연대 측정법에 따르면 그 건축 시기는 15세기 초반이다.

📝 Note Taking

Zheng He Visited America in the 15th Century

1 Bimini Road off the Bahamas
  • Seems to be underground road / dock
  • Appears to be in a Chinese pattern

2 Anchors discovered off California coast
  • Kind of anchor used by Chinese for thousands of years ➡ made of stone & have holes in the middle

3 Newport Tower in Rhode Island
  • Same shape as a Chinese lighthouse
  • Used crushed seashells for mortar ➡ was used to make Chinese lighthouses

---

Listening

Script 🎧 01-11

M Professor: I'm sure you're all aware Christopher Columbus is credited with discovering the Americas in 1492. There are, of course, competing claims for this discovery, including that of a Chinese expedition by the Chinese Admiral Zheng He in 1421. But let me assure you that any claims of a Chinese discovery of America are utterly false and without merit.

First, some cite a supposed Chinese dock or road in the waters off the Bahamas. This is actually a naturally occurring limestone formation. Geologist Eugene Shinn has stated that it's made of a kind of beach rock, a common form of limestone found in tidal waters. This rock typically forms cracks or breaks in regular patterns, which gives it a manmade appearance. There are, in fact, many other similar formations in the Bahamas, yet these are conveniently ignored by those who believe the 1421 myth.

There's also the reported 1975 discovery of Chinese anchors off the California coast. Those anchors were not ancient but were barely one hundred years old. Logically, they couldn't have come from a fifteenth-century Chinese voyage, could they have? Those anchors were used by Chinese immigrants to California who were working as fishermen. They were merely following Chinese traditions by making their anchors in the ways of their ancestors.

Now, let's get to the Newport Tower in Rhode Island. Yes, the date of construction and the purpose of the tower are unknown. But most historians agree that the shape and design resemble an English windmill more than a Chinese lighthouse. In addition, the, um, Arnold family from Newport is believed to have been the builders and original owners. And finally, carbon dating places the mortar used to bind the stones to the mid-seventeenth century, more than 200 years after Zheng He's final voyage.

해석

M Professor: 확실히 여러분 모두 크리스토퍼 콜럼버스가 1492년에 아메리카 대륙을 발견했다고 알고 있을 거예요. 물론 이러한 발견과 관련해서, 중국 제독인 정화가 이끈 중국 원정대가 1421년에 아메리카 대륙을 발견했다는 주장을 포함하여, 그와 상충되는 주장들이 있습니다. 하지만 중국인이 아메리카 대륙을 발견했다는 주장은 모두 완전히 잘못된 것이며 근거가 전혀 없는 이야기라는 점을 설명해 드리죠.

우선 몇몇 사람들은 바하마 제도의 수역에 있는, 중국의 것으로 생각되는, 부두 또는 도로를 인용합니다. 이는 사실 자연적으로 만들어진 석회암 지형이에요. 지질학자인 유진 쇤은 이것이, 조수 해역에서 흔히 발견되는 석회암의 한 형태인 해안 암석으로 만들어졌다고 설명합니다. 이 암석에서는 대개 규칙적인 패턴의 틈이나 금이 만들어지기 때문에 암석이 인위적인 행태로 보이게 되죠. 실제로 바하마 제도에는 이와 비슷한 다른 많은 지형들이 존재하지만 1421년의 잘못된 신화를 믿는 사람들은 편리하게도 이러한 점을 무시합니다.

또한 1975년 캘리포니아 해안에서 중국 닻이 발견되었다는 보고가 있었습니다. 그 닻들은 오래된 것도 아니고 기껏해야 100년 정도 된 것들이었어요. 논리적으로 생각하면 15세기 중국 원정대에서 나올 수 없는 것이죠, 그렇지 않나요? 그 닻들은 어부로 일했던 중국계 캘리포니아 이주민들에 의해 사용된 것이었어요. 선조들이 쓰던 방식으로 닻을 만들어서 중국의 전통을 따르고 있었던 것뿐이었죠.

자, 로드 아일랜드의 뉴포트 타워로 넘어가 봅시다. 네, 이 타워의 시공 날짜와 목적은 알려져 있지 않아요. 하지만 대다수 역사가들은 그 모양과 디자인이 중국식 등대라기보다는 영국식 풍차에 더 가깝다는 점에 의견을 같이합니다. 또한, 음, 뉴포트 출신의 아놀드 가가 그 구조물을 건축했으며 원 소유주였다고 생각되고 있어요. 그리고 마지막으로 탄소 연대 측정법에 따르면 돌을 붙이는데 사용된 회반죽이 정화의 마지막 항해보다 200년이나 뒤인 17세기 중반의 것으로 나타났습니다.

Note Taking

Zheng He Never Visited America

1 Formation off Bahamas = natural
   • Limestone formation ➜ often forms cracks in regular patterns like manmade ones
   • Other similar formations in Bahamas
2 Anchors ≠ very old
   • From Chinese immigrants ➜ just around 100 years old
3 Newport Tower = English windmill
   • Was built by Arnold family
   • Carbon dating: mid-17th century ➜ 200 years after Zheng He's last voyage

Writing

Sample Response

The reading passage gives credence to the claim that Chinese Admiral Zheng He's armada made it to America in 1421. The professor, on the other hand, rejects this notion completely.

The author of the passage mentions the Bimini Road, an underwater structure that looks Chinese and may have been a dock for Zheng He's fleet, in the Bahamas. However, the professor declares this is a naturally occurring formation of limestone, of which there are many more similar structures throughout the Bahamas.

The reading next describes the 1970s finding of twenty anchors in the Pacific Ocean near California. The author believes they are from Zheng He's fleet because the anchors are distinctly Chinese. However, the professor claims that the anchors came from Chinese immigrant fishermen from around one hundred years ago, so they cannot be from Zheng He's fleet.

Finally, to refute the reading passage's claim that the Newport Tower in Rhode Island was built by the Chinese, the professor declares that the Arnold family from Newport constructed it. He also states that it is not a Chinese-style lighthouse but more of an English-style windmill that is carbon-dated to the mid-seventeenth century, not the fifteenth century.

The reading passage presents much evidence to support the theory of a Chinese discovery of America, but the professor provides his own information to refute these assertions.

해석

읽기 지문은 중국 해군 제독인 정화의 함대가 1421년에 아메리카 대륙을 발견했다는 주장을 신뢰한다. 반면에 교수는 그러한 주장을 전적으로 부정한다.

읽기 지문의 저자는, 중국의 것으로 보이며 정화 함대의 부두였던 것으로 추측되는 수중 구조물인, 바하마 제도에 있는 비미니 로드를 언급한다. 하지만 교수는 이것이 자연 발생적인 석회암 지형이며, 바하마 제도 전역에 석회암 층으로 만들어진 비슷한 지형들이 보다 많이 있다고 주장한다.

다음으로 읽기 지문은 1970년대에 캘리포니아 인근 태평양에서 20개의 닻이 발견된 점을 설명한다. 저자는 닻이 분명 중국 양식을 나타내기 때문에 이들이 정화 함대에서 나온 것이라고 믿는다. 하지만 교수는 그 닻들이 약 100년 전에 이주해 온 중국 어부들의 것으로, 따라서 정화 함대로부터 나올 수가 없는 것이라고 주장한다.

마지막으로 로드 아일랜드에 있는 뉴포트 타워가 중국인들에 의해 건축되었다는 지문의 주장을 반박하기 위해 교수는 뉴포트 지역의 아놀드 가가 그것을 건축했다고 주장한다. 그는 또한 그것이 중국식 등대보다 영국식 풍차에 가까우며 탄소 연대 측정법을 통해 15세기의 것이 아니라 17세기 중반의 것으로 추정된다고 말한다.

읽기 지문은 중국인이 아메리카 대륙을 발견했다는 이론을 뒷받침하는 여러 증거들을 제시하지만, 교수는 자신이 알고 있는 내용을 제시하면서 그러한 주장을 반박한다.

Unit 06 Archaeology

Exercise 1 ·· p.49

Reading

해석

아메리카 대륙은 인간이 거주하게 된 마지막 주요 대륙이지만 언제부터 이곳에 사람이 살기 시작했는지는 알려져 있지 않다. 가장 오래된 고고학적 유적지는 칠레의 몬테 베르데에 있다. 일부 연구자들은 약 1만 2500년 전에 인간이 그곳에 거주했다고 주장한다. 하지만 여러 가지 이유에 근거해 볼 때 이러한 고고학자들의 생각은 잘못된 것이라는 점과 그처럼 오래 전에는 그 지역에 인간이 거주하지 않았다는 점이 명백하다.

최초로 아메리카 대륙에 정착한 사람들은 채집한 식물과 사냥한 동물을 먹고 산 수렵 채집민으로 알려져 있다. 그 후 수천 년이 지나서야 사람들이 농사를 알게 되었다. 하지만 몬테 베르데 유적지에는 사람들이 실제로 당시 그곳에 거주했음을 보여 주는 창촉이나 화살촉과 같은 사냥 도구가 전혀 발굴되지 않았다. 무기가 없다는 사실은 몬테 베르데에 수렵 채집 생활을 한 원시인들의 사회가 존재하지 않았음을 암시한다.

안타깝게도 몬테 베르데 주변 지역은 수 세대에 걸쳐 농지로 사용되었기 때문에 농부들이 유적지를 심하게 훼손시켰다. 밭을 갈고 농작물을 재배함으로써 고고학적인 증거들을 훼손시켰고, 그 결과 수천 년 전 그곳에서 실제로 어떤 일이 있었는지를 알기가 어렵게 되었다. 일반적으로 유적지의 땅속 가장 깊숙한 곳에 가장 오래된 유물이 있고 지표면 가까이에는 가장 최근의 유물이 있다. 하지만 몬테 베르데에서는 토양이 훼손되어 출토된 유물들의 정확한 연대를 측정하는 일이 불가능하다.

또한 도로 포장에 사용되는 타르와 비슷한 물질인 아스팔트가 존재한다. 이 역시 유적지를 훼손시켰다. 아스팔트는 연대 측정 과정 전반에 영향을 미칠 수 있기 때문에 탄소 연대 측정을 어렵게 만든다. 따라서 고고학자들은 특정 유물의 연대만 측정했을 뿐 유적에서 발견된 모든 유물의 연대를 측정하려고 하지는 않았다. 이러한 불완전한 연대 측정 과정 때문에 많은 회의론자들은 그들이 몬테 베르데 및 그곳의 최초 정착에 대한 진실을 감추려는 것이 아닌지 의문을 품는다.

Note Taking

1) Absence of weapons at dig site
2) Archaeological evidence compromised by farmers
3) cannot accurately date artifacts
4) can affect dating process
5) Not every object was dated

Listening

Script 🎧 01-12

M Professor: There's a great debate in archaeological circles concerning when people first came to the Americas. It's centered on the site at Monte Verde, Chile. In 1975, a human settlement with many artifacts was uncovered in a peat bog near a creek on some farmland. It has been dated to 12,500 years ago, which therefore proves that this small, yet well-preserved, place was the site of, well, some kind of human settlement.

The settlers consumed plants and small animals, which they hunted with stones and bones. Just because no one has found any spearheads or arrowheads there doesn't mean the settlers didn't hunt. In fact, a bone with meat still on it was found preserved in the peat bog, proving that they did, after all, hunt. Some archaeologists have also suggested that this group of settlers simply lacked the knowledge of how to make rudimentary weapons, explaining why none was found there.

Now, much of the site was farmland, which suggests that farmers destroyed the site over the years. This just isn't true. The main dig site was the bog itself, which the farmers never touched. Farming also only disturbs the upper layers of the soil. Many archaeological artifacts were found in the deeper layers that had never been disturbed by farming.

Some people also question the results of the carbon dating carried out. It's true that some artifacts weren't carbon dated. The reason is that they had to be promptly immersed into chemicals to preserve them, and the chemicals rendered any dating useless. And, yes, bitumen, which was found there, can influence these tests. However, archaeologists did more than twenty-five tests and also used different dating methods to lend them more accuracy. The majority of the results indicated that the site was occupied 12,500 years ago.

해석

M Professor: 고고학계에는 사람들이 언제 처음으로 아메리카 대륙으로 왔는지에 대한 커다란 논쟁이 존재해요. 그 논쟁의 중심에 칠레의 몬테 베르데 유적지가 있습니다. 1975년 어떤 농지의 개울가에 있던 토탄지에서 많은 유적과 함께 인간의 거주지가 발굴되었어요. 이는 1만 2500년 전의 것으로 추정되었는데, 이로써 이 작고 보존 상태가 양호한 장소는, 음, 일종의 인간 거주지 유적으로 판명되었죠.

정착민들은 식물과 작은 동물을 먹고 살았으며, 동물은 돌이나 뼈로 사냥을 했습니다. 그곳에서 창촉이나 화살촉이 발견되지 않았다고 해서 정착민들이 사냥을 하지 않았다는 의미는 아니에요. 실제로 토탄지에서 고기가 붙어 있는 뼈가 발견되었는데, 이는 어쨌거나 사냥이 이루어졌음을 증명해 줘요. 일부 고고학자들은 또한 이들 정착민 무리가 단순히 초보적인 무기를 만드는 방법을 몰랐다고 주장하는데, 이는 왜 그곳에서 아무런 무기도 발견되지 않았는지를 설명해 줍니다.

자, 유적지의 많은 부분이 농지였고, 이는 농부들이 오랜 세월에 걸쳐 유적지를 훼손시켰다는 점을 암시합니다. 이것은 사실이 아니에요. 주요 발굴 장소는 늪이었는데, 이곳은 농부들이 손을 댄 적이 없는 곳이었습니다. 또한 농사를 짓느라 훼손된 부분은 토양의 상층부에 불과해요. 다수의 고고학적 유물은 농사에 의해 결코 훼손되지 않은 심층에서 발견되었습니다.

또한 어떤 사람들은 탄소 연대 측정의 결과에 의문을 제기합니다. 일부 유물들에 대한 탄소 연대 측정이 이루어지지 않은 것은 사실이에요. 그 이유는 이들을 보존을 위해 이들을 신속히 화학 물질에 담가야 했는데, 화학 물질은 연대 측정을 무의미하게 만들기 때문이었죠. 그리고, 네, 그곳에서 발견된 아스팔트가 이러한 측정에 영향을 미칠 수도 있습니다. 하지만, 고고학자들은 25차례 이상의 실험을 실시했고, 정확성을 높이기 위해 여러 가지 연대 측정법을 사용했어요. 대부분의 결과는 1만 2500년 전 그 유적지에 인간이 거주했다는 점을 암시했습니다.

1) Hunted with stones & bones
2) Peat bog = main dig site
3) many artifacts found in deep layers
4) dipped in chemicals to preserve them
5) Employed 25 different tests & different dating methods

Comparing the Points

Reading	Listening
Stance There were never any settlers at Monte Verde 12,500 years ago.	**Stance** There was a group of people who lived at Monte Verde around 12,500 years ago.
Main point 1 Early American settlers were hunter-gatherers, but no hunting tools were found at the dig site.	**Refutation 1** The settlers hunted small animals with stones and bones, not with spears and arrows.
Main point 2 Farmers constantly plowed the land at the dig site, making it impossible to date the site accurately.	**Refutation 2** The original site was in a peat bog, which had never been disrupted by farmers.
Main point 3 Because there is bitumen at the site, only a few select artifacts could be dated.	**Refutation 3** There were many dating tests done, and most agree settlers were there 12,500 years ago.

Synthesizing

1   The author of the reading is convinced that there were no people at the site that long ago in the past, yet the professor believes at least a small group of people lived there 12,500 years ago.

2   Whereas the reading states the lack of weapons showed that no hunter-gatherers lived there, the professor asserts that this group of people may simply not have known how to make even simple weapons.

3   In contrast to the reading passage author's argument that the farming of the land ruined the value of the excavation site, the professor mentions that the primary site was in the peat bog, which had never been farmed at all.

4   While the reading claims that the presence of bitumen ruined the accuracy of any carbon dating, the professor declares that over twenty-five tests utilizing different methods were done on the artifacts.

Organization

1   The author of the reading is convinced there was no human settlement at Monte Verde over 12,500 years ago.

2   The professor, however, believes that this was not the case and that people actually were there then.

3   First, the reading declares the absence of hunting tools means no one lived there that long ago.

4   However, the professor claims that they hunted small animals with stones and bones, citing evidence that a bone with meat on it was found.

5   He further mentions that this tribe may not have known how to make even simple weapons.

6   The reading also discusses how generations of farming corrupted the land and made it useless for legitimate archaeological research.

7   But the professor points out that most of the dig occurred in the peat bog, which had never been touched by farmers.

8   Besides, a lot of artifacts were found in the deeper layers of the soil instead of in the upper layers, which had been disrupted by farming.

9   Finally, to counter the assertion in the reading that the presence of bitumen made carbon dating impossible, the professor claims that over twenty-five tests using various methods were conducted.

10 According to him, most of them confirmed the site's date as being 12,500 years old.

11 The reading strongly denies there was a settlement at Monte Verde long ago in the past; however, the professor refutes this information and provides his own proof of this very fact.

Exercise 2 ··· p.53

Reading

해석

구리 두루마리는 구리로 만들어진 두 개의 동판으로 1952년 사해 근처의 동굴에서 발견되었다. 동판이 해독되었을 때 전문가들은 동판에 오늘날 화폐 가치로 수십억 달러에 달하는 숨겨진 보물의 이야기가 적혀 있다는 것을 알게 되었다. 이 이야기는 그 후 미스터리 마니아들과 보물 사냥꾼들을 매혹시켰지만 사실 허구일 가능성이 높고 보물은 존재한 적도 없었다.

동판에 적혀 있는 언어가 가장 큰 문제 중의 하나이다. 고대 히브리어인데, 본문과 대조할 만한 알려진 문서가 존재하지 않는다. 또한 동판의 내용을 자세히 읽어보면 누군가가, 실수였는지 혹은 고의였는지, 번역에 몇몇 실수를 했다. 동판의 정확한 번역과 관련해서는 오늘날에도 여전히 논란이 분분하다.

알려진 점은 동판이 현재의 이스라엘에 해당하는 전 지역 중 특정 지역에 금과 은이 쌓여 있다는 점을 말해 준다는 것이다. 동판에 적힌 보물의 양이 너무 많기 때문에 그런 보물이 실제로 존재할 수는 없을 것으로 보인다. 더욱 확실한 증거로서 이 동판은 쿰란 종파에 의해 만들어진 것으로 생각된다. 쿰란 종파는 금욕주의를 따르는 사람들로 세속적인 재산은 바라지도 않았고 소유하지도 않았다. 그들이 그처럼 엄청난 양의 보물을 소유하지는 않았을 것이다.

일부 학자들과 보물 사냥꾼들은 보물이 숨겨진 몇몇 장소를 특정짓기까지 했다. 하지만 그러한 장소를 파 본 결과 금과 은은 발견되지 않았다. 사실 탐색자들은 이들 장소를 찾아내서 그 주변 지역을 파기 위해 엄청난 돈을 쏟아 부었다. 그것이 고대의 장난이든 예전에 발견된 보물에 관한 지도이든 간에 구리 두루마리가 새로운 보물을 드러내 주지는 않을 것이라는 점은 확실하다.

Copper Scrolls Are Not Authentic

1 No agreed-upon translation
 • Written in an ancient form of Hebrew
 • Presence of errors in the translations
2 Too much treasure to be true
 • Buried throughout modern Israel → unbelievable
 • Scrolls come from Qumran sect → they had no possessions
3 No treasures found until now
 • Dug some locations mentioned in the scrolls → found nothing
 • Unlikely any treasure will ever be found

Listening

Script 🎧 01-13

W Professor: One of the ancient world's greatest mysteries is that of the Copper Scrolls. Supposedly, they reveal the secret locations of a vast amount of treasure buried throughout modern-day Israel. Nice, huh? Now, many people believe they're a hoax. I, however, hold that the scrolls were inaccurately translated and instead reveal that the treasure was buried in Egypt, not in Israel.

The Copper Scrolls were tricky to translate because of the poor condition in which they were found and the language in which they were written. The language was actually a combination of ancient common Hebrew and an Egyptian numbering system. Not only that, but there were also many deliberate mistakes made in the translation of the scrolls. The real translations were meant only for the eyes of certain people.

A host of scholars wasted their time on the scrolls by using inaccurate Hebrew numbering systems. Robert Feather, who conducted further studies on them, concluded that the numbers were Egyptian, not Hebrew. When Egyptian numbers are applied, the amount of treasure given is considerably less and therefore more believable. The scrolls date from around 1300 B.C., a period when the Egyptians had a strong presence in that area of the Middle East, so it's possible that an Egyptian or a Hebrew scribe with Egyptian training made the scrolls.

Feather also determined that the scrolls described places in Egypt, not in Israel. The locations described in the scrolls actually correspond to places near Amarna, a city in ancient Egypt. Throughout history, most of these sites have already been, uh, located, and the treasure has been dug up and carted away. So if Mr. Feather's theories are correct, as I believe them to be, the lost treasures of the Copper Scrolls have already been found and are either in museums or personal collections.

해석

W Professor: 고대의 가장 큰 미스터리 중 하나가 구리 두루마리예요. 추측으로는 현재의 이스라엘 지역 중 엄청난 양의 보물이 묻혀 있는 비밀 장소가 그곳에 표시되어 있다고 합니다. 근사하지 않나요? 자, 많은 사람들은 그것이 날조라고 생각해요. 하지만 저는 동판이 부정확하게 번역되었으며, 이스라엘이 아닌 이집트에 보물이 묻혀 있을 것이라고 믿습니다.

구리 두루마리는 발견 당시의 열악한 상태와 그곳에 쓰여진 언어 때문에 번역하기가 까다로웠어요. 그 언어에는 사실 고대의 일반 히브리어와 이집트의 수기법이 혼합되어 있었습니다. 뿐만 아니라 동판의 번역에는 의도적인 실수들이 다수 존재했어요. 제대로 된 번역은 특정인의 눈으로만 가능하도록 의도된 것이었죠.

많은 학자들은 부정확한 히브리 수기법을 사용함으로써 동판에 시간을 낭비했습니다. 동판을 보다 자세히 연구했던 로버트 페더는 그 숫자들이 히브리 숫자가 아니라 이집트 숫자라고 결론지었어요. 이집트 숫자를 적용하면 보물의 양은 상당히 적어지는데, 그래서 신빙성이 더 높아지죠. 동판은 이집트가 중동 지역에서 맹위를 떨쳤던 기원전 1300년경에 만들어졌기 때문에 이집트인이나 이집트어 교육을 받았던 히브리인 필경사가 이 동판을 만들었을 거예요.

페더는 또한 동판에 이스라엘이 아닌 이집트의 장소가 적혀 있다고 주장했습니다. 동판에 설명되어 있는 장소들은 실제로 고대 이집트 도시인 아마르 주변 장소들과 일치하죠. 역사를 통틀어 이들 장소는 대부분 이미, 어, 발견되었고 보물은 출토되어서 옮겨졌어요. 따라서 제가 생각하는 것처럼 페더의 이론이 옳다면 구리 두루마리의 사라진 보물은 이미 발굴되어서 박물관에 있거나 개인 소장품이 되었을 거예요.

Note Taking

Copper Scrolls Are Authentic

1 Difficult to translate
 • A combination of Hebrew and an Egyptian numbering system
 • Deliberate mistakes → prevent everyone from knowing treasures' locations
2 Use of Egyptian numbering system
 • Robert Feather → reliable amount of treasure when in Egyptian units
 • Strong Egyptian influence in the area when the scrolls were made
3 Treasures already found & taken away
 • Real treasure locations = areas near Amarna
 • Most sites were already dug up

Writing

Sample Response

The reading and the lecture both discuss the Copper Scrolls. While the reading states the scrolls tell a fictitious story about buried treasure, the professor believes the treasure mentioned in the scrolls was legitimate.

It is mentioned in the reading passage that the translation of the scrolls posed a problem. According to the reading, they contained many translation errors. The professor explains this by saying that the mistakes were done purposely so that only a few people would actually be able to know the locations of the treasure.

The reading is skeptical of the existence of the treasure because not only are the sums described very huge, but the scrolls also came from the Qumran sect, a group whose members owned no possessions. However, the lecturer explains that if an Egyptian numbering system is used instead of a Hebrew one, then the treasure becomes smaller and therefore more believable.

Finally, the reading reveals that some people deciphered the locations of some of the treasure, but they found nothing when they tried digging it up. The professor argues the treasure's locations were in Egypt, and these sites were already dug up. She is convinced the treasure was taken away long ago and is now in museums or personal collections.

Both the reading and the lecture describe the secrets of the Copper Scrolls, but they come to separate conclusions as to their legitimacy.

해석

지문과 교수는 모두 구리 두루마리에 관해 논의한다. 읽기 지문은 구리 두루마리가 매장된 보물에 관해 지어낸 내용을 말하고 있다고 주장하는 반면에 교수는 구리 두루마리에 언급되어 있는 보물이 사실이라고 생각한다.

읽기 지문에는 두루마리의 번역에 문제가 있다고 언급되어 있다. 읽기 지문에 따르면 번역 상의 오류가 다수 존재한다. 교수는 그것이 소수의 사람들만 보물이 묻힌 장소를 알 수 있도록 의도적으로 만들어진 것이라고 말함으로써 그 점을 설명한다.

읽기 지문은 언급된 보물의 양이 매우 많고 두루마리가 재산을 소유하지 않았던 쿰란 종파로부터 나왔다는 점에서 보물의 존재에 대해 회의적이다. 하지만 교수는 히브리 수기법 대신 이집트 수기법을 사용하면 보물의 양이 더 적어지기 때문에 신빙성이 더 높아진다고 설명한다.

마지막으로 읽기 지문은 몇몇 사람들이 일부 보물이 묻힌 장소를 해독했지만 발굴을 시도하자 아무것도 발견되지 않았다는 점을 밝힌다. 교수는 보물이 묻힌 장소가 이집트였으며 이러한 장소들은 이미 발굴되었다고 주장한다. 그녀는 보물들이 오래 전에 빠져 나가서 지금은 박물관에 있거나 개인 소장품이 되었을 것으로 확신한다.

읽기 지문과 교수 모두 구리 두루마리의 비밀에 대해 설명하지만 그것의 진실성에 대해서는 서로 다른 결론에 도달한다.

Unit 07 Astronomy

Exercise 1 .... p.56

Reading

해석

1908년 6월 말에 러시아 시베리아의 퉁구스카 지역에서 역사상 최대 규모의 폭발이 일어났다. 대형 핵무기와 맞먹는 위력의 엄청난 폭발이었다. 이 폭발의

원인과 관련해서, 소행성이 그곳 지면과 충돌했다는 이론을 포함하여, 많은 이론이 존재한다. 하지만 가장 가능성이 높은 설명은 그것이 대규모 메탄 가스 폭발이라는 것이었다.

그 장소에 대한 첫 번째 조사가 1927년에 이루어졌다는 사실에도 불구하고 그곳에는 그 후에도 많은 탐사단이 파견되었다. 이들 중 누구도 소행성 충돌의 증거를 발견하지 못했다. 소행성에서 나온 암석이나 물질은 전혀 확인되지 않았다. 소행성 암석에는 다량의 니켈과 이리듐이 응축되어 있기 때문에 이들은 쉽게 찾아낼 수 있다. 마지막으로 소행성이 하늘을 가로지르는 것을 보았고 증언하는 목격자도 나타나지 않았다.

알려져 있는 지구의 소행성 충돌 지역에는 커다란 충돌 화구가 남아있지만 퉁구스카에는 그런 화구가 없다. 몇몇 사람들은 한 호수가 충돌 화구였다고 생각하지만 연구자들이 호수 바닥에 있는 진흙이 5천년도 더 된 것임을 밝혀냈다. 하지만 폭이 50km에 이르는 산림 지대가 황폐화되었다. 나무들이 쓰러졌고 나뭇가지와 나무껍질들이 떨어져 나갔다. 이러한 효과는 메탄과 같은 가스가 폭발할 때 더 잘 일어나는 현상이다.

퉁구스카에는 강, 호수, 늪, 그리고 토탄지가 많으며 다량의 메탄 가스가 있는 것으로 알려져 있다. 매우 신빙성 있는 한 이론에 따르면 높은 농도의 메탄 가스가 지하에 축적되었다. 이것이 그 후 인위적으로 또는 자연적으로 방출되어 숲 위쪽에서 폭발을 했고 그로 인해 많은 나무들이 파괴되었다. 실제로 일부 목격자들은 그 근처에서 번개가 치는 것을 보았다고 전했는데, 그것이 메탄 가스를 폭발시켰을 것이다.

📝 Note Taking

1) have found no rock material from asteroid
2) No impact crater in Tunguska
3) Many trees knocked down
4) High level of methane gas in the area
5) Eyewitnesses saw lightning nearby

Listening

Script 🎧 01-14

M Professor: There was a great explosion in Siberia in eastern Russia in 1908. The explosion's cause is still debated to this day. Some people claim it was a nuclear device, the crash landing of a UFO, or a gas explosion. I, however, am certain that the event was caused by an asteroid exploding above the Earth as it entered our atmosphere. Let me explain.

Many eyewitnesses reported a streak of bright light in the sky close to the Earth. One said it was, um, as if the sky had split open. Soon afterward, there was a massive explosion and a great wind, which shattered windows and knocked people to the ground. The light in the sky suggests, er, an asteroid entering the atmosphere.

Since the asteroid exploded before it struck the ground, there was no impact crater to be found. No asteroid rock has been found as well because it either washed away before scientists could get there or it existed in such small quantities that it was essentially unrecognizable. Additionally, the explosion destroyed trees in a unique pattern for fifty kilometers all around. The trees directly below the explosion were still standing but had lost their branches and bark. Those further away were knocked flat. Laboratory tests simulating an asteroid explosion conducted by the Russians revealed identical patterns of destruction.

There is also the implausibility of a methane gas explosion. The main reason is the sheer volume of gas required for an explosion of that size. The area simply doesn't—and never did—have enough methane gas to have created this kind of explosion. No way. Additionally, if there had been a gas explosion, there would have been fires nearby, but no eyewitnesses reported any fires burning in the forests.

해석

M Professor: 1908년 러시아 동부의 시베리아 지역에서 거대한 폭발이 일어났습니다. 폭발의 원인에 관한 논란은 오늘날까지 이어지고 있어요. 몇몇 사람들은 핵폭탄, UFO의 불시착, 또는 가스 폭발이 그 원인이었다고 주장하죠. 하지만 저는 그 사건이 소행성이 대기를 통과해 지구의 상공에서 폭발함으로써 일어났다고 확신합니다. 설명해 드릴게요.

많은 목격자들이 지상과 가까운 하늘에서 밝은 빛 줄기를 보았다고 전했습니다. 한 사람은 마치 하늘이, 음, 쪼개진 것 같았다고 말을 했죠. 그 후 얼마 지나지 않아 거대한 폭발과 광풍이 발생을 했고, 그로 인해 창문이 깨지고 사람들이 바닥에 쓰러졌어요. 하늘에 나타난 빛은, 어, 소행성이 대기에 진입했다는 점을 암시합니다.

소행성이 지면에 닿기 전에 폭발을 했기 때문에 충돌 화구가 발견되지 않은 것입니다. 소행성 암석이 발견되지 않은 것도 과학자들이 그곳에 도착하기 전에 다 쓸려갔거나 양이 너무 적어 사실상 식별할 수 없었기 때문이었죠. 또한 폭발로 인해 사방 50km 지역의 나무들이 독특한 형태로 파괴되었습니다. 폭발이 일어난 바로 아래에 있던 나무들은 그대로 서 있었지만 나뭇가지와 나무껍질은 없어진 상태였어요. 보다 먼 곳에 있던 나무들은 납작한 상태로 쓰러져 있었고요. 러시아인들에 의해 실행된 소행성 폭발을 시뮬레이션한 실험실 테스트에서도 동일한 패턴의 파괴가 이루어졌습니다.

또한 메탄 가스 폭발의 가능성이 없습니다. 주된 이유는 그러한 규모의 폭발에 필요한 가스의 절대량에 있어요. 그 지역에는 그러한 폭발이 일어날 정도의 충분한 메탄 가스가 존재하지 않으며, 존재했던 적도 없습니다. 전혀 없었죠. 게다가 가스 폭발이 있었다면 근처에서 화재가 발생했을 텐데, 산불이 일어났다고 말한 목격자는 한 명도 없었습니다.

📝 Note Taking

1) Eyewitnesses saw bright light in sky
2) Huge explosion & great wind
3) no impact crater / asteroid rocks
4) Trees below explosion were still standing
5) No fires seen nearby a/f the explosion

Comparing the Points

Reading	Listening
Stance The 1908 explosion at Tunguska was most likely caused by a methane gas explosion.	**Stance** An asteroid strike is the most likely cause of the Tunguska explosion.

Main point 1 There was no streak of bright light across the sky, nor were there any asteroid rocks.

Main point 2 No one has found the impact crater of an asteroid in that area.

Main point 3 Methane gas probably rose above the ground and exploded.

Refutation 1 People saw a great light in the sky, and there was a tremendous explosion afterward.

Refutation 2 The asteroid never hit the ground, thus leaving no rocks or crater, and the explosion pattern is the same as that of an asteroid hit.

Refutation 3 There was not enough methane gas there to make such a big explosion.

Synthesizing

1 The reading passage depicts the Tunguska explosion as being caused by methane gas, yet the professor expresses his certainty that an asteroid really caused the explosion.

2 In direct contrast to the reading's assertion that no witnesses ever saw a light in the sky, the professor claims many people did see a bright streak of light in the sky.

3 While the reading cites the lack of an impact crater from an asteroid at Tunguska, the professor believes the asteroid exploded above the ground, hence the lack of a crater.

4 The author of the reading passage thinks a methane gas explosion was the reason the forest was destroyed; however, the professor asserts the Tunguska area lacked enough methane to create an explosion that big.

Organization

1 The reading author presents evidence that methane gas caused the Tunguska explosion of 1908.

2 The professor, however, contests this theory and believes an asteroid caused the explosion.

3 The first evidence presented in the reading is that an asteroid could not have caused the damage because no evidence of asteroid rocks has ever been found.

4 In addition, no one saw an asteroid streaking across the sky.

5 The professor counters by saying that some people did see a streak of light in the sky, thereby suggesting an asteroid.

6 In addition, the aftereffects of the explosion mirror those caused by an asteroid.

7 Next, the reading mentions the lack of an impact site and the fact that the tree damage was similar to what a gas explosion would have caused.

8 The professor, however, indicates that the asteroid exploded in the air, explaining the absence of an impact crater and any minerals.

9 He also says that the results of the explosion are consistent with damage caused by an asteroid.

10 Finally, while the reading author believes a large concentration of methane gas built up and finally exploded, the professor disregards this theory since there was not enough methane there, nor were there any forest fires later.

11 While the reading supports a methane gas explosion, the professor believes an asteroid caused the Tunguska event.

Exercise 2 .... p.60

Reading

해석

수 세기 동안 사람들은 우주에 인간만 존재하는 것인지에 대해 궁금해했다. 생명체가 존재할 가능성이 가장 큰 곳 중 하나는 화성이다. 실제로 수십 년 동안 화성에 생명체가 존재하거나 혹은 존재했는지를 알아내는 것이 여러 과학 탐사와 관찰의 목적이었다. 현재 기본적인 형태의 생명체가 그 행성에 실제로 존재할 수도 있다는 징후가 있는 것으로 보인다.

이러한 믿음의 한 가지 근거는 화성에 존재하는 메탄 가스이다. 메탄은 동식물 사체로부터 자연적으로 발생하는 기체이며 지구의 탄광이나 늪지에서 흔히 발견된다. 메탄은 수백 년 동안만 존재한 후 흩어져 버리기 때문에, 크기가 박테리아 정도로 작더라도, 살아 있는 유기체에 의해 다시 채워져야 한다. 화성에 메탄이 있다는 것은 그 기체를 다시 채워 주는 일종의 살아 있는 유기체가 존재한다는 점을 강력히 암시한다.

최근에 발견된, 화성에서 온 것으로 추정되는 운석에서 박테리아 화석의 흔적을 볼 수 있다. 운석에 긴 사슬 모양으로 된 자철광 결정이 들어 있다. 이 광물은 박테리아에 의해서만 만들어질 수 있다. 연구자들은 이 운석을 1990년대에 남극에서 발견된 유사한 화성 운석과 비교했다. 이 운석 역시 박테리아의 흔적을 보여 준다.

상당 기간 동안 천문학자들은 화성의 두 극지방에서, 대부분 얼음으로 되어 있긴 하지만 생명을 이루는 기본 구성 요소인, 수소가 존재한다는 증거를 확인했다. 더욱이 최근의 우주 탐사에서는 화성 표면 아래에 자유로이 흐르는 듯한 다량의 물이 존재한다는 증거가 발견되었다. 자유로이 흐르는 물이 존재하면, 아무리 기본적인 것일지라도, 생명체가 살 수 있을 것이다. 따라서 화성에 생명체가 존재할 가능성은 다소 높아 보인다.

Note Taking

Life Exists on Mars

1 Existence of methane gas
   • Dead animals & plants ➡ methane
   • Methane gas on Mars ➡ existence of living organisms
2 Specimens of meteorites from Mars
   • Made of magnetite crystals ➡ formed by bacteria
   • Similar meteorite from Mars in Antarctica ➡ also shows signs of bacteria

3 Existence of hydrogen & water
   • Martian poles ➡ frozen ice
   • Free-flowing underground water ➡ could support life

Listening

Script 🎧 01-15

W Professor: Does life exist on other planets? Well, Mars is the most obvious place to look because of its similarity to the Earth and the fact that it has shown signs of possible life in recent explorations. Unfortunately, none of the scientists' findings has been proven with one-hundred-percent certainty, so our search for extraterrestrial life must, regrettably, continue.

One report mentions that the presence of methane gas on Mars proves life exists there since only dead life forms produce it. Wrong. Methane also comes from other sources, including volcanic activity. Mars has plenty of volcanoes. And all indications are that volcanic activity on Mars still continues and has not entirely ceased.

I know many people have pointed at those meteorites with the supposed bacteria from Mars. First, it's uncertain that those meteorites really came from Mars. They could just as easily be from the Earth. You see . . . We don't know for sure. Additionally, the testing on these bacteria forms is still in its initial stages, so it may prove to be something else. Since there are only two specimens, not too many scientists are willing to claim life exists on Mars based upon such a small sampling from meteorites that might not even be from that planet.

While it seems clear-cut that water has been discovered on Mars, this isn't as important as it may seem. Yes, water is necessary for life on the Earth. But most of Mars's water is frozen, and life has difficulty surviving in frozen water. And let's not forget that the existence of underground free-flowing water hasn't been verified. Even if true . . . and that's a long shot . . . it will take some time before we can get underground to see what's going on beneath the Martian surface.

해석

W Professor: 다른 행성에도 생명체가 존재할까요? 음, 화성은 지구와 비슷하다는 점과 최근 탐사에서 생명체의 존재 가능성을 나타내는 징후들이 나타났기 때문에 화성을 가장 먼저 살펴볼 필요가 있습니다. 하지만 안타깝게도 과학자들이 알아낸 어떤 것도 100% 확실한 것으로 입증되지는 않았으며, 따라서 외계 생명체를 찾기 위한 노력은, 유감스럽게도, 계속되어야만 하죠.

한 보고에 따르면 메탄 가스는 생물의 사체에서만 발생하기 때문에 화성에 존재하는 메탄 가스는 그곳에 생명체가 있다는 점을 입증해 줍니다. 틀렸어요. 메탄 가스는 화산 활동을 포함하여 다른 원인에 의해서도 만들어집니다. 화성에는 화산이 많아요. 그리고 모든 징후를 볼 때 화성에는 여전히 화산 활동이 계속되고 있으며 화산 활동이 완전히 멈춘 적은 없습니다.

많은 사람들이 화성에서 온 박테리아라고 생각되는 물질이 들어 있는 운석을 지적한다는 점은 저도 알고 있어요. 먼저 그 운석들이 정말로 화성에서 온 것인지는 확실하지 않습니다. 지구에서 나온 것일 수도 있어요. 그러니까… 확실하지가 않습니다. 게다가 이 박테리아 형태에 관한 조사는 아직 초기 단계라서 다른 존재로 판명될 수도 있어요. 표본이 두 개밖에 없기 때문에 화성에서 왔는지도 확실하지 않은 운석에서 나온 그런 소량의 표본을 근거로 화성에 생명체가 존재한다고 주장하는 과학자는 그다지 많지 않습니다.

화성에서 물이 발견되었다는 점은 분명하지만 이것이 생각만큼 그렇게 중요한 것은 아니에요. 네, 지구상의 생명체에게 물은 필수적입니다. 하지만 화성의 물은 대부분 얼음 상태이며 생명체가 얼음 상태의 물에서 살아남기는 힘들어요. 그리고 지하에서 자유로이 흐르는 물의 존재도 확인된 바가 없다는 사실을 잊지 맙시다. 사실이라고 하더라도… 전혀 그렇지는 않겠지만… 지하에 도달해서 화성 표면 아래에서 어떤 일이 일어나고 있는지 알아내기까지는 시간이 꽤 걸릴 거예요.

📝 **Note Taking**

It's Not Certain that Life Exists on Mars

1 Methane has other sources
- Existence of methane ≠ evidence of life
- Many active volcanoes on Mars ➡ methane gas

2 Not sure of meteorites' origins
- May not be from Mars ➡ may be from Earth
- Only 2 samples ➡ not enough to determine if life exists on Mars

3 Martian water ➡ not favorable to life
- Mostly frozen ➡ hard to live in frozen water
- Free-flowing underground water ➡ not verified

Writing

Sample Response

Although the author of the reading passage is convinced there is life on Mars, the professor is not so certain that this is the case.

The reading first points out the presence of methane gas on Mars. Since methane disappears after some time, it must be replenished by living creatures, even something as small as bacteria. However, according to the professor, methane can be created by volcanoes, of which Mars still has many active ones.

To contrast the reading passage's claim that two meteorites from Mars have been found to contain fossilized bacteria, the professor mentions that no one is even positive that the meteorites actually came from Mars. He thinks that they could be from the Earth and that there is not enough evidence to make a definitive claim.

The reading then describes the presence of frozen hydrogen on the surface of Mars and free-flowing water underneath the surface. The author believes life could exist in this water. The professor, on the other hand,

dismisses the importance of water since most of Mars's water is frozen. She also says that no one has proven that free-flowing water on Mars actually exists.

While the professor wants to wait for further proof of the existence of life on Mars, the reading passage's author believes this proof has already been established.

해석

읽기 지문의 저자는 화성에 생명체가 존재한다고 확신하지만 교수는 그렇게 생각하지 않는다.

읽기 지문은 먼저 화성에 존재하는 메탄 가스를 지적한다. 메탄은 시간이 어느 정도 경과하면 사라지기 때문에 박테리아처럼 작은 생명체일지라도 생물체에 의해 다시 보충되어야 한다. 하지만 교수에 따르면 메탄은 화산 활동으로도 만들어지며 화성에는 여전히 많은 활화산들이 존재한다.

화성에서 온 두 개의 운석에 박테리아 화석이 포함되어 있었다는 읽기 지문의 주장을 반박하기 위해 교수는 그 운석들이 실제로 화성에서 온 것인지는 아무도 장담할 수 없다고 말한다. 그는 그 운석이 지구에서 나온 것일 수도 있으며 단정적인 주장을 하기에는 증거가 충분하지 않다고 생각한다.

이후 읽기 지문은 화성 표면에 냉동 상태의 수소가 존재하고 화성 표면 아래에는 자유로이 흐르는 물이 존재한다고 설명한다. 저자는 이러한 물에 생명체가 존재할 수 있다고 믿는다. 반면에 교수는 화성의 물이 대부분 얼어 있는 상태라서 물의 중요성을 일축한다. 그녀는 또한 아무도 화성에 자유로이 흐르는 물이 실제로 존재한다는 것을 증명하지 못했다고 말한다.

교수는 화성에 생명체가 존재한다는 증거가 더 나타날 때까지 기다려야 한다는 입장이지만 읽기 지문의 저자는 그러한 증거가 이미 확정적이라고 믿는다.

Unit 08 Business

Exercise 1 .... p.63

Reading

해석

비즈니스 분야에서의 최신 마케팅 경향 중 하나는 버저들을 이용하는 것인데, 이들은 제품 홍보를 위해 기업들이 고용하는 사람들이다. 버저들은 흔히 공공 장소에서 제품을 사용한 뒤 이 제품이 얼마나 마음에 드는지를 사람들에게 이야기함으로써 제품을 홍보한다. 하지만 안타깝게도 이러한 마케팅 방법에는 많은 문제가 있다.

버저를 이용한 마케팅은 기업의 제품을 홍보하는 댓가로 돈을 받는다는 점에서 본질적으로 부정직하다. 더욱이 그들 중 대부분은 자신이 버저라는 사실을 누구에게도 말하지 못하도록 강요하는 비밀 유지 계약을 고용주와 체결한다. 이는 그들이 기업의 직원이며 실제 자신의 의견을 표현하지는 않는다는 점을 의미한다. 이들 중 일부는 자신이 홍보하는 제품을 좋아하지 않을 수도 있지만, 그럼에도 불구하고 가족, 친구, 그리고 전혀 모르는 타인들에게 시중에서 그 제품이 최고라고 말한다.

또한 버저는 구매 제품에 대해 소비자들이 덜 객관적이 되도록 만든다. 요즘에는 대부분의 사람들이 광고를 잘 믿지 않는다. 기업들이 버저들을 고용한 주된 이유가 바로 그러한 점 때문이다. 끊임없는 버저의 과대 포장에 노출되면 사람들은 제품에 대해 덜 비판적이 될 수 있다. 문제의 사람들이 버저의 친인척이거나 친구인 경우일 때 훨씬 더 그러하다. 그들은 있을 수 있는 제품의 단점을 쉽게 무시하고 제품의 품질이 실제보다 더 좋다고 믿을 수도 있다.

따라서 버저는 사회 구성원 사이에 불신을 초래함으로써 전체적으로 사회에 해를 끼친다. 버저가 자발적으로 제품을 홍보하고 있는 것처럼 보이기 때문에 사람들은 쉽게 버저를 믿는 경향이 있다. 하지만 소비자가 일단 버저에 관한 진실을 알고 나면 버저뿐만 아니라 다른 사람들도 전반적으로 불신하기 시작한다. 다른 사람에 대한 신뢰도가 떨어짐으로써 사회 전반이 흔들리기 시작한다.

📝 Note Taking

1) receive money from companies
2) Confidentiality agreement
3) Make people less objective
4) 2 friends / family
5) don't trust anyone else

Listening

Script 🎧 01-16

W Professor: Nowadays, people are doing a lot of talking about buzzers, you know, those guys hired to tell you some product is great. There's a lot of negative reaction to them, and many people maintain buzzers only promote a product since they're getting financial compensation. In actuality, many buzzers like the products they're promoting, which makes them much more easily trustworthy than other forms of advertising.

Companies don't just hire anyone to be a buzzer. They conduct tests to find people who genuinely like their products. The buzzers then spend time using the products to learn everything about them. Testing has shown people can often tell when another person is being deceitful, so companies want buzzers who really love the products they're trying to sell. For example, I once worked as a buzzer myself. I loved the product and tried to encourage others to buy it. There was nothing deceitful in that.

Consumers often ask many questions about new products. They don't become less critical. Unless potential customers receive the answers they're looking for, they won't buy a product. This is how buzzers can be of, uh, valuable assistance. Buzzers have to learn all about a product to describe its features and benefits; otherwise, they won't make any sales. As a result, they can impart valuable information to the public.

I completely disagree with the notion that buzzers affect society negatively. As a matter of fact, their influence is rather positive. For example, they help build trust in society by telling others about good quality products. This, um, word-of-mouth marketing then spreads widely, letting people learn about new products from their friends and family members. In fact, if buzzers weren't helpful and harmed societal relationships,

companies wouldn't hire them in the first place. So they must be doing some good, right?

해석

W Professor: 요즘에 사람들이 버저에 대해, 아시다시피 제품이 좋다는 말을 하도록 고용된 사람들에 대해, 많은 이야기를 하고 있어요. 이들에 대해서는 부정적인 반응이 많으며 많은 사람들은 버저가 금전적인 보상을 받는다는 이유만으로 제품을 홍보한다고 주장하죠. 실제로는 많은 버저들은 자신이 홍보하는 제품을 좋아하는데, 이러한 점 때문에 버저들은 다른 형태의 광고에서보다 훨씬 더 많은 신뢰를 얻습니다.

기업들이 아무나 버저로 고용하는 것은 아니에요. 테스트를 진행해서 자사 제품을 진정으로 좋아하는 사람을 찾아냅니다. 그 다음에는 버저가 오랫동안 제품을 사용하면서 제품에 대한 모든 것을 알게 되어요. 조사에 따르면 사람들은 다른 사람이 자신을 속이려 하는 것을 금방 알아차릴 수가 있기 때문에 기업들은 판매하려는 제품을 진정으로 좋아하는 버저를 원합니다. 예를 들어 저도 한때 버저로 활동했던 적이 있었어요. 저는 그 제품을 정말 좋아해서 다른 사람들에게도 구입을 권했죠. 그러한 과정에서 거짓은 전혀 없었어요.

소비자들은 종종 신제품에 대해 많은 질문을 합니다. 비판적인 태도가 줄지는 않죠. 잠재 고객은 원하는 대답을 얻지 못하면 제품을 구매하지 않습니다. 이러한 점 때문에 버저가, 어, 값진 도움이 될 수 있어요. 버저는 제품의 특성과 장점을 설명하기 위해 제품에 관한 모든 것을 알아야 합니다. 그렇지 않으면 제품을 판매할 수 없을 테니까요. 따라서 이들은 대중들에게 값진 정보를 나누어 줄 수 있습니다.

저는 버저가 사회에 부정적인 영향을 끼친다는 주장에 전적으로 동의하지 않습니다. 실제로 이들의 영향은 다소 긍정적인 것이에요. 예를 들어 버저는 양질의 제품을 다른 사람에게 소개함으로써 사회적인 신뢰가 형성되는데 도움을 주죠. 이러한, 음, 입소문 마케팅이 널리 퍼지면서 사람들은 가족과 친구를 통해 신제품에 대해 알게 됩니다. 사실 버저가 도움이 되지도 않고 사회적 관계에 해를 끼친다면 우선적으로 기업들이 버저를 고용하지 않을 거에요. 그러니 버저가 어느 정도 도움을 주고 있다는 것은 확실합니다, 그렇죠?

📝 Note Taking

1) Companies conduct tests to see who qualifies
2) very critical & demand good answers
3) provide valuable information to public
4) use word-of-mouth marketing to tell others about good products
5) companies wouldn't use them

Comparing the Points

Reading	Listening
Stance Buzzers have negative effects on consumers and society in general.	**Stance** Buzzers actually provide valuable services for potential customers.
Main point 1 Buzzers often work just for the money and might not even like the products they promote.	**Refutation 1** Companies only hire buzzers who really like their products.
Main point 2 The constant hyping of products by buzzers makes people less critical of products.	**Refutation 2** Since consumers are so critical, buzzers must learn much about their products, and they can then share this knowledge with the public.

Main point 3 Once people become suspicious of buzzers, they begin to distrust everyone else in general.	Refutation 3 Buzzers help build trust in society by getting people to share their feelings about products through word-of-mouth discussions.

Synthesizing

1 While the reading passage says that buzz marketing is not admirable, the professor thinks buzzers actually like their products, which makes them easier to trust than other advertisers.

2 Whereas the reading passage thinks that since buzzers are getting paid, they are not honest, the professor mentions that people usually know when others are lying, so companies need buzzers who like their products.

3 The reading passage declares that people tend to be less critical of products because of the influence of buzzers; however, the professor says that customers will not purchase a product if they fail to receive the information they are looking for.

4 In contrast to the reading, which claims buzzers are making people develop a distrust for society, the professor believes that buzzers are helping people learn to trust one another.

Organization

1 The author of the reading is very much against buzzers, yet the lecturer feels that buzzers actually provide a positive service for consumers.

2 The reading mentions that buzzers are deceitful because they work for the money and do not tell others they are buzzers.

3 They may not even like the product they are promoting.

4 However, the lecturer declares that buzzers do like the products they are promoting.

5 She claims to have worked as a buzzer herself because she really loved a certain product.

6 While the reading passage declares that the continual hyping by buzzers makes consumers less critical of products, the lecturer believes customers actually are critical enough.

7 She also notes that since buzzers must be well versed in how to use their products, they provide important services to people when they talk about various products.

8 Finally, the reading passage believes buzzers are causing society to break down because people do not know whom they can actually trust.

9 The lecturer, on the other hand, feels that buzzers build up trust in society by using word-of-mouth marketing.

10 She points out that if buzzers were really harmful, companies would not hire them at all.

11 In conclusion, the reading passage feels buzzers are harmful to society, yet the lecturer believes they are helping customers and society alike.

Exercise 2 ⋯⋯⋯⋯⋯⋯⋯⋯⋯⋯⋯⋯⋯⋯⋯⋯⋯⋯ p.67

Reading

해석

요즘 점점 더 많은 사람들이 창업을 하기 위해 회사를 떠나고 있다. 이러한 경향은 급격히 확산되고 있다. 이제 일부 회사의 경우 직원들을, 특히 가장 유능하고 똑똑한 직원들을 지키기가 힘든 상황이 되었다. 회사에 다니는 것의 부정적인 측면이 보다 확실해지고 있기 때문에 그러한 점은 놀랄 일이 아니다.

대기업에는 여러 단계의 관료 체제가 있어서 하급 직원이 높은 직위에 있는 사람과 접촉하는 일이 거의 불가능한 경우가 많다. 기업 서열의 꼭대기까지 올라가는 것이 개인의 목표가 아닐 수도 있지만, 모든 직원들은 자신의 아이디어가 경청되고 실행되기를 바란다. 이런 일은 기업에서 불가능한 경우가 많다. 심지어 직원들이 세운 공로를 때때로 상급 관리자가 가로채기도 한다. 직장인에게 창업은 종종 자신의 아이디어가 확실히 빛을 볼 수 있도록 만들 수 있는 유일한 방법이다.

끊임없이 변하는 경제 상황에서 고용 보장은 과거의 일이 되었다. 한때 안정적이라고 생각되었던 기업들도 재무상의 계산 착오와 스캔들의 무게를 견디지 못해 무너져 내렸다. 지난 몇 년 동안 수만 명의 사람들이 해고를 당했다. 자신이 책임을 지는 사업을 운영함으로써 개인은 재정적으로 더 큰 안정감을 느낄 수 있다. 이러한 사람들은 스스로를 보호하기 위해서만 노력할 뿐이다.

사람들은 보험, 퇴직 연금, 그리고 퇴직 연금 투자에 의존하여 어려움에 처했을 때 스스로를 보호하며 미래를 대비한다. 하지만 보험료는 점점 인상되고 있고, 연금 기금은 문제를 겪고 있으며, 회사가 파산을 하는 경우에는 많은 퇴직 연금 투자가 무용지물이 된다. 따라서 개인 사업주가 되면 사업주의 미래의 안정성이 보장된다. 이 모든 것을 종합해 볼 때 창업은 매력적인 일이다.

📝 Note Taking

Owning a Business = Good Idea

1 Big companies = too bureaucratic
  • New ideas ➜ difficult to act upon
  • Senior managers ➜ take credit for hard work

2 No more job security at companies
  • Companies thought to be safe ➜ now going bankrupt & firing workers
  • Owning a business ➜ more financially secure

3 Unstable pension plans & retirement investments
  • Worthless when company fails
  • Owning a business ➜ can be stable

Listening

Script 🎧 01-17

M Professor: Okay, everyone wants to be the boss, but starting a business on your own is like traveling down a road filled with trouble. Sure, there are many successful businesses, and everyone dreams of being the next Bill Gates or Steve Jobs. But most businesses ultimately fail. It's far better to be an employee than to be a boss.

Starting the business itself is a bureaucratic nightmare. You have to deal with state and federal laws and get permits, licenses, and all other sorts of things. You may have a great idea, but someone else might have had the same one and have already patented it. And let's not forget about taxes, rents, and employee wages. If you don't succeed in your first six months, chances are that you never will.

While job security isn't really present at big corporations anymore, running your own business is even less secure. Take, um, restaurants for example. Nine out of ten restaurants go out of business within five years of opening. You may have to sell your car or home to pay off the business debts you incur. You won't get fired, of course, but you may lose everything, even the proverbial shirt off your back.

You also need to take the issues of insurance, pension plans, and retirement investments into account. If you're a business owner, you'll have to provide for all of these and set your employees up with them, too. And your insurance costs will be greater since you'll require insurance for your property, inventory, and, er, employees. And if everything falls apart, I mean if the pension plan fails or the retirement investments disappear, people are going to take action against you. No, running your own business isn't as easy as it sounds.

해석

M Professor: 좋아요, 모두들 사장이 되고 싶어하지만 자신의 사업을 시작한다는 것은 고생길에 들어서는 것과 같습니다. 물론 성공하는 경우도 많으며 모든 이들이 제2의 빌 게이츠나 스티브 잡스가 되기를 꿈꾸죠. 하지만 대다수 사업들은 결국 실패로 끝납니다. 사장이 되기보다는 사원으로 있는 편이 훨씬 낫습니다.

창업 자체가 관료주의를 상대해야 하는 끔찍한 경험이에요. 주법과 연방법을 마주해야 하고 허가, 면허, 그리고 기타 여러 가지를 받아야 하죠. 여러분들이 대단한 아이디어를 가지고 있을 수도 있지만, 다른 누군가가 똑같은 아이디어로 이미 특허를 출원했을 수도 있습니다. 그리고 세금, 임대료, 그리고 직원 임금도 잊지 말아야 해요. 처음 6개월 만에 성공하지 못하면 결코 성공하지 못할 확률이 큽니다.

더 이상 대기업에서 고용 안정성이 보장되는 것은 아니지만 개인 사업을 하는 쪽이 더 불안정합니다. 음, 식당을 예로 들어 보죠. 열 개의 식당 중 아홉은 개업 후 5년 안에 문을 닫습니다. 사업에서 생긴 빚을 갚기 위해 자동차나 집을 팔아야 할 수도 있어요. 물론 해고를 당하는 일은 없겠지만 가진 것 모두를 잃게 될 수도 있습니다.

또한 보험, 퇴직 연금, 그리고 퇴직 연금 투자도 고려해야 합니다. 여러분이 회사의 사장이라면 이 모든 것을 여러분이 준비해서 직원들에게 제공해야 할 거예요. 그리고 여러분의 재산, 재고, 그리고, 어, 직원들을 위한 보험을 들어야 하기 때문에 여러분의 보험료가 더 올라갈 것입니다. 그리고 모든 것이 실패할 경우, 그러니까 퇴직 연금이 지급되지 않거나 퇴직 연금 투자금이 사라지면 사람들이 여러분을 상대로 행동을 취할 거예요. 그래요, 자기 사업을 한다는 것은 생각만큼 쉬운 일이 아닙니다.

📝 **Note Taking**

Owning a Business = Risky

1 Difficult at start
- Too much bureaucracy ➡ laws, permits, & licenses
- Must pay rent, taxes, & salaries

2 Not safe
- 90% of restaurants fail within 5 years
- Go out of business ➡ may lose everything to pay debts

3 Must pay extra benefits
- Insurance, pension, & retirement investments for employees
- Go out of business ➡ employees will come demanding their money

Writing

Sample Response

The reading passage mentions why running one's own business is a much better choice than working for a corporation. However, the professor feels that owning a business is risky and advises against it.

The reading first mentions that it is difficult for many corporate employees to have their ideas acted upon. They simply get lost in the bureaucracy of large companies. However, the professor notes that simply beginning a business involves a lot of bureaucratic procedures. One has to go through red tape to deal with laws, taxes, and licenses and must also pay rents and salaries.

The reading next states that corporations are no longer safe places to work since many of them have gone bankrupt lately. However, the professor says that the large majority of startups fail, which could cost a person many of his possessions to pay off his debts.

The reading then declares that many corporations' pension plans and retirement investments are becoming worthless, so people with their own companies can get some security. The professor counters by saying that a business owner must pay for all of these expenses, and if the company fails, the employees will pursue the owner to get their money.

While the reading passage's author feels that owning a business is a good idea, the professor believes owing a business is a bad idea.

해석

읽기 지문은 자기 사업을 하는 것이 직장 생활을 하는 것보다 훨씬 더 나은 이유를 설명한다. 하지만 교수는 사업체를 소유하는 것이 위험하다고 생각하고 그에 대한 반대 의견을 제시한다.

읽기 지문은 먼저 회사에 다니는 많은 직장인들이 자신의 아이디어를 실현시키기가 힘들다고 언급한다. 그들은 대기업의 관료 제도 내에서 어떻게 할 수가 없다. 하지만 교수는 창업에도 많은 관료주의적인 절차가 수반된다고 지적한다. 법률, 세금, 그리고 면허와 관련된 형식적인 절차를 거쳐야 하고 임대료 및 직원 임금도 지불해야 한다.

다음으로 읽기 지문은 최근에 많은 회사들이 파산했기 때문에 회사가 더 이상 안전한 곳이 아니라고 말한다. 하지만 교수는 대다수의 스타트업 기업들이 실패로 끝나는데, 이로써 개인 재산의 상당 부분이 빚을 갚기 위해 처분될 수도 있다고 말한다.

이후 읽기 지문은 회사의 퇴직 연금 및 퇴직 연금 투자의 가치가 줄고 있기 때문에 자기 사업체를 가지고 있는 사람들이 어느정도 안정성을 얻을 수 있다고 주장한다. 교수는 사업주가 이 모든 비용을 직접 지불해야 하고, 만약 회사가 실패로 끝날 경우, 직원들이 돈을 받기 위해 사업주를 괴롭힐 것이라고 말함으로써 읽기 지문을 반박한다.

읽기 지문의 저자는 자기 사업을 하는 것이 좋은 아이디어라고 생각하는 반면에 교수는 자기 사업을 하는 것이 좋지 않은 아이디어라고 생각한다.

Unit 09 Biology II

Exercise 1 .... p.70

Reading

해석

대부분의 거미들은 몇 가지 형태로 거미집을 짓는다. 이러한 거미집은 거미가 자연적으로 만들어 내는 끈적한 명주실 같은 물질로 만들어진다. 거미집에는 두 가지 유형, 즉 원형 거미집과 깔때기형 거미집이 있다. 두 가지 모두 먹이를 포획하여 붙잡아 둘 수 있지만 원형 거미집이 훨씬 더 효율적으로 그렇게 한다.

원형 거미집은 평면에 만들어진 일차원적인 거미집이다. 이는 중심에서 바깥쪽으로 원이 점점 커지는 나선형의 거미줄로 이루어진다. 이 거미집은 1차원적이라는 사실과 거미줄이 밤에는 말할 것도 없고 환한 대낮에도 잘 보이지 않을 만큼 가늘다는 사실 때문에 눈에 잘 띄지 않는다. 따라서 대다수의 거미들은 원형 거미집을 짓는데, 그 이유는 곤충들은 이러한 거미집 안으로 날아오거나 순진하게 걸어 들어와서 손쉬운 먹잇감이 되기 때문이다.

원형 거미집의 납작한 형태와 일차원적인 구조 또한 거미줄을 보다 효율적으로 사용할 수 있게 만든다. 이러한 형태의 거미집은 구조가 비교적 단순하기 때문에 거미가 거미줄을 최소한으로 쓸 수 있다. 이처럼 단순한 구조 덕분에 거미는 빠르게 거미집을 만들 수 있다. 실제로 원형 거미집을 완성하기까지 30분에서 45분밖에 걸리지 않는다. 이러한 효율성은 중요한 점인데, 그 이유는 많은 종의 거미들이 새벽녘에 자신의 거미집을 파괴해서 먹어 치운 후 밤이 되면 새로운

거미줄로 다시 집을 짓기 때문이다.

마지막으로 원형 거미집은 거미에게 언제 먹이가 접근하고 잡히는지 알려 준다. 거미는 거미집 한가운데 있기 때문에 먹이가 걸려 들면 모든 방향에서 곤충의 진동을 감지할 수 있다. 진동은 실제로 먹이가 가까이 있음을 거미에게 알려 주는 신호이다. 그러면 거미는 먹이의 위치를 쉽게 파악한 후 먹이에 접근해서 먹이를 잡아먹는다.

📝 Note Taking

1) difficult to see
2) Easy to build with little spider silk
3) takes 30-45 min. to build
4) Can know when prey is caught
5) feel vibrations from captured prey

Listening

Script 🎧 01-18

W Professor: As you probably know, spiders use webs to catch their prey. They may use either orb webs or cobwebs to do so. Some believe orb webs are better. I, on the other hand, favor the cobweb as the spider's ideal kind of web for a number of different reasons.

The cobweb is a three-dimensional web built in the shape of a cone or triangle and is located in the branches of trees or plants or in manmade structures. Unlike an orb web, a cobweb is generally made of irregular strands of spider silk and has a much denser structure. Therefore, ensnared insects cannot escape as easily as they can from an orb web. Remember that the spider's food source is integral to the production of its web, so it can ill afford to allow any prey to escape lest it die.

Cobwebs are much stronger than orb webs. Orb webs only consist of one flat layer of web strands, and these may easily be broken by the wind, birds, or even, you know, large insects. Once an orb web breaks, a spider must start again from scratch to rebuild it. Cobwebs, however, are denser and stronger, meaning they break much less easily. Because they're three-dimensional, damage to one section doesn't mean the spider must rebuild the entire structure. It only needs to repair that one section.

Last, but not least, cobwebs are much safer than orb webs. Because the spider must lie in the center of an orb web to feel the vibrations of captured prey, it is easy to be spotted by its natural enemies like birds. Cobwebs, on the other hand, are not so vulnerable to attack. The spider can lie deep in its dense folds and remain hidden from outside enemies.

해석

W Professor: 아마 여러분도 알고 있겠지만 거미는 거미집을 이용해서 먹이를 잡습니다. 원형 거미집이나 깔때기형 거미집 둘 중 하나를 이용할 수 있죠. 어떤 사람들은 원형 거미집이 더 낫다고 생각해요. 하지만 저는 여러 가지 다양한 이유로 깔때기형 거미집이 거미에게 이상적인 거미집이라고 생각합니다.

깔때기형 거미집은 원뿔 모양이나 삼각형으로 지어진 3차원적인 거미집으로 나무나 식물의 가지 또는 인공 구조물 내에 만들어져요. 원형 거미집과 달리 깔때기형 거미집은 일반적으로 불규칙하게 생긴 거미줄로 만들어지며 훨씬 더 빽빽한 구조를 갖추고 있죠. 그래서 덫에 걸린 곤충이 원형 거미집에서처럼 쉽게 탈출할 수가 없어요. 거미의 먹이는 거미집을 만들어 내는데 필수적이므로 거미가 죽지 않기 위해서는 먹이를 놓치는 일이 없어야 하죠.

깔때기형 거미집은 원형 거미집보다 훨씬 튼튼해요. 원형 거미집은 단지 평평한 한 층의 거미줄로 이루어져 있기 때문에 바람, 새, 혹은 심지어, 아시다시피, 몸집이 큰 곤충에 의해서도 쉽게 망가집니다. 원형 거미집은 망가지면 거미가 처음부터 이를 다시 만들어야 해요. 하지만 깔때기형 거미집은 보다 빽빽하고 튼튼한데, 이는 이들이 훨씬 망가지기가 어렵다는 점을 의미하죠. 3차원적인 형태를 띠고 있기 때문에 한 부분이 망가지더라도 전체를 다시 만들 필요가 없어요. 그 한 부분만 수리하면 됩니다.

마지막이지만 중요한 점으로, 깔때기형 거미집이 원형 거미집보다 훨씬 더 안전합니다. 원형 거미집에서는 거미가 걸려든 먹이의 진동을 느끼기 위해 거미집의 한 가운데 앉아 있어야 하기 때문에 새와 같은 천적의 눈에 띄기가 쉬워요. 반면에 깔때기형 거미집은 공격에 그다지 취약하지 않습니다. 거미는 겹겹이 쌓인 거미줄 깊숙한 곳에 들어가 외부의 적으로부터 몸을 숨길 수가 있죠.

📝 **Note Taking**

1) Difficult
2) must be completely rebuilt
3) only small sections to repair
4) Safer from predators than orb webs
5) hard for predators to attack it

Comparing the Points

Reading	Listening
Stance Orb webs are more efficient webs than cobwebs.	**Stance** Cobwebs are more efficient types of webs than orb webs.
Main point 1 Because orb webs are hard to see, they can capture prey easily.	**Refutation 1** The density of cobwebs makes it hard for prey to escape from them.
Main point 2 The orb web is easy to build with little spider silk thanks to its simple structure.	**Refutation 2** Cobwebs are stronger and, when damaged, do not need to be repaired completely.
Main point 3 The spider in the middle of the orb web can easily know when prey gets caught.	**Refutation 3** Spiders can hide deep in their cobwebs so that enemies cannot attack them.

Synthesizing

1 According to the reading passage, orb webs are efficient at capturing and keeping hold of prey, yet the professor favors cobwebs as the ideal type of web for spiders.

2 While the reading points out that most spiders build orb webs because the webs allow for the easy capture of prey, the professor states that the dense structure of cobwebs means that insects trapped in them cannot escape very easily.

3 In response to the reading, which reads that building

orb webs requires spiders to use a small amount of web substance, the professor says that when orb webs break, spiders must completely rebuild them.

4 The reading mentions that spiders in the centers of orb webs can detect vibrations from captured prey; however, the professor declares that the fact that spiders must be in the center of orb webs leave them vulnerable to attack by birds and other predators.

Organization

1 The reading passage's author believes orb webs are best for spiders, yet the professor opines that cobwebs are much better.

2 The reading cites the fact that orb webs are one dimensional, which makes them difficult to be spotted by potential prey, so insects get captured easily.

3 Meanwhile, the professor says the three-dimensional aspect of cobwebs makes it more difficult for insects to escape from cobwebs than from orb webs.

4 Next, the author of the reading believes the orb web's structure is an efficient use of the spider's web substance.

5 Spiders can make orb webs in less than an hour and spin new ones each day.

6 However, the professor claims a damaged orb web must be remade completely, which wastes valuable web substance.

7 She says that when cobwebs are damaged, the spider just repairs one particular section, not the entire web.

8 Finally, the reading mentions that the spider, which sits in the orb web's center, can feel the web vibrating when prey get trapped, so it can capture them immediately.

9 However, the professor feels that spiders in the centers of orb webs can be attacked easily by birds whereas spiders in cobwebs can sit deep in their webs and be protected from outside attacks.

10 Both the reading passage's author and the professor have differing opinions of the best type of web for spiders.

Exercise 2 ⋯⋯⋯⋯⋯⋯⋯⋯⋯⋯⋯⋯⋯⋯⋯⋯⋯⋯⋯⋯ p.74

Reading

해석

인간 및 영장류, 원숭이, 고릴라, 그리고 침팬지 등은 많은 특성을 공유한다. 영장류는 모든 동물 중에서 가장 지능이 높은 것으로 알려져 있지만 대부분의 연구자들은 이들에게 언어 구사 능력이 없다고 믿는다. 하지만 1970년대 조지아 대학에서 진행된 한 연구에 의하면 침팬지에게 마치 어린 아이와 같은 언어 학습 능력이 존재할 가능성도 있다.

이 프로젝트는 몇 마리의 침팬지를 실험 대상으로 삼았는데, 그중 암컷인 라나에 실험의 초점이 맞춰졌다. 영장류에게는 인간과 같은 언어 형태를 만들어 낼 수 있는 발성 구조가 없기 때문에 연구자들은 소리와 단어를 나타내는 기호로 이루어진 여키시라는 기호 문자를 만들었다. 키보드에 125개의 기호를 표시했고 라나에게는 키보드를 사용해서 연구자들과 의사소통을 하는 법을 가르쳤다. 라나는 여러 다른 키를 연속으로 눌러 자신의 생각을 성공적으로 표현했다. 어떤 경우에는 한 번에 최대 7개의 키를 사용하기도 했다.

키보드 사용으로 라나의 의사소통 능력이 약간 제약을 받기는 했지만 연구자들은 이 침팬지가 기초적인 언어 능력을 갖출 수 있었다고 주장했다. 라나는 단어를 조합할 수도 있었으며 심지어 명사와 형용사를 구별하기도 했다. 예를 들어 반지에 해당되는 기호 문자가 없었기 때문에 라나는 반지를 설명하기 위해 "손가락 팔찌"라는 말을 사용했다. 라나는 "손가락"을 명사로 배웠지만, 그 경우에는 형용사로 사용을 했다.

라나는 연구자들의 질문을 받는 경우 대답을 할 수 있었다. 질문을 단어 문자 기계에 입력하면 라나는 질문 내용을 이해하는 것처럼 보였다. 그런 다음 라나는 키보드를 사용해서 논리적으로 보이는 대답을 했다. 의사소통이 제한적이기는 했지만 연구자들은 라나의 실험을 통해 일부 영장류에게 언어로 의사소통하는 법을 익힐 수 있는 능력이 있다는 점이 입증되었다고 생각했다.

📝 Note Taking

Chimps Can Learn Language

1 Learned symbol language
 • Yerkish: new language that uses symbols
 • Used symbols 2 communicate ➜ esp. Lana
2 Formed the basis of language ability
 • Combined words to express thought ➜ e.g. "finger bracelet" to mean "ring"
 • Learned grammar ➜ distinguish nouns from adjectives
3 Responded to questions
 • Gave logical answers
 • Proved primates' ability to learn language

Listening

Script 🎧 01-19

M Professor: It's a well-documented fact that animals have the ability to communicate with one another by using sounds and pheromones. However, the notion that animals can actually talk with humans has yet to be fully proved. While there have been some minor breakthroughs in communications with primates, they are limited in nature and have been treated with skepticism by most of the scientific community.

Lana, a female chimp from the University of Georgia, is the most celebrated case. Lana learned the new language Yerkish, which was comprised of symbols, and managed to communicate with the researchers. Or so it appeared. Remember that Lana was limited in her ability to learn and was in fact conditioned by endless repetition of the same words and symbols. Unlike a human child, which can learn multiple languages if exposed to them, Lana had difficulty learning even one.

Lana could understand some grammar, but it was so basic that she could only manage to create, um, a few short sentences. She and the other test subjects never even advanced beyond the beginning level of language learning. The chimps couldn't form sentences on their own unless first exposed to them by the research team. Unlike humans, who can absorb and understand complex grammar, the primates in the study never did the same.

The primates did learn to respond to human questions, but these answers weren't in speech form; they were translated in Yerkish as symbols. These so-called "conversations" were passive, with primates like Lana responding yet not being able to form their own questions or to have long conversations. Nor could the primates communicate with one another. At least, there was no recognizable form of communication. This is much unlike human children, who can do so at an early age.

해석

M Professor: 동물들도 소리와 페로몬을 사용해 서로 의사소통을 할 수 있다는 사실과 관련해서는 많은 근거들이 있어요. 하지만 동물이 실제로 인간과 이야기를 나눌 수 있다는 주장은 아직 완전히 입증되지 않았습니다. 영장류와의 의사소통에 관한 몇 가지 작은 진전이 있었지만, 이러한 진전은 사실상 제한적인 것으로 대다수의 과학계 인사들에게 회의적인 적으로 비춰지고 있죠.

조지아 대학의 암컷 침팬지인 라나가 가장 유명한 케이스입니다. 라나는 기호로 이루어진 여키시라는 새 언어를 배워서 연구자들과 의사소통을 했습니다. 적어도 그렇게 보였죠. 라나는 학습 능력은 제한적인 것이었고 실제로 동일한 단어와 기호를 끊임없이 반복하여 조건이 형성되었다는 점을 기억하세요. 다양한 언어에 노출되면 다양한 언어를 배울 수 있는 인간의 아이와 달리 라나는 한 가지 언어를 배우는 것에도 어려움을 겪었습니다.

라나가 어느정도 문법을 이해할 수도 있었겠지만 이는 너무 기초적인 것이어서 라나는, 음, 짧은 문장 몇 개만 만들 수 있었어요. 라나와 다른 실험 대상들은 언어 학습에 있어서 초보적인 수준을 벗어난 적이 없었습니다. 침팬지들은 먼저 연구팀이 보여 주지 않는 이상 스스로 문장을 만들어 내지 못했어요. 복잡한 문법을 받아들여서 이해할 수 있는 인간과 달리 실험에 나오는 영장류는 결코 그렇게 하지 못했죠.

영장류들이 인간의 질문에 반응하는 법을 배우긴 했지만 이 응답들은 말로 된 형태가 아니었어요. 기호의 형태인 여키시어로 번역되었죠. 이러한 소위 "대화"들은 수동적인 것이었고, 라나와 같은 영장류들이 응답을 하긴 했지만 스스로 질문을 만들거나 긴 대화를 할 수는 없었어요. 영장류들끼리 의사소통을 할 수도 없었고요. 적어도 인식할 수 있는 형태의 의사소통은 이루어지지 않았습니다. 이는 어린 나이에 그렇게 할 수 있는 인간의 아이와 크게 다른 점이죠.

📝 Note Taking

Chimps Cannot Learn Language

1 Only appeared to learn language
 • Conditioned by repetition
 • Had trouble learning 1 language unlike human children

2 Limited language ability
- Couldn't make sentences unless exposed to them first
- Couldn't understand complex grammar

3 No recognizable communication
- Didn't answer with speech
- Passive → couldn't form questions → couldn't have long conversation
- Couldn't communicate with other primates

Writing

In the reading passage, the author is certain that some primates have the ability to learn human language. However, the professor is not convinced that what the chimps learned was actually language.

The reading passage first points out that the chimps, especially Lana, learned to use the new language Yerkish and could express their thoughts by using pictures on the keyboard. The professor, however, says that the chimps only appeared to be communicating. Instead, he thinks that they were conditioned to respond because they did the same things again and again.

The reading next points out that Lana was able to make new words by combining those words that she already knew. While the professor admits Lana learned the language a bit, he notes that she could not make new sentences unless first exposed to them, and she was also unable to comprehend complex grammar.

Finally, the reading mentions that Lana appeared to understand the questions she was asked and then gave logical answers on the lexigram machine. The professor points out that she did not learn speech but only learned to communicate with symbols. Additionally, he says Lana could not ask her own questions or have long conversations.

While the reading passage's author thinks Lana exhibited some of language, the professor disagrees with this assessment.

해석

읽기 지문에서 저자는 일부 영장류에게 인간의 언어를 학습할 능력이 있다는 점을 확신한다. 하지만 교수는 침팬지들이 배운 것이 실제로 언어였다는 점을 확신하지 않는다.

읽기 지문은 먼저 침팬지들이, 특히 라나가, 여키시라는 새 언어를 사용하는 법을 배웠으며 키보드에 있는 그림을 이용해 자신의 생각을 표현할 수 있었다고 주장한다. 하지만 교수는 침팬지들이 의사소통을 하는 것처럼 보였을 뿐이라고 말한다. 대신 그는 침팬지들이 똑같은 것을 계속 반복했기 때문에 조건이 형성되어 반응을 한 것이라고 생각한다.

다음으로 읽기 지문은 라나가 이미 알고 있는 단어들을 조합해 새로운 단어들을 만들어 낼 수 있었다는 점을 지적한다. 교수는 라나가 그러한 언어를 약간 익혔다는 점은 인정하지만 라나가 접한 적이 없는 새로운 문장은 만들지 못했으며 복잡한 문법을 이해할 수도 없었다고 말한다.

마지막으로 읽기 지문은 라나가 받은 질문을 이해하는 것처럼 보였고 기호 문자 기계로 논리적인 답을 했다고 언급한다. 교수는 라나가 말을 배운 것이 아니라 기호를 이용해 의사소통을 하는 법을 배웠을 뿐이라고 지적한다. 또한 그는 라나가 자기 나름대로의 질문을 하거나 긴 대화를 하지는 못했다고 말한다.

읽기 지문의 저자는 라나가 어느정도 언어를 구사했다고 생각하지만 교수는 그러한 의견에 동의하지 않는다.

Unit 10 Environmental Science II

Exercise 1 ·········· p.77

Reading

해석

어류 양식은 사람들의 소비를 목적으로 포획 상태의 물고기를 번식시키고 키우는 것이다. 이는 종종 호수, 강, 그리고 바다로 이어지는 만 및 강어귀에 있는 대규모 우리 안에서 이루어진다. 물고기는 알 단계부터 사육되며 충분히 자라면 대중에게 판매된다. 이는 처음에 좋은 아이디어처럼 보였지만 어류 양식은 어류와 인간 모두에게 여러 가지 안전상의 문제를 가져다 주기 때문에 위험한 행위이다.

물고기는 우리에서 밀착된 상태로 갇혀 키워지는데, 이는 물고기에게 자연적으로 적합한 환경이 아니다. 이 때문에 포획 상태에서는 야생 상태에서보다 질병이 발생할 가능성이 더 높아진다. 또한 물고기들이 서로 가까이 있기 때문에 자연 상태에서보다 질병이 더 빨리 확산된다. 일부 질병이 발견되지 않고 퍼져서 그 물고기의 소비가 많아지는 경우에는 질병이 대중에게 전파될 가능성도 있다.

양식업자들은 질병의 확산을 예방하기 위해 물에 여러 가지 화학 물질들을 첨가한다. 또한 물고기가 야생 상태일 때 도달하는 크기보다 더 커지도록 물고기의 먹이에도 화학 첨가제를 넣는다. 이러한 화학 물질들은 일단 물고기의 몸속에 흡수되면 그 물고기를 먹는 사람에게도 위험을 가져다 줄 수 있다.

물고기들은 주로 다른 물고기를 먹는데, 이들은 양식장 물고기들의 먹이가 되기 전에 죽어서 처리 과정을 거친 물고기들이다. 하지만 먹이로 사용되는 물고기는 바다에서 잡기 때문에 야생에서 많은 양의 먹이를 빼앗아오는 셈이다. 이들은 다른 해양 생물의 잠재적 단백질원이기 때문에 이러한 먹이 자원이 사라지면 전 세계 해양 생태계에 부정적인 영향이 미칠 수도 있다.

Note Taking

1) spread disease rapidly
2) Some diseases get passed on to public
3) Chemicals added to water & fish food
4) Get absorbed into fish's bodies
5) Need to catch other fish for fish food

Listing

Script 🎧 01-20

M Professor: Fish farming is one of the most important sources of fish protein for many people nowadays. There are, sadly, many critics of fish farming who oppose its use. However, it's quite necessary because many fish raised on fish farms can no longer be harvested in the wild, and, fortunately, fish farming can provide fish that are safe to eat.

Many critics of fish farming point out the possibility of diseases running rampant throughout the farms due to the nearness of the fish. However, let me point out that fish live very close together in the wild. You've seen pictures of big schools of fish, haven't you? How's this different from a fish farm? Anyway, in the wild there is no rapid spread of disease despite fish living close together. And studies have shown the incidence of disease in the wild and on farms is identical.

Chemical usage on fish farms has raised some, hmm, red flags as to the safety of the fish, but even ocean fish absorb large amounts of chemicals from pollution. In fact, farmed fish may be even safer than ocean-caught fish. Besides, virtually every meat we consume, including beef and pork, has been chemically enhanced to help the animals grow bigger. Yes, it's true. Fish is much healthier than these meats, having less fat and healthier oils, like omega-3's.

While some fish species are killed to produce the feed needed for fish on the farms, most of these fish are not even consumed by humans or many sea creatures. One such fish is the menhaden. Humans find its taste to be bad, so it's caught in large quantities to produce animal feed. Therefore, by using the menhaden and others to feed fish on farms, we can increase the number of fish raised for human consumption.

해석

M Professor: 어류 양식은 요즘 많은 사람들에게 어류 단백질을 제공해 주는 가장 중요한 공급원 중 하나입니다. 하지만 안타깝게도 어류 어업의 활용을 반대하고 이를 비판하는 사람들이 많습니다. 하지만 어류 양식장에서 양식되는 많은 어류들이 더 이상 야생에서 잡히지 않기 때문에 양식 어업은 매우 필요하며, 다행스럽게도, 양식 어업으로 안전하게 먹을 수 있는 물고기들이 공급될 수 있습니다.

어류 양식을 비판하는 많은 사람들은 물고기들이 서로 가까이 있어서 양식장 전체에 질병이 만연할 가능성을 지적합니다. 하지만 저는 물고기들이 야생에서도 서로 가까이 붙어 지낸다는 점을 지적하고 싶군요. 여러분들도 거대한 무리의 물고기 사진을 본 적이 있을 거예요, 그렇죠? 어류 양식장과 다른 점이 있을까요? 어쨌든, 야생에서는 물고기들이 가까이 모여 살아도 질병이 급속히 확산되는 경우가 없습니다. 그리고 연구에 따르면 야생과 양식장에서의 질병 발생률은 동일합니다.

양식장에서 화학 물질을 사용하는 것 때문에, 음, 어류 양식의 안전성에 빨간 불이 들어오긴 했지만, 바다에 사는 물고기도 오염으로 인해 다량의 화학 물질을

흡수합니다. 실제로 양식되는 어류가 바다에서 잡힌 물고기보다 훨씬 더 안전할 수도 있어요. 또한 소고기와 돼지고기를 비롯해 우리가 먹는 사실상 모든 육류에도 가축들의 빠른 성장을 돕는 화학 물질이 들어갑니다. 네, 사실이에요. 지방도 적고 오메가3와 같은 건강에 이로운 기름도 있어서 어류가 육류에 비해 훨씬 건강에도 좋습니다.

양식 어류에게 필요한 사료를 만들기 위해 일부 물고기들이 희생되지만 이러한 대부분의 물고기들은 인간이나 다른 해양 동물이 먹지 않는 것들이에요. 그런 물고기 중 하나가 그물눈청어죠. 그물눈청어는 인간의 입맛에 맞지 않기 때문에 동물 사료 생산을 위해 대량으로 포획됩니다. 따라서 그물눈청어 및 기타 물고기를 양식 어류의 먹이로 사용함으로써 인간이 먹는 물고기의 수를 늘릴 수가 있어요.

📝 **Note Taking**

1) fish in wild = fish on fish farms
2) Same disease rates
3) Ocean fish & meat
4) safer & healthier
5) Menhaden: bad tasting

Comparing the Points

Reading	Listening
Stance Fish farming may appear good but is actually dangerous to fish and people.	**Stance** Fish farming is beneficial to many people around the world.
Main point 1 The fish live closely together, which makes diseases more likely.	**Refutation 1** Fish in captivity do not get diseases more easily than those in the wild.
Main point 2 Chemicals are used to grow fish, which is harmful to humans who eat them.	**Refutation 2** Even ocean-caught fish and other meats have chemicals, but fish is the healthier food.
Main point 3 The fish used for fish food are taken from the ocean, which disrupts ocean ecosystems.	**Refutation 3** The fish used for fish food is not eaten either by people or by sea creatures.

Synthesizing

1 The reading passage's author believes fish farming is dangerous to the fish and the people who eat them; however, the professor thinks fish farming benefits people by providing fish that are all right to eat.

2 In direct contrast to the reading, which claims fish in captivity suffer from more diseases than those in the wild, the professor states that they both suffer from diseases at an equal rate.

3 While the reading passage mentions that the chemicals absorbed into fish's bodies make them dangerous to eat, the professor says that even ocean fish are exposed to large quantities of chemicals due to pollution.

4 According to the reading, the catching of fish to make fish feed takes a lot of food out of the oceans, yet the professor asserts that people and sea creatures do not eat most of these fish.

Organization

1 Although the author of the reading passage writes against fish farms, the professor feels they provide an important service for people around the world.

2 According to the reading, because fish in captivity live so close to each other, there is a higher likelihood they will get diseases that they may pass on to humans.

3 The professor, however, opposes this theory by saying that fish in the wild also live close together and that fish on farms and in the wild get diseases at the same rate.

4 In response to the accusation that fish farms use chemical additives that could harm people, the professor cites the fact that even ocean fish absorb chemicals into their bodies.

5 He also says that all meat people eat has been injected with chemicals, yet people are still safe.

6 The reading passage's author then expresses concern that too many fish in the wild are being caught and processed into food for the fish on farms to eat.

7 The author thinks this takes food sources out of the wild.

8 However, the professor says that many of these food fish, like the menhaden, are often not eaten by people or sea creatures as well.

9 He believes it is a good thing to use these food fish to increase the number of edible fish for humans.

10 In conclusion, while the reading passage opposes the existence of fish farms, the professor thinks they are beneficial to humans.

Exercise 2 ··· p.81

Reading

해석

많은 조류학자들이 최근 충격적인 경향에 주목하고 있다. 많은 종의 새들이 사라지고 있는 것이다. 실제로 지난 두 세기 동안 100여 종이 넘는 조류종이 자취를 감추었고 1,200종은 멸종 위기에 처해 있다. 증거들에 의하면 새들이 느리기는 하지만 확실히 사라져 가고 있는 이유는 인간 때문이다.

인간이 주로 거주하는 도시 지역이 확장됨에 따라 새들 및 기타 동물들의 자연 서식지가 침범을 당하고 있다. 세계 인구의 거의 절반 가량이 어떤 형태로든 도심지에 살고 있기 때문에 대다수 지역에서 녹지는 후순위로 밀려나 있다. 이러한 도시 스프롤과 함께 도시에서 생산되는 오염 물질의 양도 증가하고 있다. 이러한 요소들이 결합되어 조류 서식지를 빼앗고 새들이 사는 장소를 오염시키고 있다.

지구의 인구가 증가하면서 식량에 대한 수요가 계속 늘고 있기 때문에 이러한 식량을 생산할 농지를 마련할 목적으로 많은 땅이 개간되고 있다. 농작물을 경작하기 위해 산림 지대가 개간되고 있는데, 이러한 산림에 서식하는 새들의 운명은 거의 고려되지 않는다. 해마다 약 5만에서 17만 제곱킬로미터의 숲에서 나무들이 잘려나가고 있으며, 이로 인해 많은 조류 종이 위기를 맞고 있다.

농부들은 곤충의 창궐을 막기 위해 종종 화학 살충제를 사용한다. 이러한 화학 물질 역시 다른 동물뿐만 아니라 많은 새들을 죽음으로 내몰고 있다. 이는 미국에서 거의 40년간 살충제인 DDT 사용이 금지되었던 한 가지 이유이다. DDT는 너무 많은 새들을, 특히 흰머리수리를 죽게 만들었다. 안타깝게도 지구의 나머지 지역에서는 여전히 DDT 및 기타 강력한 화학 물질들이 농사에 사용하고 있으며 그 결과 많은 새들이 죽음을 맞이하고 있다.

📝 Note Taking

Birds Are Becoming Endangered

1 Humans encroaching on birds' territory
   • Urban areas → expanding rapidly
   • Pollution in cities ↑
2 Land being cleared for farming
   • Deforestation → birds losing their habitats → many endangered species
3 Use of chemical insecticides
   • For farming → kills birds & animals
   • e.g. DDT banned in America but not in other countries

Listening

Script 🎧 01-21

W Professor: Many people have noted that large numbers of birds are endangered, but, uh, don't worry, for the overall situation is not nearly as dire as it's often made to appear. Birds may be found everywhere, and some reports even suggest that their numbers are increasing rather than declining. Let me give you a few examples as to why you shouldn't worry.

Many people live in urban areas these days, yet they want their cities to be as green as possible. Parks, playgrounds, and tree-lined rivers and streams are appearing for all to enjoy. Take Berlin for example. At times, you can't even see any buildings because of all the trees. And birds are making the most of these areas. While pigeons are not the most beautiful of birds, New York City is famous for them. Birds are clearly adapting to life in the cities.

While the increase in agriculture may be destroying some bird habitats, farmland doesn't cover the Earth's entire surface. Not by a long shot. Massive forests still stand in Canada, Russia, Brazil, uh, Southeast Asia, and many other places. And agricultural methods are more developed, so the land is much more productive. This means less land is needed to produce the same or a greater amount of food.

No one disputes that insecticides kill birds. However, many recent crops have been genetically engineered to resist disease and insects, so insecticides are being used less and less. Outside the U.S., some harmful chemicals like DDT are still used, but they are utilized to kill mosquitoes, not for insects on farms. After the ban on

DDT, deaths from mosquito-borne malaria leaped, so governments decided a few bird deaths were worth risking if they could save the lives of humans instead.

해석

W Professor: 다수의 새들이 멸종 위기에 놓여 있다는 사실은 많은 사람들이 알고 있지만, 어, 종종 보이는 것만큼 전체적인 상황이 끔찍한 것은 아니니까 걱정하지는 마세요. 새는 어디에서나 찾아볼 수 있고, 일부 보고서에 따르면 새의 수는 줄기는커녕 오히려 늘어나고 있습니다. 왜 걱정할 필요가 없는지에 관한 몇 가지 예를 들어 드리죠.

요즘에는 많은 사람들이 도시 지역에서 살지만 그들은 도시가 되도록 푸르기를 원해요. 모두가 즐길 수 있는 공원, 운동장, 그리고 나무가 늘어선 강가와 시냇가가 생기고 있죠. 베를린을 예로 들어 볼게요. 때때로 나무들 때문에 건물이 보이지 않는 경우도 있어요. 그리고 새들은 이러한 지역을 최대한 활용하고 있습니다. 비둘기가 가장 아름다운 새는 아니지만 뉴욕시는 비둘기로 유명해요. 새들은 도시 생활에 확실히 적응하고 있습니다.

농업의 증가로 조류의 서식지가 파괴될 수도 있지만 농지가 지구 표면 전체를 덮고 있지는 않습니다. 전혀 그렇지 않아요. 캐나다, 러시아, 브라질, 어, 동남아시아 및 기타 여러 지역에는 여전히 거대한 삼림 지대가 존재합니다. 또한 농법이 더욱 발전해서 토지의 생산성이 훨씬 증가되었어요. 이는 동일하거나 더 많은 양의 식량을 생산하는데 필요한 토지 면적이 줄어들었다는 뜻입니다.

아무도 살충제 때문에 새가 죽는다는 점을 부정하지는 않아요. 하지만 최근에는 많은 농작물들이 유전자 조작을 거쳐 질병이나 곤충에 대한 저항력을 갖고 있기 때문에 살충제는 점점 덜 쓰이고 있죠. 미국 밖에서는 여전히 DDT와 같은 유해한 화학 물질이 사용되고 있지만, 이는 농장의 곤충이 아니라 모기를 죽이기 위해 사용됩니다. DDT 사용을 금지한 후 모기가 옮기는 말라리아로 인한 사망률이 급격히 증가하자 정부들은 인간의 목숨을 구할 수 있다면 소수의 새가 희생되는 위험을 감수할 만하다는 결정을 내렸습니다.

Note Taking

Birds Are Not in Any Danger

1 Green zones in urban areas
   • Parks, playgrounds, & areas with trees → good areas for birds
   • e.g. Berlin & New York

2 Farmland doesn't cover the Earth
   • Are still many forests in countries around the world
   • Agriculture improving → use less land

3 Less use of insecticides nowadays
   • Genetically engineered crops → less insecticide
   • Still use DDT → helps fight malaria & save human lives

Writing

Sample Response

While the author of the reading passage expresses concern for the declining number of birds throughout the world, the lecturer feels that birds are in no danger and that their numbers are actually going up.

According to the reading, because the Earth's population is increasing, so is the size of its cities. There are therefore fewer green areas but more pollution, which is causing birds to decrease in numbers. On the contrary, the lecturer mentions that many cities like Berlin actually have green zones and that birds are learning to adapt to city life like the pigeons in New York City.

The reading then asserts that much forested land is being cleared for agriculture to feed the Earth's population. This activity is endangering many birds. However, the lecturer maintains that the Earth still has many forested areas and that agricultural methods have advanced so much that less land is needed to farm on.

Finally, the author of the reading states that insecticides and chemicals like DDT are being used around the world, and they are killing many birds. The lecturer agrees but says that insecticides are being used less and less nowadays. In the case of DDT, it is only used to kill malaria-carrying mosquitoes these days.

All in all, the reading feels strongly that birds' numbers are declining; on the other hand, the lecturer believes there is nothing to worry about.

해석

읽기 지문의 저자는 전 세계에서 조류의 수가 감소하는 것에 대해 우려를 나타내지만 교수는 새들이 위험에 처한 것이 아니며 실제로는 그 수가 증가하고 있다고 생각한다.

읽기 지문에 따르면 지구의 인구가 늘고 있기 때문에 도시도 점점 커지고 있다. 따라서 녹지는 줄어드는 반면 오염은 증가하고 있는데, 이로 인해 조류의 수가 감소하고 있다. 반면 교수는 베를린과 같은 많은 도시에 실제로 녹지대들이 존재하며 뉴욕시의 비둘기처럼 새들이 도시 생활에 적응하는 법을 익히고 있다고 언급한다.

이후 읽기 지문은 많은 삼림 지대가 지구의 인구를 부양하기 위해 농지로 개간되고 있다고 주장한다. 이러한 활동으로 많은 새들이 멸종 위기에 놓이고 있다. 하지만 교수는 지구에 여전히 많은 삼림 지대가 존재하며 농법이 크게 발전하여 보다 적은 땅으로 농사를 지을 수 있다고 주장한다.

마지막으로 읽기 지문의 저자는 전 세계에서 DDT와 같은 살충제 및 화학 물질이 사용되고 있고, 이로 인해 많은 새들이 목숨을 잃고 있다고 주장한다. 교수도 이에 동의하지만 요즘에는 살충제 사용이 점점 줄고 있다고 말한다. DDT의 경우, DDT는 현재 말라리아를 옮기는 모기를 없애기 위한 용도로만 쓰이고 있다.

전체적으로 읽기 지문은 조류의 수가 줄고 있다고 굳게 믿고 있지만, 교수는 걱정할 것이 전혀 없다고 생각한다.

Exercise 1 ·· p.90

Brainstorming & Outlining

A

Professor Nelson

해석

오늘날 환경 보호는 많은 사람들에게 중요한 이슈입니다. 어떤 사람들은 공장들이 제조 공정을 보다 깨끗하게 함으로써 환경에 가장 큰 영향을 끼칠 수 있다고 주장해요. 하지만 개인들이 각자의 활동으로 환경에 더 큰 영향을 미칠 수 있다고 생각하는 사람들도 있죠. 여러분이 다음과 같은 질문에 대해 생각해 보면 좋을 것 같습니다. 환경에 누가 더 큰 영향을 미칠 수 있다고 생각하나요? 그렇게 생각하는 이유는 무엇인가요?

✕ Outline for Brainstorming

The More Important Factor on the Environment			
Factories		**Individuals**	
Reason 1	**Reason 2**	**Reason 1**	**Reason 2**
- Run all day and night - Spew lots of pollution	- Create large amounts of air, water, and ground pollution	- Can get companies and governments to change	- Can recycle and lead cleanup efforts

B

Jeff

해석

공장들이 개인보다 환경에 훨씬 더 큰 영향을 미칩니다. 어쨌거나 많은 공장들이 하루에 24시간 동안 가동되면서 다량의 매연과 해로운 화학 물질들을 내뿜으니까요. 공장들이 보다 깨끗해지려는 노력을 한다면 지구에서 대기 오염, 수질 오염, 그리고 토양 오염의 정도가 크게 줄어들 수 있습니다.

☑ Summary Notes: Jeff

1) greater influence
2) 24 hours
3) smoke
4) harmful chemicals
5) become cleaner
6) air, water, and ground pollution

Stephanie

해석

두 가지 이유로 개인들이 환경에 강력한 영향을 미칠 수 있습니다. 예를 들어 개인들은 재활용 및 쓰레기 처리를 통해 환경에 도움을 줄 수 있는데, 이로써 지구가 더 깨끗해 질 수 있어요. 또한 공해를 일으키는 기업에 대해 보이콧을 함으로써 기업으로 하여금 오염 물질을 덜 배출하도록 만들어 환경을 개선시킬 수 있습니다.

☑ Summary Notes: Stephanie

1) protect the environment
2) clean up waste
3) Earth cleaner
4) boycotts of companies
5) produce less pollution
6) environment improve

Organization

Supporting Jeff's Opinion

1 Both Jeff and Stephanie make good points, but I believe factories have a greater impact on the environment than individuals.

2 I agree with Jeff that factories run continuously, during which time they expel smoke and dangerous chemicals.

3 Let me add that these factories cause enormous amounts of air pollution by spewing out harmful gases.

4 Factories also dump chemicals into waterways, creating water pollution, and damage the land.

5 Stephanie brought up a good point that people can boycott companies to make them change their operating methods, but that just proves how influential factories are.

6 When factories reduce the amount of pollution they create, the environment can become cleaner.

7 Although individuals can influence the environment, factories have a greater effect on it.

Supporting Stephanie's Opinion

1 While Jeff makes some good points, I have to agree with Stephanie more.

2 Individuals are definitely more influential regarding the environment than factories are.

3 To build on what Stephanie wrote, if everyone on the Earth acted by recycling and cleaning up around them, then the Earth would look completely different within a week.

4 I also believe that people can force the government to make laws protecting the environment.

5 In addition, they can protest any companies and organizations that break these laws.

6 Jeff is right that factories produce large amounts of pollution.

7 However, individual people are running those factories, and if they can be persuaded to change their actions, then factories will produce less pollution.

Professor Jackson

해석

도시 지역에서는 대중 교통을 이용할 수 있음에도 불구하고 사람들이 종종 개인용 차량을 타고 직장, 학교, 그리고 기타 장소에 갑니다. 이는 심각한 문제인데, 그 이유는 차량들이 다량의 연료를 소비하고, 오염 물질을 배출하며, 시내의 교통 체증을 유발하기 때문이에요. 이로써 도시에 사는 사람들에게 많은 문제가 발생합니다. 여러분의 생각으로 더 많은 사람들이 대중 교통을 이용하도록 만들 수 있는 최선의 방법은 무엇인가요?

✗ Outline for Brainstorming

How to Encourage Public Transportation Usage	
Method 1	Method 2
- Lower prices	- Restrict driving in some areas
Details	Details
- Would take the bus every day	- Lighter traffic, easier to breathe, and would enjoy walking outdoors

Lisa

해석

저는 대충 교통 이용이 지역 주민들에게 보다 매력적인 것이 되도록 도시들이 만들어야 한다고 생각합니다. 예를 들어 버스나 지하철 이용 요금을 인하할 수도 있을 거예요. 저는 버스를 이용하고자 하는 사람들을 알고 있는데, 그들은 버스 요금이 너무 비싼 것을 좋게 생각하지 않습니다. 요금을 내림으로써 도시는 사람들로 하여금 대중 교통을 보다 자주 이용하도록 유도할 수 있습니다.

Theodore

해석

차를 가진 대부분의 사람들은 환경에 대한 영향을 고려하지 않고 차를 사용해요. 따라서 저는 정부가 일부 지역에서 차량 운행을 금지해야 한다고 생각합니다. 시 정부는 특정 도심지에서의 차량 운행을 금지시킬 수 있을 것입니다. 그러한 지역에서 버스 및 기타 대중 교통 수단만 운행을 허가한다면 사람들은 더 이상 차를 끌고 다니는 대신 대중 교통을 이용해야 할 거예요.

☑ Summary Note

Lisa

1 Make public transportation more appealing
  • Lower price of bus or subway
  • People want to take but too expensive
2 Lowering prices will encourage people to use public transportation

Theodore

1 Restrict vehicular usage in some areas
  • Ban driving downtown
  • Only buses and other public transportation allowed in places
2 People have to stop driving and must use public transportation

Sample Response 1 Supporting Lisa

I like the points each person makes, but I believe Lisa makes the better argument. I fully agree with Lisa that governments should reduce the price of taking public transportation. I try to take the bus as often as possible, but it can be expensive at times. If the government would lower the price, I would probably ride on the bus every day. Governments could also make public transportation cleaner. Some subways in the city are so dirty, and the seats look like they have not been cleaned in a long time. Nobody wants to sit on those seats, so people avoid the subway. I like Theodore's argument about banning cars in some places. But we should consider that a full ban on vehicles in certain places is simply not realistic. For that reason, I like Lisa's argument more than Theodore's.

해석

나는 각각의 주장이 모두 마음에 들지만 Lisa의 주장이 보다 타당하다고 생각한다. 나는 정부가 대중 교통 이용 요금을 인하해야 한다는 Lisa의 말에 전적으로 동의한다. 나는 최대한 자주 버스를 타려고 하지만 때때로 비용이 많이 들 수가 있다. 정부가 요금을 인하한다면 나는 아마도 매일 버스를 타게 될 것이다. 정부는 또한 대중 교통을 더 깨끗하게 만들 수 있다. 시내의 일부 지하철은 매우 더러우며 좌석은 오랫동안 청소가 되지 않은 것처럼 보인다. 아무도 그러한 자리에는 앉고 싶어하지 않기 때문에 사람들은 지하철을 피하게 된다. 나는 일부 지역에서 차량 운행을 금지하는 것에 대한 Theodore의 주장이 마음에 든다. 하지만 특정 장소에서 전면적으로 차량 운행을 금지하는 것은 현실적이지 못하다는 점을 고려해야 한다. 이러한 이유들로 나는 Theodore보다 Lisa의 주장이 더 마음에 든다.

Sample Response 2 Supporting Theodore

Of the two arguments, I support Theodore's more than Lisa's. In my opinion, we are in a major environmental crisis these days, so the government needs to take serious action. By banning cars from driving in some downtown areas, the government could show people that it is determined to do something about the environment. In addition, traffic in these areas would instantly become much better. With only public transportation on the roads, people would breathe more easily and would probably enjoy walking outdoors more. I like Lisa's argument in favor of lower prices and wish the government would make taking the subway cheaper. However, I do not believe her solution would solve the pollution and traffic jam problems, so we need a stronger method like the one proposed by Theodore.

해석

두 가지 주장 중에서 나는 Lisa의 주장보다 Theodore의 주장을 더 지지한다. 내 생각에는 오늘날 우리가 커다란 환경 위기를 겪고 있기 때문에 정부가 강력한 조치를 취해야 한다. 일부 시내 중심지에서 차량 운행을 금지함으로써 정부는 환경에 관해 정부가 단호한 조치를 취하고 있다는 점을 사람들에게 보여 줄 수 있다. 또한 이러한 지역의 교통도 그 즉시 크게 좋아질 것이다. 도로에 대중 교통 수

단만 존재한다면 보다 숨을 쉬기가 편해질 것이고 아마도 야외에서 걷는 것이 더 즐거워질 것이다. 나는 요금 인하를 선호하는 Lisa의 주장이 마음에 들며 정부의 지하철 요금 인하를 바라고 있다. 하지만 그녀의 해결 방안으로는 오염 및 교통 체증 문제가 해결될 것이라고 생각하지 않기 때문에 우리에게는 Theodore가 제안한 해결 방안과 같은 보다 강력한 방안이 필요할 것이다.

Unit 12 Sociology I

Exercise 1 .... p.96

Brainstorming & Outlining

A

Professor Rendon

해석

과학 기술은 매년 발전하고 있으며 사람들의 삶에 막대한 영향을 끼치고 있어요. 따라서 수학 및 과학과 같은 학문들이 그 어느 때보다 중요합니다. 하지만 대부분의 고등학교들은 여전히 미술 및 음악과 같은 과목들의 수업을 강조하고 있죠. 고등학교들이 수학 및 과학 수업을 보다 강조하고 미술 및 음악과 같은 과목들의 수업은 중단해야 한다고 생각하나요? 왜 그럴죠?

✖ Outline for Brainstorming

Teach Only Science and Math or Teach Other Subjects			
Teach Only Math and Science		Teach Art and Music as Well	
Reason 1	Reason 2	Reason 1	Reason 2
- High-tech society - Need people who can do math and science	- Can learn art and music in free time - Focus on important topics at school	- Need students to have balanced educations	- Some students might become great artists or musicians

B

Daniel

해석

과학 기술은 우리의 삶에서 매우 큰 부분을 차지하고 있지만 수학 및 과학 분야에서 유능한 사람들은 많지가 않습니다. 이곳에서 얼마나 많은 학생들이 수학 및 기타 과학 과목을 전공하고 있는지 보세요. 그 수가 충분하지 않습니다. 고등학교는 수학과 과학을 강조해야 하며 미술과 음악은 무시해야 해요. 그럼으로써 우리의 과학 기술 사회를 계속 유지시킬 수 있는 충분한 수의 사람들이 생기게 될 것입니다.

☑ Summary Notes: Daniel

1) modern life
2) competent people
3) major in math and science
4) math and science
5) ignore
6) technological society operational

Emily

해석

미술과 음악은 중요한 분야이기 때문에 고등학생들에 이를 가르치는 것이 중요합니다. 저는 고등학교 때 그러한 수업을 들었던 것이 기억나요. 제가 그림을 잘 그리지도 못하고 노래를 잘 하거나 악기를 연주할 수 있는 것이 아니지만, 저는 그러한 수업들로 혜택을 받았습니다. 학생들에게 균형 잡힌 교육을 제공하고자 한다면 고등학교들이, 수학과 과학뿐만 아니라, 모든 과목들을 계속 가르치도록 요구해야 합니다.

☑ Summary Notes: Emily

1) teach art and music
2) classes in high school
3) art or music well
4) benefitted from classes
5) balanced educations
6) high schools teach all subjects

Organization

Supporting Daniel's Opinion

1 Daniel clearly understands what we need to keep modern society running.

2 Almost everything we do all day depends on technology, and we need people educated in the fields of math and science to guarantee that society does not collapse.

3 I wish that high schools would abandon teaching art and music and focus almost exclusively on math and science.

4 If students want to learn about art and music, they can use the Internet to study it on their own or hire private tutors.

5 I like the fact that Emily wants students to have well-rounded educations, but they can accomplish this in their free time, not when they are attending school.

Supporting Emily's Opinion

1 I understand the point that Daniel is making, but I cannot bring myself to agree with him.

2 Instead, I believe that Emily understands something important; it is necessary for students to study a wide variety of topics and not just focus on a couple of different ones.

3 High schools should definitely teach art and music in addition to math and science.

4 After all, some students might be inspired by these classes and go on to become great artists or musicians.

5 If students want to learn more in the fields of math and science, they can teach themselves by borrowing books from the library or by watching online lectures.

6 That is something they can easily do.

Exercise 2 ·· p.99

Professor Martin

해석

과거에 그랬던 것과 달리 이제는 가족들이 같은 장소에서 수십 년 동안 살지를 않습니다. 대신 오늘날에는 이사하는 경우가 상당히 빈번하죠. 그 결과 아이들의 학교가 종종 바뀌게 되는데, 이는 아이들이 친구를 새로 사귀어야 하고 새로운 학습 환경에 적응해야 한다는 점에서 문제가 될 수도 있어요. 학교측은 이러한 학생들이 새로운 환경에 적응할 수 있도록 어떤 도움을 줄 수 있을까요?

✖ **Outline for Brainstorming**

How Schools Can Help New Students	
Method 1	Method 2
- Have mentors for new students	- Have orientation session
Details	Details
- Can show new students around - Can introduce new students to friends	- Show students around campus - Let students meet instructors

Carla

해석

저희 가족이 주기적으로 이사를 다녀서 개인적으로 그러한 경험을 했는데, 저는 일곱 군데의 학교에 다녔습니다. 저로서는 결코 유쾌한 경험이 아니었어요. 제 생각으로는 학교측이 새로 온 학생에게 단짝이나 멘토 역할을 할 수 있는 학생을 배정해 주어야 합니다. 그 학생이 새로 온 학생에게 학교 주변을 안내해 주고 다른 학생들도 소개시켜 줄 수 있을 거예요.

Russell

해석

새로 온 학생을 돕기 위해 학교측이 할 수 있는 가장 좋은 일은 오리엔테이션 프로그램을 실시하는 것입니다. 학기 초에 새로 온 학생들에게 캠퍼스를 구경시켜 주고 선생님들을 만날 기회를 주는 것이죠. 그들은 어떤 수업을 들을 수 있는지, 그리고 어떤 과외 활동에 참석할 수 있는지 알게 될 것입니다. 학교측은 또한 새로 온 학생들에게 적극적으로 나서서 친구들을 사귀라고 독려할 수도 있을 거예요.

📝 **Summary Note**

Carla	Russell
1 Family moved regularly • Attended several schools • Unpleasant experience 2 Schools should assign mentor to newcomer • Help newcomer find way around school • Introduce to other students	1 Have orientation program • Give students tour of campus and meet instructors 2 Inform students about classes and extracurriculars • Encourage students to be active and to make friends

Sample Response 1 Supporting Carla

Carla and Russell both make some good suggestions on how schools can help students get used to their new environments. I particularly like Carla's suggestion that schools assign each new student a mentor who is a current student. Taking it one step further, the mentor should be a popular student, so when other students see the new student hanging out with the mentor, they will be eager to meet that student. I also like Russell's suggestion of having a new student orientation because that will enable students to learn about their new schools. Something else that I feel schools could do is have teachers check up on new students. The teachers could make sure the students are keeping up with their assignments and are getting along well with their classmates.

해석

Carla와 Russell 모두 학생들이 새로운 환경에 적응할 수 있도록 학교측이 어떤 도움을 줄 수 있는지에 대해 좋은 제안을 하고 있다. 나는 학교측이 새로 온 각각의 학생들에게 기존 학생을 멘토로 지정해 주자는 Carla의 제안이 특히 마음에 든다. 더 나아가서 멘토는 인기 있는 학생이어야 하는데, 그 이유는 새로 온 학생이 멘토와 어울리는 것을 다른 학생들이 보면 그들도 그 학생을 만나고 싶어할 것이기 때문이다. 나는 오리엔테이션으로 학생들이 학교에 대해 배울 수 있기 때문에 새로 온 학생에게 오리엔테이션을 받게 하자는 Russell의 제안도 마음에 든다. 학교측이 할 수 있을 것으로 생각되는 또 다른 일은 교사들이 새로 온 학생들의 상황을 확인하는 것이다. 교사들은 해당 학생들이 과제를 잘 수행하고 있는지, 그리고 급우들과 잘 어울리고 있는지 확인할 수 있을 것이다.

Sample Response 2 Supporting Russell

I really like Russell's idea of having a new student orientation. I changed schools once, and an orientation program like that would have helped me a considerable amount. Since I was left to fend for myself, it took me a couple of weeks to learn about my new school. Carla's idea about a mentor is good, but schools need to make sure that the mentor is actually interested in doing a good job, or else the new student might get a bad impression of the school. Something that neither student mentions is that schools could have social activities such as dances at the beginning of the school year. These activities would allow new students to meet their classmates in a relaxed environment and give them the opportunity to make friends, which would help them adjust to their new environments.

해석

나는 학생들에게 오리엔테이션을 받게 하자는 Russell의 아이디어가 정말로 마음에 든다. 나는 전학을 여러차례 했는데, 그와 같은 오리엔테이션 프로그램이 있었으면 나에게 상당한 도움이 되었을 것이다. 나는 알아서 하도록 내버려졌기 때문에 새로운 학교에 대해 알기까지 2주일이 걸렸다. 멘토에 관한 Carla의 아이디어는 좋지만 학교측은 멘토가 실제로 일을 잘 하고 있는지, 혹은 새로 온 학생이 학교에 대해 나쁜 인상을 갖고 있지는 않은지 확인해야 한다. 두 사람 모두 언급하지 않은 점은 학교측이 학년 초에 댄스와 같은 사교 활동의 기회를 마련할 수도 있다는 점이다. 이러한 활동으로 새로 온 학생들은 편안한 환경에서 급우들을 만나고 친구를 사귈 수 있는 기회를 갖게 될 것인데, 그러면 그들이 새로운 환경에 적응하는데 도움이 될 것이다.

Unit 13 Sociology II

Exercise 1 .... p.102

Brainstorming & Outlining

A

Professor Donaldson

해석

모두들 행복을 생각해 보시기 바랍니다. 행복을 느끼게 만드는 요인은 사람마다 다른 경향이 있어요. 하지만 많은 사람들의 경우 자신의 일이 행복에 중요한 영향을 미칩니다. 반면에 가족이 중요한 역할을 하는 경우도 있죠. 여러분의 생각으로는 개인의 행복을 결정하는데 일과 가족 중 무엇이 중요한가요? 그 이유는요?

✖ Outline for Brainstorming

The More Important Factor for Happiness			
Career		Family	
Reason 1	Reason 2	Reason 1	Reason 2
- Spend most of time at job	- Happy with job = happy with other things	- Focus on family = makes people happy	- Family life = unhappy → all other things unhappy, too

B
Eric

해석

저로서는 개인의 행복을 결정하는 것에 있어서 일이 훨씬 더 중요합니다. 많은 사람들이 깨어 있는 시간 중 절반 이상을 직장에서 보내고 있으며 일을 하지 않는 때에도 일에 대해 생각을 하죠. 만약 자신의 일에 만족하지 않는다면 행동에서 드러납니다. 또한 자신의 일을 싫어하는 사람들은 종종 불행한 삶을 살며 우울증을 겪기도 해요.

☑ Summary Notes: Eric

1) more than half waking hours at jobs
2) when not working
3) shows in actions
4) unhappy with careers
5) miserable lives
6) depression

Rachel

해석

사람들을 행복하게 만드는 것에 관해서는 분명 일보다 가족이 더 중요합니다. 가

족과 함께 지내면서 행복을 느끼는 경우, 돈을 많이 벌지 못하거나 혹은 무능하거나 짜증나는 상사가 있는 경우라도, 일은 그다지 중요하지 않아요. 많은 부모들이 자신의 일에 대해 그다지 많이 생각하지 않고 가족에게 초점을 맞추는데, 그럼으로써 그들은 행복을 느낍니다.

☑ Summary Notes: Rachel

1) w/families
2) particularly important
3) make much money
4) bad supervisor
5) about jobs too much
6) family
7) happy

Organization

Supporting Eric's Opinion

1   I can understand the arguments for both sides, but to me, the choice is obvious.

2   A person's career is more important in determining a person's level of happiness.

3   I therefore agree more with the argument that Eric made.

4   I like that Eric pointed out people spend so much of their time awake either at work or thinking about work.

5   That is precisely what my parents do.

6   Fortunately, they love their jobs, so they are happy when they arrive home.

7   I have also noticed that people unhappy with their careers tend to have depressing personal lives.

8   Families even split up due to a person's unhappiness at work.

9   So while Rachel makes a good point about the importance of family, I think family is not as important as a career in determining happiness.

Supporting Rachel's Opinion

1   Although Eric and Rachel each makes legitimate points, I find myself more in agreement with Rachel.

2   Rachel is right in stating that when people have happy family lives, their jobs are not especially important.

3   I would take that one step further and add that when people's family lives have a low level of happiness—or they are unhappy—their careers are of no importance to them.

4   People unhappy because of their jobs resign and find new jobs.

5   But quitting a family is harder and requires a greater level of unhappiness.

6   Many of my friends have joyful lives because they love their families and enjoy spending time with them.

7   Their parents' jobs are not of great importance to their happiness.

Professor Cleveland

해석

요즘 인터넷과 특히 소셜 미디어 덕분에 사람들이 예전보다 유명 인사들에 대해 많이 알고 있습니다. 실제로 현재 유명 인사들은 그 어느 때보다 큰 영향력을 지니고 있죠. 하지만 유명 인사들이 사회에 끼치는 영향이 긍정적인 것일까요, 아니면 부정적인 것일까요? 어떻게 생각하나요? 그 이유는요?

✕ Outline for Brainstorming

Celebrities Have a Positive or Negative Influence	
Positive Influence	Negative Influence
- Encourage people to help others	- No talents or skills but tell others what to do
Details	Details
- Register to vote, help after tornado, help kids, sick, and homeless	- Promote violent or criminal behavior

Andrea

해석

오늘날 유명 인사들이 매우 중요하다는 점은 부정할 수 없습니다. 종합적으로 저는 사회에 대한 그들의 영향이 부정적인 것이라기보다 긍정적인 것이라고 말하고 싶어요. 예를 들면 많은 유명 인사들이 다양한 명분을 지지하며 소셜 미디어에 이를 홍보하고 있죠. 제가 가장 좋아하는 유명 인사 중 한 명은 사람들에게 건강에 좋은 음식을 먹고 운동할 것을 장려하고 있어요. 열심히 공부하는 것, 좋은 가족관을 갖는 것, 그리고 기타 긍정적인 행동들을 지지하는 유명 인사들도 있습니다.

Peter

해석

소셜 미디어의 가장 나쁜 점 중 하나는 사람들이 유명 인사들로부터 영향을 받는 것인데, 이들 대부분은 끔찍한 행동을 일삼는 형편 없는 사람들입니다. 리얼리티 TV 프로그램들은 유명 인사들을 보여 주며 이들의 가치관이 얼마나 저급한지, 그리고 이들의 성격이 얼마나 나쁜지 알려 줍니다. 더 나쁜 것은 많은 사람들이 유명 인사들을 따라할 가치가 있는 사람으로 여긴다는 점이에요. 사실은 전혀 그렇지가 않은데 말이죠.

✎ Summary Note

Andrea	Peter
1 Celebrities have more positive influence than negative • Support various causes and promote on social media 2 One encourages people to eat healthy food and exercise • Others support other positive behaviors	1 Influence of celebrities on social media is bad • Many celebrities terrible • Do awful activities 2 Celebrities promoted on reality TV • Poor values and character • Not people worth emulating

Sample Response 1 Supporting Andrea

Even though Peter is right in that some celebrities who act poorly are often promoted on social media, I support Andrea's argument more. Andrea notes that many celebrities support various causes, which is a valid point. My favorite actor is constantly encouraging people to register to vote and to get involved in politics no matter what their beliefs. Recently, another celebrity made news by visiting a town that had been destroyed by a tornado. He assisted in the relief effort, which inspired others to help. Surely, positive actions like these outweigh the negative actions often seen on reality TV, as Peter points out. Let me add that I have seen many celebrities assist sick children and the poor and the homeless. By bringing attention to these issues, celebrities have engaged in positive behavior worthy of praise.

해석

행동이 좋지 못한 몇몇 유명 인사들이 종종 소셜 미디어에서 주목받는다는 점에서 Peter의 생각은 옳지만 나는 Andrea의 주장을 더 지지한다. Andrea는 다수의 유명 인사들이 다양한 대의 명분을 지지한다는 점에 주목하는데, 이는 타당한 점이다. 내가 가장 좋아하는 배우는 항상 사람들에게 자신의 신념이 무엇이든 투표를 해서 정치에 참여하라고 독려한다. 최근 또 다른 유명 인사는 토네이도가 휩쓴 한 마을을 방문함으로써 뉴스에 등장했다. 그는 구호 활동을 도왔는데, 이로 인해 다른 사람들도 도움을 주게 되었다. 분명 이러한 긍정적인 행동이, Peter가 지적한 리얼리티 TV에서 종종 보여지는 부정적인 행동보다 더 많다. 첨언하자면 나는 많은 유명 인사들이 아픈 아이들과 빈곤층 및 노숙자들을 돕는 것을 보았다. 이러한 이슈에 주의를 기울이도록 만듦으로써 유명 인사들은 칭찬받을 만한 긍정적인 활동을 하고 있다.

Sample Response 2 Supporting Peter

I agree with Peter one hundred percent and wish social media had never been invented because I am tired of seeing the antics of various celebrities. Peter is right when he states that people erroneously believe they should imitate certain celebrities. Many celebrities are only famous because they can act or sing well or because they are attractive. They have no other talents or abilities, yet they think they should tell other people what to do. When I see a singer talking about a topic that he knows nothing about, I just want to tell him to shut up and sing. I will admit that as Andrea writes, some celebrities help others, but the percentage of those who do so is small. Overall, celebrities have a much more negative effect on society than a positive one.

해석

나는 Peter의 생각에 백 퍼센트 동의하며, 여러 유명 인사들의 별난 행동을 보는 것이 지겹기 때문에 소셜 미디어가 발명되지 않았으면 좋았을 것이라고 생각한다. 사람들이 특정 유명 인사들을 따라야 한다고 잘못 알고 있다는 Peter의 주장은 옳다. 많은 유명 인사들은 노래나 연기를 잘하기 때문에, 혹은 매력적이기 때문에 유명할 뿐이다. 그들은 다른 재능이나 능력은 가지고 있지 않으면서도 다른 사람들에게 무엇을 하라고 말을 해야 한다고 생각한다. 나는 자신이 아무것도 모르는 주제에 대해 이야기하는 가수를 보면 그에게 입다물고 노래나 하라고 말해 주고 싶다. 나는 Andrea가 쓴 것처럼 몇몇 유명 인사들이 다른 사람들을 돕는다는 점은 인정하겠지만, 그렇게 하는 사람들의 비율은 적다. 전체적으로 볼 때 유명 인사들은 사회에 긍정적인 영향보다 부정적인 영향을 훨씬 더 많이 끼친다.

<table>
<tr><td colspan="2" style="background:#1a1a1a;color:white">Unit 14 Environmental Science II</td></tr>
</table>

Exercise 1 ···························· p.108

Brainstorming & Outlining

A

Professor Cromartie

해석

다음 수업에서 우리는 인간이 다른 종에 미치는 영향에 대해 논의할 거예요. 아시다시피 인간의 행동 때문에 일부 동물들은 멸종 위험에, 그리고 일부 동물들은 멸종에 처해 있습니다. 여러 차례, 예컨대 주간 고속 도로와 같은 대규모 기반 시설 공사로 동물들이 피해를 입고 있어요. 생각해 봅시다. 멸종 위기종에게 피해를 줄 기반 시설 공사들을 취소해야 할까요? 이에 동의하나요, 동의하지 않나요? 그 이유는요?

✗ Outline for Brainstorming

<table>
<tr><th colspan="4">Cancel Large Infrastructure Projects or Not</th></tr>
<tr><th colspan="2">Agree</th><th colspan="2">Disagree</th></tr>
<tr><th>Reason 1</th><th>Reason 2</th><th>Reason 1</th><th>Reason 2</th></tr>
<tr><td>- Must protect animals since can't protect themselves</td><td>- Stop killing animals → don't want more to go extinct</td><td>- Can adapt projects to accommodate animals</td><td>- Can relocate animals to other places</td></tr>
</table>

B

Irene

해석

인간은 자연의 관리자이며, 많은 경우 동물들은 스스로를 지킬 수가 없기 때문에, 인간이 동물들을 보호해야 합니다. 기반 시설 공사가 멸종 위기종에게 피해를 줄 위험이 된다면 그러한 공사는 즉시 취소되어야 해요. 필요한 경우 우리의 필요보다 동물을 우선시함으로써 동물계의 구성원들에 대한 우리의 책임을 강조해야 합니다.

✎ Summary Notes: Irene

1) stewards of environment
2) cannot protect themselves
3) cancel project immediately
4) animal kingdom
5) ahead of our needs

Chad

해석

일부 동물들 때문에 기반 시설 공사가 취소되어야 한다는 주장에 저는 전적으로

반대합니다. 우리가 동물들을 무시해야 한다는 말은 아니에요. 인간은 임기응변적으로 행동해서 자신과 동물들을 보호할 수 있습니다. 예를 들어 동물의 이동 경로를 가로지르는 주간 고속도로 위쪽에 육교형 생태 통로를 건설하고 아래쪽에는 터널형 생태 통로를 만들 수가 있어요. 이러한 것들이 지어진 곳에서는 동물들이 이를 이용한다고 알려져 있죠.

✎ Summary Notes: Chad

1) cancel infrastructure projects
2) ignore animals
3) improvise to help humans and animals
4) bisect animal migration routes
5) animal bridges over them
6) tunnels
7) use them

Organization

Supporting Irene's Opinion

1 While Chad makes a good point about animal bridges and tunnels, I side with Irene and agree that infrastructure projects which could potentially harm endangered species should canceled.

2 In the past few centuries, humans have been directly responsible for the extinction of numerous animal species.

3 We need to stop killing so many animals, and the best way to do that is to cancel certain projects.

4 New projects taking the lives of animals into consideration can be proposed in their place, but anything guaranteed to kill animals should be terminated.

5 I would really hate to see more animals go the way of the dodo and disappear from the face of the planet due to human carelessness.

Supporting Chad's Opinion

1 Although I sympathize with the plight of animals like Irene does, I do not believe progress should be impeded, so I find myself in agreement with Chad.

2 He is correct in that designers and engineers should make an effort to accommodate animals.

3 There is a highway in Africa with special paths allowing migrating elephants to cross busy roads.

4 We should be inspired by that and make infrastructure projects more considerate of animals.

5 Something else we should consider is that the world is a big place with plenty of empty land where people do not live.

6 Some animals could be relocated to places where no humans are.

7 Then, there would be no need to worry about canceling infrastructure projects.

Professor Hopewell

해석

지난 몇 년에 걸쳐 전기 자동차의 품질이 크게 개선되어 이제는 전 세계에서 전기 자동차가 대량으로 생산되고 있습니다. 휘발유 차량에서 배출되는 오염 물질의 양을 감안하면서 다음과 같은 질문에 대해 생각해 보았으면 해요. 정부가 새로 생산되는 모든 차는 전기 자동차가 되도록 강제해야 할까요? 여러분 생각은 무엇인가요? 그 이유는요?

✖ Outline for Brainstorming

Mandating All New Cars Be Electric Vehicles	
Agree	Disagree
Reason	Reason
- Gas-powered cars = huge polluters	- Electric vehicles = very expensive
Details	Details
- More electric vehicles = cleaner air	- Many people can't afford → transportation problems

Wilson

해석

가솔린 자동차와 트럭은 주요 오염원이며 저는 환경이 그로 인해 피해를 입는다는 점을 참을 수가 없습니다. 그러한 이유로 저는 전기 자동차만 생산되도록 만드는 법을 지지하고자 합니다. 자동차를 운행하기 위해 더 이상 휘발유를 연소시키지 않는다면 대기가 얼마나 빨리 다시 숨쉬기에 적합하게 될지 생각해 보세요. 현재의 상황이 크게 개선될 것입니다.

Amanda

해석

저는 전기 자동차를 적극적으로 지지하며 전기 자동차가 미래에 필수적인 것이 될 것으로 생각하지만, 정부가 모든 신차는 전기 자동차이어야 한다고 명령을 내려서는 안 된다고 생각해요. 먼저 전기 자동차는 엄청나게 비싸기 때문에 그러한 상황에서는 많은 사람들이 개인용 차량을 구입하지 못하게 될 것입니다. 또한 저는 정부가 사람들에게 무엇을 해야 하는지, 그리고 무엇을 하지 말아야 하는지에 대해 말을 한다는 아이디어를 반대합니다.

☑ Summary Note

Wilson	Amanda
1 Gas-powered cars = huge polluters • Damage environment 2 Support law only letting EVs be made • Air will become breathable quickly • Improvement over current situation	1 Governments shouldn't make this order • EVs = expensive • Many can't afford to purchase personal vehicle 2 Disapprove of government telling people what to do

Sample Response 1 Supporting Wilson

Wilson's and Amanda's answers are both insightful; however, I believe Wilson's argument is correct. The quality of the air in urban centers is atrocious, mainly because so many cars and trucks are burning gas and spewing noxious toxins into the air. A world in which only electric vehicles were sold would be incredible. I understand and share Amanda's feelings about the government. I despise being told what to do by bureaucrats, but in this case, there really is an environmental crisis we must do something about. One additional point I want to make is that if there only electric vehicles, then drilling for oil would cease being so important. This would make a positive contribution to the health of the entire Earth.

해석

Wilson과 Amanda의 답변 모두 통찰력 있는 것이지만 나는 Wilson의 주장이 옳다고 생각한다. 도시 중심지의 대기 상태는 끔찍한 편으로, 이는 주로 많은 자동차와 트럭이 휘발유를 연소시켜 유해 독성 물질을 대기 중으로 뿜어내기 때문이다. 전기 자동차만 판매되는 세상은 정말 좋을 것이다. 나는 정부에 대한 Amanda의 생각을 이해하며 동감하는 편이다. 나는 관료주의자들에 의해 무엇을 해야 한다는 말을 듣는 것을 경멸하지만, 이 경우 정말로 우리가 조치를 취해야만 하는 환경적인 위기가 존재한다. 내가 추가로 주장하고 싶은 것은 전기 자동차만 존재한다면 석유 시추의 중요성이 사라질 것이라는 점이다. 이로써 지구 전체의 건강에 긍정적인 영향이 미치게 될 것이다.

Sample Response 2 Supporting Amanda

I wholeheartedly agree with Amanda as I do not think there should be a law requiring all vehicles manufactured to be electric vehicles. As she pointed out, due to the high costs of these vehicles, few people would be able to afford them. This would cause all kinds of problems, including preventing people from commuting to school and work. I understand there is an environmental problem like Wilson mentioned, but let me point out something important. Electric vehicles get electricity from power plants, many of which run on coal. If more cars were electric vehicles, even more coal would be burned than now. Burning more coal instead of gas would not improve the environment in any way since both of them produce harmful emissions.

해석

나는 생산되는 모든 차량이 전기 자동차일 것을 요구하는 법이 존재해서는 안 된다고 생각하기 때문에 Amanda의 의견에 전적으로 동의한다. 그녀가 지적한 대로 전기 자동차의 높은 가격 때문에 이를 구입할 수 있는 사람은 거의 없을 것이다. 이로써 통학 및 통근 문제를 포함하여 온갖 문제들이 나타날 것이다. 나는 Wilson이 언급한 것처럼 환경 문제가 존재한다는 점은 인정하지만 중요한 점 하나를 지적하고 싶다. 전기 자동차는 발전소에서 생산되는 전기를 이용하는데, 이들 중 다수는 석탄으로 가동된다. 전기 자동차가 더 많아지면 지금보다 훨씬 더 많은 석탄이 연소될 것이다. 둘 다 해로운 물질을 배출하기 때문에 휘발유 대신 석탄을 더 많이 연소시키는 경우에도 환경이 개선되지는 않을 것이다.

Unit 15 Child Studies

Exercise 1 ·········· p.114

Brainstorming & Outlining

A

Professor Robinson

해석

미국의 거의 7천만에 이르는 가구가 최소한 한 마리의 개를 기르고 있으며 약 4천 5백만 가구에서 한 마리 이상의 고양이를 기르고 있습니다. 애완 동물은 많은 미국인들의 삶에서 필수적인 부분이에요. 그럼에도 불구하고 어린 아이들이 종종 가정에서 기르는 애완 동물로 인해, 특히 덩치가 크고 공격성을 지닌 개들에 의해 다치거나 목숨을 잃을 수 있습니다. 아이들이 애완 동물과 함께 있는 것에 대한 여러분들의 생각은 어떤가요? 부모에 의해 허용되어야 할까요? 왜 그렇게 생각하나요?

✗ Outline for Brainstorming

Children Owning Pets			
Should Be Allowed		Should Not Be Allowed	
Reason 1	Reason 2	Reason 1	Reason 2
- Have owned big dogs → no biting	- Teach chidren to care for others	- Can get bitten → hurt or killed	- Children get bored → ignore pets

B

Linda

해석

저는 평생 애완 동물을 길러 왔고 아이들과 애완 동물이 있는 경우 문제가 된 것을 본 적이 없어요. 저는 독일 셰퍼드와 같은 커다란 개를 길렀지만 개가 제 남동생이나 저를 위협한 적은 한 번도 없었습니다. 제 부모님들께서는 개 주변에서 저희가 어떻게 행동해야 하는지, 그리고 그들을 괴롭히거나 때려서는 안 된다는 점을 가르쳐 주셨어요. 저희 개들은 온순하게 행동했고 누구도 문 적이 없었습니다. 아이들은 애완 동물로부터 많은 것을 배울 수 있으며 그러한 혜택은 잠재적인 위험성을 뛰어 넘습니다.

☑ Summary Notes: Linda

1) large dogs all life
2) threatened brother or me
3) behave around dogs
4) tease or hit
5) well behaved
6) bit anyone

Fred

해석

저는 친구의 집을 방문한 적이 있었습니다. 친구가 기르던 개는 그 가족들에 의해 방치되어 있었고 줄에 묶여 있었어요. 불행하게도 개가 줄에서 빠져나와 저를 물었습니다. 그때 물린 상처가 아직도 남아 있죠. 그 개는 덩치가 컸던 반면에는 몸집이 작았고 제 자신을 방어할 능력이 없었습니다. 저는 아이들이 사나운 동물들로부터 스스로를 보호할 수 있을 정도로 충분히 크기 전까지는 애완 동물로부터 떨어져 있어야 한다고 생각합니다.

☑ Summary Notes: Fred

1) friend's house
2) neglected dog kept on chain
3) bit me
4) scar
5) away from pets
6) big enough

Organization

Supporting Linda's Opinion

1 I am similar to Linda in that I grew up with multiple dogs and cats as pets, and nobody in my family ever felt threatened by them.

2 Linda is correct in observing that children can learn greatly from owning pets.

3 For example, I learned not to think only about myself but to consider others thanks to my pets.

4 I had to feed them daily, take them for walks, and clean up after them.

5 Without me, they would not have been able to survive.

6 I do feel bad for Fred, but it sounds like his friend's parents were bad owners.

7 Most people treat their pets like family members these days, so animal attacks are not particularly common.

Supporting Fred's Opinion

1 I see both sides of this argument, but I lean more toward supporting Fred.

2 When I was three, I was badly scratched by my family's cat.

3 She had always been nice, but then, for no reason, she suddenly attacked me and clawed my legs.

4 My parents realized that pets and young children do not mix well, so we did not have another pet until I turned thirteen.

5 I guess I missed out on some of the benefits of owning a pet Linda mentioned, but at least no animals attacked me again.

6 A final point is that many children become bored with pets.

7 As a result, they stop taking care of their animals, which leads to neglect.

Exercise 2 ·········· p.117

Professor Durham

해석

많은 부모들이 여러 가지 이유로 학교 시스템에 대한 불만을 나타내기 시작했는데, 그 결과 공립 학교 및 사립 학교에서 자녀들을 자퇴시키고 그 대신 홈스쿨링을 실시하고 있어요. 최근 몇 년 동안 홈스쿨링을 하는 사람들의 수는 수백만 명으로 늘어났습니다. 홈스쿨링에 대한 여러분의 생각은 무엇인가요? 장점이 더 많다고 생각하나요, 아니면 단점이 더 많다고 생각하나요? 그 이유는요?

✗ Outline for Brainstorming

Homeschooling	
Advantages	Disadvantages
Reason	Reason
- Advanced learning	- Poor social skills
Details	Details
- Learn at own pace → take college-level classes in high school	- Can't hang out w/peers anymore

Kevin

`해석`

저는 홈스쿨링을 하지 않았지만 제 친구들 중 몇 명은 홈스쿨링을 했어요. 저는 그들이 받은 교육의 질에 큰 인상을 받았습니다. 그들은 같은 나이의 대부분의 사람들보다 훨씬 더 많이 알고 있으며 일반 학생들보다 훨씬 더 적은 시간을 공부하는데 썼어요. 또한 그들은 스포츠 팀 활동 및 과외 활동에도 참여할 수 있었는데, 그들의 사교성은 뛰어난 편입니다.

Molly

`해석`

저는 홈스쿨링이 아이들을 친구들로부터 떼어놓기 때문에 정말로 홈스쿨링 운동을 반기지 않습니다. 홈스쿨링을 하는 많은 아이들은 하루 종일 집에 머물면서 부모로부터 수업을 듣는데, 부모들 중 대부분은 교사가 아닙니다. 이는 아이들을 교육하는 좋은 방법이 될 수 없어요. 홈스쿨링을 하는 아이들은 같은 나이의 다른 아이들과 만나서 그들과 사회적인 교류를 할 수 있는 기회를 잃고 있습니다.

🖉 Summary Note

Kevin	Molly
1 Friends were homeschooled • Got high-quality education • Know more than people their ages • Spent less time studying than regular students **2** Could participate in other activities • Played on sports teams • Did extracurricular activities • Remarkable social skills	**1** Dislike homeschooling • Separates kids from peers • Stay home all day • Taught by parents → not usually teachers **2** Losing opportunities to meet others their age • No social interactions w/peers

`Sample Response 1` **Supporting Kevin**

Similar to Kevin, I am a big supporter of the homeschooling movement. Students who are homeschooled learn very much and are also able to pursue topics they are interested in much more than they could at school. One benefit of homeschooling is that the students study at their own pace. Many homeschoolers are smart, so they can take college-level classes when they are in high school or even middle school. I understand Molly's fear that homeschoolers do not always get to socialize with other students. However, they are also not subjected to bullying, which is a major problem at many schools. They also do not have to worry about teachers who try to indoctrinate them with views that go against their parents' values. It is therefore clear to me that homeschooling has many more benefits than drawbacks.

`해석`

Kevin과 마찬가지로 나는 홈스쿨링 운동의 열렬한 지지자이다. 홈스쿨링을 하는 학생들은 매우 많은 것을 배우며, 학교에 다니는 경우보다 관심이 가는 주제에 대해 훨씬 더 많은 탐구를 할 수가 있다. 홈스쿨링의 한 가지 혜택은 학생들이 자신의 속도에 맞춰 공부를 한다는 것이다. 홈스쿨링을 하는 많은 사람들이 똑똑하기 때문에 고등학교 혹은 심지어 중학교 학생인 경우에도 대학 수준의 수업을 들을 수 있다. 나는 홈스쿨링을 하는 사람들이 항상 다른 학생들과 교류를 하는 것은 아니라는 Molly의 우려를 이해한다. 하지만 그들은 많은 학교에서 중대한 문제인 집단 괴롭힘을 겪지 않는다. 또한 부모의 가치와 상반되는 견해를 주입시키려는 교사에 대해 걱정할 필요도 없다. 따라서 홈스쿨링에 단점보다 장점이 더 많이 존재한다는 점은 내게 명확하다.

`Sample Response 2` **Supporting Molly**

There are both advantages and disadvantages of homeschool, and Kevin and Molly do an effective job of describing them. I actually have personal experience with homeschooling, and that makes me agree with Molly. When I was in middle school, my parents withdrew me from my school and started homeschooling me. While I did learn a lot, like Kevin mentions, I felt so isolated studying at home. My friends from school were suddenly not interested in hanging out with me anymore. This caused me to ignore my studies. I actually became so depressed that my parents enrolled me in school the following semester. Had I remained a homeschooler, I believe I would have received a superior education. Nevertheless, I would have missed out on other benefits of school, such as sports and clubs, and that would have been a drawback.

`해석`

홈스쿨에는 장점과 단점 모두 존재하며 Kevin과 Molly는 홈스쿨링에 대해 효과적으로 설명하고 있다. 사실 나는 개인적으로 홈스쿨링을 한 경험을 가지고 있기 때문에 Molly의 의견에 동의한다. 내가 중학생이었을 때 우리 부모님께서는 나를 중퇴시키신 후 내게 홈스쿨링을 시키셨다. Kevin이 언급한 것처럼 나는 많은 것을 배웠지만 집에서 공부하면서 고립감을 느꼈다. 학교 친구들은 갑자기 더 이상 나와 어울리려 하지 않았다. 그로 인해 나는 공부를 소홀히 하게 되었다. 실제로 너무 우울해져서 우리 부모님께서는 그 다음 학기에 다시 학교에 등록시키셨다. 내가 계속 홈스쿨링을 했다면 나는 더 우수한 교육을 받았을 것으로 생각한다. 그럼에도 불구하고 나는 학교의 기타 혜택들, 예컨대 스포츠 및 동아리 활동을 놓쳤을 것인데, 이는 단점에 해당되는 것이다.

Unit 16 Economics I

Exercise 1 ·· p.120

Brainstorming & Outlining

A

Professor Redding

해석

다음 수업 시간에는 다양한 상황에서의 사람들의 쇼핑 행태에 대해 생각해 볼 것입니다. 그러니 이에 대한 여러분의 생각을 제게 알려 주세요. 오늘날 식품을 구입하려는 사람들은 대형 수퍼마켓 체인과 집 근처의 소규모 식품점 중 하나를 선택할 수가 있습니다. 여러분은 두 가지 유형의 매장 중 어디에서 식품을 구입하고 싶으세요? 그 이유는요?

✕ Outline for Brainstorming

Preferred Shopping Location			
Large Chain Supermarkets		Small Local Grocery Stores	
Reason 1	**Reason 2**	**Reason 1**	**Reason 2**
- Lots of foods to choose from	- Fresh fruits and vegetables all year	- Sell locally sourced foods	- Receive personal touch from employees

B

Rose

해석

쇼핑에 대해 말하자면 저는 대형 수퍼마켓 체인의 편리함을 선호합니다. 일반적으로 선택할 수 있는 식품이 다양해요. 예를 들면 저는 다수의 브랜드 파스타 소스를 구입할 수 있으며 1년 내내 전 세계에서 온 다양한 과일과 채소를 구입할 수가 있습니다. 제가 선택할 수 있는 것이 매우 많다는 점은 제게 필요한 모든 것을 한 군데의 매장에서 구입할 수 있다는 점을 의미하죠.

✎ Summary Notes: Rose

1) choices of food
2) brands of pasta sauce
3) fruits and vegetables
4) throughout year
5) shop at one store

Anthony

해석

소규모 동네 식품점이 대형 수퍼마켓 체인보다 훨씬 더 낫습니다. 저희 동네 식품점에서는 모두 인근 지역에서 생산된 신선한 과일, 채소, 그리고 육류를 판매하는데, 이는 환경에 이상적인 일입니다. 물론 다른 곳보다 가격이 약간 더 비쌀 수는 있지만 저는 친근함을 느끼는 것을 좋아하고 그 매장은 저희 집에서 도보로 3분 거리에 있습니다.

✎ Summary Notes: Anthony

1) fruits, vegetables, and meat
2) locally sourced
3) environment
4) personal touch
5) three-minute walk

Organization

Supporting Rose's Opinion

1. I am actually a fan of both large chain supermarkets and small local grocery stores, so I like the reasons that Rose and Anthony provide.
2. Still, if I had to pick one of them, I would support large chain supermarkets.
3. I love how they provide so many food choices.
4. I sometimes go shopping at them with no solid plans for dinner.
5. I merely look around until I see something I like and then purchase it.
6. Anthony is right that local grocery stores often have a personal touch since the employees come to know their shoppers well.
7. But that is not enough to convince me to abandon shopping at large supermarkets.

Supporting Anthony's Opinion

1. While Rose accurately notes that large supermarkets provide numerous choices, Anthony makes stronger observations that I agree with.
2. He points out that small neighborhood grocery stores normally sell locally sourced foods.
3. I prefer buying them because doing that supports nearby farmers.
4. It also means that food does not have to be shipped thousands of miles from distant places, which is both costly and bad for the environment.
5. I can also ask my local grocer for special orders, and he is willing to accommodate my requests.
6. That is a level of service which supermarkets cannot aspire to.
7. I am not saying that I never shop at large supermarkets, but my preference is small grocery stores.

Exercise 2 ·· p.123

Professor Holmes

해석

어디를 보더라도 온갖 상품을 광고하는 광고들이 있습니다. 사람들에게 필요하던 필요하지 않던 최대한 많은 제품을 구입하라고 권장을 하죠. 우리 사회는 소비지상주의에 기반한 사회가 되고 있습니다. 이로써 중요한 질문이 제기됩니다. 사람들이 지나친 소비를 하고 있다고 생각하나요? 그 이유는요?

✗ Outline for Brainstorming

Do People Consume Too Much	
Agree	Disagree
Reason	Reason
- Buy things don't need	- Only buy necessary things
Details	Details
- Have wardrobe full of clothes almost never wear	- Can overcome urge to consume too much

Claude

`해석`

제 기숙사 방을 둘러보면 구입은 했지만 필요는 없는 제품들이 많이 있습니다. 마찬가지로 제 친구들의 방에 가 보면 그들도 저와 똑같은 일을 한 것을 알게 되죠. 과소비는 상당히 많은 사람들이 상대해야 하는 문제입니다. 천문학적 숫자의 인쇄 광고, TV 광고, 유명 인사 광고, 그리고 기타 구매 유도를 의한 광고들이 너무 많아서 대부분의 사람들은, 저를 포함해서, 저항을 하지 못하고 있어요.

Rebecca

`해석`

사람들에게 소비가 권장되고 있는 것은 사실이지만 저는 대부분의 사람들이 과소비를 하고 있다는 것을 사실로 받아들이지 않습니다. 예를 들어 제 옷장에는 옷이 그렇게 많이 있지는 않은데, 제 친구들의 옷장도 마찬가지에요. 저는 또한 책을 구입하는 것보다 도서관에서 빌리는 것을 더 선호합니다. 실제로 저는 구매하는 횟수를 줄이기 위해 의도적으로 노력을 하고 있어요.

✎ Summary Note

Claude	Rebecca
1 Dorm room has items bought but don't need • Friends' rooms = same • Overconsumption = huge problem **2** Astronomical numbers of ads, commercials, celebrity endorsements, and other inducements • Too much for most people to resist	**1** Don't believe most people overconsume • Wardrobe doesn't have too many clothes • Friends' wardrobes = same **2** Borrows books from library • Doesn't purchase them • Makes conscious effort to limit number of purchases

Sample Response 1 Supporting Claude

I admire people like Rebecca who can control the urge to make purchases, but that is a miniscule number of people. Claude and his friends are much more representative of the average person than Rebecca is. Claude remarks that he and his friends have made large numbers of unnecessary purchases. I have done the same as I have bought clothes I have worn a single time and books I have never read. Whenever I visit the shopping mall, I see people carrying numerous bags and with shopping carts piled sky high. I doubt they need everything they are buying. But since our culture is one based on consumption, they have been trained to buy, buy, and buy some more. I wish our culture would change, but that may not happen for a long time.

`해석`

나는 구매 충동을 억누를 수 있는 Rebecca와 같은 사람들을 존경하지만 그러한 사람은 소수이다. Rebecca보다는 Claude와 그 친구들이 훨씬 더 평범한 사람들의 모습을 나타낸다. Claude는 자신과 자신의 친구들이 필요하지 않은 물품을 다수 구입했다고 언급한다. 내게도 사고서 한 번만 입은 옷과 사고서 읽지 않은 책들이 있기 때문에 나도 마찬가지이다. 나는 쇼핑몰을 방문할 때마다 많은 봉투를 들고 물건이 산처럼 쌓인 쇼핑 카트를 끌고 다니는 사람들을 보게 된다. 나는 그들이 구입한 모든 제품이 필요한 것인지 의심이 든다. 하지만 우리의 문화가 소비에 기반해 있기 때문에 그들은 구입하고, 구입하고, 그리고 더 구입하도록 훈련이 되어 있다. 나는 우리 문화가 바뀌기를 바라지만 한동안 그런 일은 없을 것 같다.

Sample Response 2 Supporting Rebecca

While there are some people who engage in overconsumption in the manner described by Claude, but I do not believe this constitutes the majority of consumers. Where I come from, most people are like Rebecca and avoid spending too much money. The only time that I make a purchase is when I absolutely need a specific item I am getting. I actually have a strong dislike for the culture of consumption that some people engage in. Many of these items, especially shoes and clothes, are manufactured by children working in sweatshops. That is morally wrong, so people should not support companies that utilize sweatshops by purchasing their products. Fortunately, most people are able to control their urges, so they do not consume too much.

`해석`

Claude가 말한 방법으로 과소비를 하는 사람들이 있기는 하지만, 나는 이것이 대다수 소비자들에게 해당되는 이야기라고 생각하지는 않는다. 내가 사는 곳의 대부분의 사람들은 Rebecca와 마찬가지로 지나치게 많은 돈을 쓰지 않는다. 내가 물건을 구입하는 경우는 내가 사려는 제품이 절대적으로 필요한 때이다. 실제로 나는 일부 사람들이 따르는 과소비 문화를 정말로 싫어한다. 그러한 많은 제품들은, 특히 신발과 옷은, 노동 착취 공장에서 일하는 아동들에 의해 생산된다. 이는 도덕적으로 옳지 않은 일이기 때문에 사람들은 이러한 제품을 구입함으로써 노동 착취 공장을 이용하는 기업들을 도와서는 안 된다. 다행히도 대부분의 사람들은 충동을 억제할 수 있기 때문에 소비를 그다지 많이 하지 않는다.

Exercise 1 · p.126

Brainstorming & Outlining

A

Professor Reynolds

해석

구입을 하기 전에, 특히 사람들이 많은 돈을 써야 하는 제품을 구입하기 전에, 사람들은 종종 다른 사람들의 의견을 구합니다. 일부 사람들에게 이는 친구로부터 구매와 관련된 조언을 구한다는 점을 의미해요. 다른 경우로 특정 제품에 대한 온라인 리뷰를 읽어 보는 것을 좋아하는 사람들도 있죠. 이 두 가지 방법 중에서 어떤 것을 선호하나요? 그 이유는요?

✖ Outline for Brainstorming

Getting Opinions before Making Large Purchases			
Asking Friends for Advice		Reading Online Reviews	
Reason 1	Reason 2	Reason 1	Reason 2
- Friends know preferences	- Friends have best interests in mind	- Reviews written by knowledge-able people	- Can help change mind and buy something else

B

Orlando

해석

가끔 비싼 제품을 구입하는 경우 저는 항상 제가 소중하게 생각하는 의견을 지닌 한두 명의 친구들에게 물어봅니다. 먼저 그들은 저와 저의 선호도를 알고 있기 때문에 제가 사려는 제품에 대한 통찰력을 제시해 줄 수 있어요. 또한 저한테 최선인 것이 무엇인지 알고 있기 때문에 그들이 제가 무엇을 사야 하고 무엇을 사지 말아야 하는지 이야기할 때 저는 그들의 말을 믿을 수 있습니다.

📝 Summary Notes: Orlando

1) one or two friends
2) opinions
3) me and my preferences
4) insight
5) making purchase
6) my best interests
7) buy or avoid something

Sally

해석

저는 제가 사려고 생각 중인 제품에 대해 항상 온라인 리뷰를 자세히 읽어보려고 해요. 리뷰를 쓴 사람은 보통 그 제품에 대한 상당한 지식을 가지고 있기 때문에 제품을 제대로 평가할 수 있습니다. 온라인 리뷰는 또한 종종 두 개 이상의 제품의 유사점과 차이점을 보여 줍니다. 그 결과 저는 온라인 리뷰를 읽은 후 때때로 마음을 바꾸어서 제가 사려고 했던 것과 다른 제품을 구입하게 되죠.

📝 Summary Notes: Sally

1) considerable amount of knowledge
2) excellent evaluations
3) compare and contrast
4) change my mind
5) different purchases

Organization

Supporting Orlando's Opinion

1 Even though I sometimes read online reviews like Sally, there is nothing better than getting an honest opinion from a friend.

2 Orlando is correct in observing that friends have your best interests in mind.

3 On occasion, my friends have recommended items that I later purchased, and I loved them.

4 They have also suggested not buying other things, and I followed their advice.

5 While it is true that online reviews can impart some valuable information, they lack the personal knowledge that the opinions of friends have.

6 In fact, the last time I relied only on online reviews before making a purchase, I came to regret my decision.

7 That has never once happened after I received advice from a friend.

Supporting Sally's Opinion

1 I make most of my purchases online, so it is only natural that I rely upon online reviews before clicking on an item to buy it.

2 Sally makes a good point in stating that online reviewers are typically knowledgeable about the items they are reviewing.

3 Thanks to them, I have avoided purchasing items that I wanted when I read a review and subsequently learned about a problem a certain product had.

4 By the same token, friends can provide valuable guidance in the manner suggested by Orlando.

5 Yet my friends might not know anything about certain products that I want to purchase.

6 It would therefore make no sense to request their opinions on those items.

Exercise 2 · p.129

Professor Sullivan

해석

개인 행동의 중요한 측면에 대해 생각해 보았으면 해요. 학교에 오지 않고 집에서 머무르는 경우 어떤 식으로 식사를 하는 것을 선호하나요? 집에서 혼자서 혹은 가족들과 식사를 하는 것을 좋아하나요? 아니면 식당에 가서 식사하는 것을 좋아하나요? 그 이유는요?

⊠ Outline for Brainstorming

Eating Meals at Home or at Restaurants	
At Home	At Restaurants
Reason	Reason
- Parents are great cooks	- Not much time
Details	Details
- Can have delicious and nutritious meals at home	- Too busy to buy food, prepare it, and cook

Mary

해석

저희 어머니는 매우 요리를 잘 하시고 아버지는 온갖 구이를 도맡아 하시기 때문에 저로서는 선택이 수월하네요. 저는 식당에 가기보다 집에서 식구들과 식사를 하는 편이 훨씬 더 좋습니다. 우선 식당에 가면 돈이 많이 들고 종종 서비스가 좋지 못한 경우도 있죠. 또한 저는 집에서 자리에 앉아 식사를 하면서 부모님 및 여동생과 이야기를 나누는 것이 정말 좋습니다.

Douglas

해석

저는 집에서 요리를 하는 것보다 식당에서 식사를 하는 것을 선호합니다. 집에 있을 때에는 항상 무언가에 몰두해 있어서 제게 식사를 준비할 수 있는 한두 시간이 없습니다. 저로서는 식당을 방문해서 식사를 주문하는 것이 더 편해요. 저는 저렴한 가격으로 건강에 좋고 포만감을 주는 음식을 제공하는 식당을 몇 군데 알고 있는데, 저는 그곳의 단골입니다.

☑ Summary Note

Mary	Douglas
1 Parents both cook well • Stay home and eat dinner 2 Restaurants = expensive + poor service 3 Love being at home, eating dinner, and chatting with family	1 Always occupied at home • Lack time to prepare meal 2 Convenient to visit restaurant to order dinner • Get wholesome, filling food • Pay low prices

Sample Response 1 Supporting Mary

Douglas is correct in that some restaurants provide quality inexpensive food, yet I resemble Mary in that I would rather remain home for dinner. My father does the cooking in my family, and he is an outstanding cook. In addition, because he cooks, he controls the ingredients. My father avoids adding anything harmful to the food, which is something that is not guaranteed at a restaurant. Of course, I enjoy going out to eat on occasion, and I search for restaurants like those that Douglas describes. But it brings me great pleasure to aid my father in the kitchen and then to eat the food that we worked so hard

to prepare. That makes the food taste better than anything I could order at a five-star restaurant.

해석

일부 식당에서 뛰어나고 저렴한 음식을 제공한다는 Douglas의 말은 맞지만 나는 집에서 식사하는 것을 더 좋아하기 때문에 Mary와 의견이 같다. 우리 아버지는 집에서 요리를 하시며 요리를 매우 잘 하신다. 게다가 아버지가 요리를 하시기 때문에 재료도 아버지가 정하신다. 아버지는 음식에 해로운 것은 첨가하지 않으시는데, 이는 식당에서 보장되지 않는 점이다. 물론 나도 때때로 외식을 좋아하고 Douglas가 이야기한 것과 같은 식당을 찾는다. 하지만 주방에서 아버지를 도와 열심히 준비한 음식을 먹는 것이 내게는 큰 즐거움을 가져다 준다. 그러면 5성 식당에서 주문할 수 있는 그 어떤 음식보다 음식 맛이 더 좋아진다.

Sample Response 2 Supporting Douglas

Mary's argument is rather convincing, but so is Douglas's. As a matter of fact, he brings up a point that is true for me. I do not have time to go shopping, to cut up and mix ingredients, and then to cook them. It is much easier for me to walk down the street to a restaurant near my home and to order an inexpensive yet delicious meal. The restaurants that I frequent list all the ingredients in each dish they serve, and they also note how many calories each dish contains. This enables me to avoid eating unhealthy food and also to keep my weight down. Furthermore, I am not talented in the kitchen, so the food I prepare for myself is unappetizing. That is why I would rather eat out than eat at home.

해석

Mary의 주장도 다소 설득력이 있지만 Douglas의 주장도 마찬가지이다. 실제로 그가 제기한 한 가지 논점은 나에게 딱 들어맞는다. 내게는 쇼핑을 해서, 재료를 자르고 섞고, 그리고 요리를 할 시간이 없다. 나로서는 거리에 나가 집 근처의 식당에 가서 비싸지 않고 맛있는 음식을 주문하는 편이 훨씬 더 수월하다. 내가 자주 다니는 식당은 그곳에서 제공되는 모든 요리의 성분을 목록으로 보여 주며 또한 각 요리의 칼로리가 어느 정도인지 알려 준다. 이로써 나는 건강에 좋지 않은 음식을 피할 수 있고 체중도 감량할 수 있다. 게다가 나는 주방일에 소질이 없기 때문에 내가 직접 준비하는 음식은 맛이 없다. 바로 그런 이유 때문에 나는 집보다 밖에서 식사를 하고 싶다.

Unit 18 Urban Development

Exercise 1 .... p.132

Brainstorming & Outlining

A

Professor Carlton

해석

수많은 도시의 도로들이 상태가 좋지 못해서 보수가 필요합니다. 하지만 시 정부는 종종 보수할 필요한 예산이 부족하다고 주장을 해요. 도로 보수를 위해 지방세를 인상하는 것에 찬성하나요? 아니면 역내 모든 차량 소유자들이 도로 개선에 사용될 비용을 매년 부담해야 한다고 생각하나요? 그러한 선택을 한 이유는요?

✗ Outline for Brainstorming

Who Pays for Road Repairs			
Taxpayers		Vehicle Owners	
Reason 1	Reason 2	Reason 1	Reason 2
- Okay to use taxes for good purpose	- All taxpayers benefit, so all should pay	- Use roads the most so should pay	- Not fair to make people who don't use roads pay

B

Kaye

해석

두 가지 선택 사항 중에서 저는 전자를 선택하겠습니다. 돈이 어떻게 쓰일지 납세자들이 아는 한 지방세 인상에는 아무런 문제가 없습니다. 도로와 같은 기반 시설의 개선은 가치가 있는 일이며 정부가 해야 할 일이에요. 판매세를 1% 인상시키면 도로 보수에 필요한 자금이 마련될 것입니다.

✎ Summary Notes: Kaye

1) raise taxes
2) money will be spent
3) infrastructure
4) worthy cause
5) one percent
6) road repairs

Scott

해석

시에 거주하는 모든 사람들이 본인은 사용하지도 않는 것에 비용을 부담해야 한다는 점은 제게 상당히 불공정하게 비춰집니다. 차량 소유주들이 도로를 이용하는 사람들이기 때문에 그들이 보수 비용을 부담해야 해요. 저는 운전을 하지도 않으며 버스조차 타지 않습니다. 저는 모든 곳을 걸어서 다니기 때문에 제게 아무런 소용이 없는 것에 비용을 부담하고 싶지는 않아요.

✎ Summary Notes: Scott

1) Unfair
2) don't use
3) use roads
4) cost of repairs
5) takes bus
6) Walks
7) of no use

Organization

Supporting Kaye's Opinion

1 I believe that Scott's response is misguided whereas Kaye understands the situation perfectly.
2 Like she mentions, governments are responsible for taking care of roads, so I would be willing to pay higher taxes to facilitate repairs.
3 It is important to note that everyone uses the roads either directly or indirectly.
4 I am sure that Scott has items delivered to him by trucks driving on city roads.
5 And he likely buys food that was shipped to supermarkets on busy roads.
6 Everyone living in a city benefits from the roads in some way, so all of the residents have the joint responsibility to help pay for their upkeep.

Supporting Scott's Opinion

1 Scott has the right idea even though I understand the argument Kaye is making.
2 While I acknowledge that I utilize the roads by taking the bus and by riding my bike on it, I do not believe I am personally responsible for a lot of wear and tear on the roads.
3 Therefore, there is no reason for me, who has no car, to pay for the maintenance of the city's roads.
4 In addition, cities should do a better job constructing the roads.
5 Then, they would not be in dire need of repairs.
6 Cities themselves created these problems, and now they are demanding that taxpayers bail them out.
7 That is unacceptable to me.

Exercise 2 ·· p.135

Professor Reyes

해석

공공 도서관 및 소장 도서에 대해 생각해 보죠. 많은 도서관들이 공간 부족에도 불구하고 여전히 인쇄된 서적을 구입하고 있습니다. 새로운 도서를 위한 공간을 마련하기 위해서는 소장 도서 중 오래된 책들을 종종 처분해야 합니다. 하지만 전자책을 구입한다면 공간을 고려할 필요가 없을 거예요. 도서관이 인쇄된 서적 대신 전자책을 구입하는 것에 집중해야 한다고 생각하나요? 그 이유는요?

✗ Outline for Brainstorming

What Books Libraries Should Buy	
E-books	Printed Books
Reason	Reason
- Convenient for users	- Can store old printed books
Details	Details
- Don't have to visit library but can borrow online	- Shouldn't get rid of books out of print and hard to find

Donald

해석

저는 공공 도서관을 좋아하지만 공간이 부족해서 소장 도서들을 처분하는 것은 싫어합니다. 그들이 버리는 도서 중 많은 것들이 절판되어 구하기가 힘든 것들이에요. 도서관은 최대한 많은 도서들을 소장해야 하며 그럴 수 있는 최선의 방법은, 현대 과학 기술 덕분에, 이용객들에게 빌려 줄 수 있는 전자책을 구입하는 것입니다.

Wendy

해석

저는 전자책을 크게 불신하며 인쇄된 책을 읽는 것만 좋아합니다. 그 이유는 전자책이 소유자의 동이 없이 업데이트될 수 있고 심지어 때로는 소유자의 소장 도서에서 삭제될 수도 있기 때문이에요. 인쇄된 책은 결코 바뀌지 않기 때문에 도서관은 이를 소장해야 합니다. 공간이 문제가 되는 경우, 사람들이 거의 읽지 않는 책은 주로 창고에 보관해 두었다가 요청이 있을 때만 꺼내 주면 됩니다.

✏ Summary Note

Donald	Wendy
1 Abhor how public libraries dispose of books • Discard books out of print • Discard books hard to find **2** Should try to build up collections • Best way = acquire e-books that can lend to patrons	**1** Has strong distrust of e-books • Can update e-books without owner's consent • E-books may be deleted from collection at times **2** Printed books = never change • Can put books seldom read in storage • Take them out upon request

Sample Response 1 Supporting Donald

Donald has the right idea when he remarks that libraries ought to increase the sizes of their collections and not remove and dispose of books that they already possess. Since thousands of e-books can fit on a single computer, libraries that embrace e-books will never have to be concerned with space considerations again. I like Wendy's idea of storing books that are not often used by patrons and bringing them out when they are requested. I think that would provide more room for libraries. An additional advantage of having libraries lend e-books is that patrons could borrow books online, so they would never even have to visit the library. That would be a great advantage to people far from the library or without access to transportation.

해석

도서관은 소장 도서의 규모를 늘려야 하며 이미 소장 중인 도서들을 폐기 및 처분해서는 안 된다는 주장과 관련해서 Donald의 생각은 옳다. 수천 권의 전자책이 단 한 대의 컴퓨터 안에 들어갈 수 있기 때문에 전자책을 도입한 도서관은 공간 문제에 대한 걱정을 또 다시 할 필요가 없을 것이다. 이용객들이 자주 찾지 않는 도서들은 창고에 보관했다가 요청이 있는 경우에 꺼내 줄 수 있다는 Wendy의 아이디어는 마음에 든다. 그러면 도서관에 더 많은 공간이 마련될 것으로 생각된다. 도서관에서 전자책을 대여하는 경우의 또 다른 이점은 이용객들이 온라인으로 책을 대출할 수 있기 때문에 도서관을 방문할 필요조차 없게 될 것이라는

점이다. 이는 도서관에서 멀리 떨어져 사는 사람들이나 교통 수단을 이용할 수 없는 사람들에게 큰 이점이 될 것이다.

Sample Response 2 Supporting Wendy

I am a traditionalist and only read books that I can hold in my hands and physically turn the pages, so I love Wendy's argument. She is right in that e-books can be altered without the owner's consent. I would hate for one of my books to be changed without my permission. We should also remember that not everyone has a computer at home, and reading a book on a cell phone is hard for people with poor vision. These individuals require physical books if they want to be able to read. Donald's argument is good for members of the younger generation, who are comfortable with e-books. But older people, who use libraries more than younger people, are more hesitant to adopt new technology, so they are less likely to read e-books.

해석

나는 전통주의자로서 손에 들 수 있고 물리적으로 페이지를 넘길 수 있는 책을 읽는 것만 좋아하기 때문에 Wendy의 주장이 마음에 든다. 전자책은 소유자의 동의 없이 바뀔 수 있다는 점에서 그녀의 주장은 옳다. 내 책들 중 하나가 내 허락 없이 바뀐다면 싫을 것이다. 또한 모든 사람들의 집에 컴퓨터가 있는 것은 아니라는 점과 시력이 나쁜 사람들에게 휴대 전화로 책을 읽는 것은 힘든 일이라는 점을 기억해야 한다. 그러한 사람들이 책을 읽고 싶어하는 경우에는 물리적인 책이 필요하다. 전자책에 친숙한 보다 젊은 세대에 속하는 사람들에게는 Donald의 주장이 타당하다. 하지만 젊은 사람보다 도서관을 더 많이 이용하는 나이든 사람들은 새로운 기술을 받아들이는 것을 보다 꺼리기 때문에 그들이 전자책을 읽을 가능성은 낮다.

Unit 19 Economics II

Exercise 1 .... p.138

Brainstorming & Outlining

A

Professor Robinson

해석

경기는 순환하기 때문에 때때로 호황기가 있을 수도 있지만 경기가 하강하는 경우에는 경기 침체나 심하면 불황이 찾아올 수도 있습니다. 경기가 좋지 않은 시기에는 사람들이 종종 정부가 조치를 취해서 시민들을 도울 것을 요청하기도 하죠. 토론 게시판의 주제를 알려 드릴게요. 경기가 좋지 않을 때 정부가 취할 수 있는 최선의 조치는 무엇일까요?

✕ Outline for Brainstorming

Government Actions during a Poor Economy			
Provide Loans to Companies		Provide Extended Unemployment Benefits	
Reason 1	Reason 2	Reason 1	Reason 2
- Get money → cannot fire employees	- Fewer people lose jobs → helps during bad economy	- Lose job → get benefits for 6 months	- Hard to find work → extend for 1 year

B

Allen

해석

정부가 취할 수 있는 조치는 많지만 최선책은 자금난을 겪고 있는 기업에게 정부가 융자를 해 주는 것입니다. 융자를 받기 위한 한 가지 조건은 기업이 직원을 해고하지 않는다는 것이 될 거예요. 기업은 융자금을 이용해서 직원들의 급여를 지급할 수가 있겠죠. 그 결과로 일자리를 잃는 사람이 적어질 것인데, 그러면 경기가 좋지 않은 기간에 도움이 될 것입니다.

✎ Summary Notes: Allen

1) suffering financially
2) receive loan
3) loaned money
4) lose jobs
5) economic times

Robyn

해석

경기가 좋지 않은 국면에 있으면 사람들은 종종 일자리를 잃습니다. 또한 다른 일자리를 구하는데 어려움을 겪는 경우도 흔하죠. 사람들이 해고를 당하면 보통 6개월 정도 실업 급여를 받을 수가 있습니다. 하지만 경기 침체나 불황의 시기에는 그 정도의 기간 동안 새로운 일을 찾기가 힘듭니다. 따라서 정부는 실업 급여를 받는 기간을 1년으로 늘려야 하며, 이는 사람들에게 막대한 도움이 될 것입니다.

✎ Summary Notes: Robyn

1) replacement positions
2) six months
3) recession or depression
4) Extend benefits
5) immeasurably

Organization

Supporting New Ideas: Decreasing Taxes

1 While I like the ideas that Allen and Robyn present, I have a different opinion from them.

2 In my view, the best action the government can take during a bad economy is to decrease taxes.

3 For instance, income taxes, sales taxes, and property taxes could all be lowered temporarily.

4 One result of people paying less taxes is that they would have more money in their pockets.

5 They could use that money in various ways.

6 For instance, unemployed people could use the money they saved since they do not have any income coming in.

7 People who remained employed could spend some of the money that they saved from lower taxes.

8 This would help the economy by injecting more money into it.

9 As a result, it is possible that the economy could improve more quickly.

Supporting New Ideas: Doing Nothing

1 Personally, I dislike the suggestions made by Allen and Robyn.

2 My solution to the problem is quite simple as I believe the government should do absolutely nothing.

3 As Professor Robinson mentions in her question, the economy is cyclical.

4 This means there will be both good and bad economic times.

5 In some cases, government interference in the economy can actually cause poor economic conditions to persist for a long period of time.

6 This is exactly what happened in the United States during the Great Depression of the 1930s.

7 The government took actions which made the depression much longer by a factor of several years.

8 Instead of lowering taxes or bailing out companies, the government should do nothing and let the economy naturally heal itself.

9 This would guarantee that the economy would improve at the fastest possible rate.

Exercise 2 .... p.141

Professor Kennedy

해석

대부분의 학생들은 졸업 후에 취직을 해서 경력을 쌓기 시작할 것입니다. 대다수의 학생들은 대기업 입사를 선택하겠지만 소수의 학생들은 사업가가 되어 자신의 사업을 시작하게 되죠. 여러분은 학업을 마친 후에 어떻게 할 건가요? 대기업에 취직하고 싶나요, 아니면 자신의 사업을 하고 싶나요? 그 이유는요?

✕ Outline for Brainstorming

A Large Corporation or an Entrepreneur	
Large Corporation	Entrepreneur
Reason	Reason
- Foreign offices	- Personally profit
Details	Details
- Get transferred to another country	- Reap rewards of hard work → work harder

Wanda

해석

저는 쉽게 선택할 수 있어요. 저는 대기업 입사를 선택하겠습니다. 우선 대기업은 대부분 재정적으로 안정적이기 때문에 제가 업무를 열심히, 그리고 잘 하는 한 아마도 제 일자리는 보장될 것입니다. 다른 이유로 대기업은 직원들에게 승진의 기회를 부여해요. 이로써 저는 제 직급과 급여를 모두 높일 수가 있죠.

Stuart

해석

저는 대학 졸업 후에 사업가가 되고자 합니다. 사업주가 되면 누군가를 위해서 일하는 경우에 결코 누릴 수 없는 자유가 생기게 되죠. 게다가 제가 독창적인 생각을 떠올리거나 제 분야에서 선구자가 되는 경우, 저는 엄청난 성공을 거둘 수도 있고 아마도 억만장자가 될 수도 있을 거예요. 열심히 일하고 약간의 운만 따라 주면 됩니다.

Summary Note

Wanda	Stuart
1 Large corporations financially stable • Guaranteed job • Work hard and competently 2 Can be promoted • Improve rank • Get higher salary	1 Entrepreneur after college • Get freedom • No freedom if work for other 2 Have original idea or be pioneer in industry • Have phenomenal success • Become billionaire • Work hard and be fortunate

Sample Response 1 Supporting Wanda

I like Stuart's response, but I do not have the right personality to become an entrepreneur. Instead, like Wanda, I would take the safer choice and acquire a job at a large corporation. Wanda is correct in writing that large corporations offer financial stability. For instance, both of my parents have worked at big companies for decades. Neither has ever lost a job even during bad economic times. I love that kind of security. Something else I should mention is that many companies have branch offices in foreign lands. I would relish the opportunity to live in another country. If I worked for a big business, I could request a transfer to another country. Then, I would get paid to live somewhere else. That would be a dream come true for me.

해석

Stuart의 답변도 마음에 들지만 나는 성격상 기업가가 되기 힘들다. 대신 Wanda와 마찬가지로 나는 보다 안전한 선택을 택해서 대기업에 취직을 하고 싶다. 대기업이 재정적인 안정성을 제공한다고 한 Wanda의 말이 맞다. 예를 들면 우리 부모님들은 모두 수십 년 동안 대기업에서 일을 하고 계신다. 심지어 경기가 좋지 않은 시기에도 두 분 중 누구도 일자리를 잃은 적은 없으셨다. 나는 그러한 안정성을 좋아한다. 내가 언급하고 싶은 또 다른 점은 많은 기업들이 해외에 지점을 두고 있다는 것이다. 나는 다른 나라에서 살 수 있는 기회를 누리고 싶다. 내가 대기업에서 일을 한다면 해외 근무를 신청할 수 있을 것이다. 그러면 다른 곳에서 살면서 급여를 받게 될 것이다. 그렇게 되면 내 꿈이 실현될 것이다.

Sample Response 2 Supporting Stuart

Both Wanda and Stuart make some valid points in their arguments, but I am more convinced by Stuart. I hope to be like him as I would love to start my own business. Like Stuart, I have no desire to work for someone else. I know so many people who dislike their bosses, and I am sure I would be identical to them. I would therefore prefer to become my own boss at my own company. Another point to consider is that so many people work hard at their jobs, but they do not personally benefit. Instead, their boss or their company profits from their work. If I have my own company and work very hard, I will be able to reap the rewards of my hard work. And that will inspire me to work even harder.

해석

Wanda와 Stuart의 주장 모두 일리가 있지만 내게는 Stuart의 의견이 보다 설득력이 있다. 나도 Stuart처럼 내 사업을 시작해 보고 싶다. Stuart와 마찬가지로 나 역시 다른 누군가를 위해 일을 하고 싶지는 않다. 나는 자신의 사장을 싫어하는 사람들을 너무 많이 알고 있으며 나도 그들과 똑같이 될 것이다. 그러므로 나는 내 회사에서 내 자신이 사장이 되고 싶다. 고려해야 할 또 다른 점은 너무나 많은 사람들이 직장에서 힘들게 일을 하지만 개인적인 이득을 취하지 못한다는 것이다. 그 대신 그들의 사장이나 회사가 그들의 업무로부터 이익을 취한다. 내가 회사를 가지고 있고 열심히 일을 한다면 내 노고에 대한 보상은 내가 받게 될 것이다. 그리고 그러한 점은 내가 보다 열심히 일하도록 만들 것이다.

Unit 20 Environmental Science III

Exercise 1 .... p.144

Brainstorming & Outlining

A

Professor Davis

해석

귀중한 천연 자원을 보존할 수 있는 한 가지 방법은 유리, 플라스틱, 종이, 그리고 금속 제품을 재활용하는 것입니다. 또한 이러한 재료들을 재활용함으로써 폐기물과 오염을 줄일 수도 있죠. 하지만 재활용은 의미가 없으며 거의 도움이 되지 않는다고 주장하는 사람들이 있어요. 여러분께 질문을 하나 하겠습니다. 사람들이 의무적으로 재활용을 해야 할까요? 그렇게 생각하는 이유는요? 왜 그렇게 생각하나요?

× Outline for Brainstorming

Being Obligated to Recycle			
Agree		Disagree	
Reason 1	Reason 2	Reason 1	Reason 2
- Can reduce garbage in landfills	- Preserve natural resources	- Government shouldn't force people to do anything	- Recycling often requires too much energy

B

Henry

해석

저는 모든 사람들이 의무적으로 재활용을 해야 한다는 점에 전적으로 동의합니다. 일주일에 대다수의 사람들이 얼마나 많은 플라스틱 병을 사용하는지 생각해 보세요. 이러한 병을 버린다면 쓰레기 매립지가 금방 꽉 차게 될 것입니다. 이들을 재활용함으로써 우리는 쓰레기 발생량을 줄일 수 있고, 또한 이들 제품의 원료를 추가적으로 사용할 수도 있어요. 이는 재활용이 가능한 다른 제품들에도 적용되는 사실입니다.

☑ Summary Notes: Henry

1) each week
2) garbage dumps
3) plastic bottles
4) Decrease
5) additional usage
6) recyclable items

Geena

해석

저는 재활용이 환경에 이롭다고 믿지만 그럼에도 불구하고 재활용을 강요해서는 안된다고 생각해요. 저는 공익을 위한 것이라고 해도 정부가 사람들에게 특정 행동을 강요하는 것은 반대합니다. 일반적으로 대다수의 사람들은 강요를 받지 않고서도 올바른 일을 하려고 하죠. 소수의 사람들이 재활용을 하지 않는다고 해도 그것은 용인할 수 있는 일이에요.

☑ Summary Notes: Geena

1) forcing people to recycle
2) government
3) common good
4) do the right thing
5) Small minority

Organization

Supporting Henry's Opinion

1 I understand the thought process behind Geena's response, but I think Henry has the right idea.
2 Recycling is simply too important of an issue to ignore, so the government must take steps to ensure that everyone recycles.
3 As Henry noted, recycling can reduce the amount of garbage created.
4 It will additionally reduce litter because people will take the time to dispose of recyclable items in special bins rather than just tossing them on the ground.
5 Let me add that making people recycle will cause many individuals to think about the environment as a whole.
6 So they might make other efforts to help the environment, such as by conserving forests, by protecting endangered animals, and by finding ways to eliminate water, air, and ground pollution.
7 Overall, there are so many advantages to requiring people to recycle.

Supporting Geena's Opinion

1 Like Geena, I cannot support people being forced to do certain activities by the government, so I support her argument and disagree with Henry's comments.
2 Governments that force their citizens to do certain activities are oppressive, and the leaders who make those kinds of decisions are tyrants.
3 Required recycling is something that should never be implemented by any government.
4 In addition, we should consider that recycling itself has many drawbacks.
5 For example, items made with recycled paper are often of very poor quality, and recycling plastic often uses a very large amount of energy, making it wasteful.
6 So there is really no need to recycle certain products because we are just making more problems instead of solving them.

Exercise 2 ·· p.147

Professor Montague

해석

인간이 새로운 부지를 개발하면 야생 동물들은 서식지를 잃습니다. 이로써 일부 동물들은 멸종 위기종이 되고 일부 동물들은 멸종을 해서 영원히 사라지게 되죠. 대부분의 사람들은 동물의 개체수를 정상적인 상태로 유지시키기 위해 이들을 보호해야 할 필요성을 인정합니다. 여러분의 생각으로 인간이 다양한 동물종의 멸종을 방지하기 위해 취할 수 있는 가장 좋은 방법은 무엇인가요?

× Outline for Brainstorming

Ensuring Animals Do Not Go Extinct	
Feeding Wild Animals	Restricting Land Development
Reason	Reason
- Establish wildlife preserves	- Pass laws protecting land
Details	Details
- Let animals live in peace → stress-free lives	- Don't let nesting grounds be developed

Lee Anne

해석

제 생각에는 전 세계의 국가들이 다양한 장소에 대규모의 야생 동물 보호 구역을 만들어야 합니다. 이곳에서는 인간의 토지 개발이 허용되지 않을 것이며 동물들은 자신의 서식지에서 안전하게 살아갈 수 있을 거예요. 충분히 많은 국가들이 야생 보호 구역을 만든다면 동물들은 스트레스를 받지 않고 살아갈 수 있을 것인데, 그러면 번식을 통해 그 수가 더 많아질 것입니다.

Anthony

해석

최근 역사를 보면 많은 동물들이 인간 때문에 멸종을 하거나 멸종 위험에 처해 있어요. 한때 그 수가 10억 마리에 이르렀던 여행비둘기와 같은 동물들은 사냥에 의해 더 이상 존재하지 않게 되었습니다. 정부는 특정 동물의 사냥을 제한하거나 금지하는 법을 통과시켜야 해요. 사냥 금지 조치는 특정 동물종, 예컨대 퓨마와 늑대들의 개체수 증가에 도움이 될 것입니다.

☑ Summary Note

Lee Anne	Anthony
1 Establish wildlife preserves • Humans can't develop land • Animals live safely in natural environments 2 Nations make enough wildlife preserves • Animals have stress-free lives • Can reproduce in greater numbers	1 Humans make animals go extinct or be endangered • Hunting → animals like passenger pigeon go extinct 2 Governments should restrict or ban hunting of animals • Help animals increase populations → mountain lions and wolves

Sample Response 1 Supporting New Ideas: Feeding Wild Animals

Both Lee Anne and Anthony have excellent ideas, but their solutions are actions which only governments can take. I would like to propose a method which regular people such as myself can use to help animals. I believe people should make an effort to feed and provide clean water for animals. For instance, we live in an area where numerous species of birds reside. Migratory birds fly through this region twice each year, too. Some of these birds have trouble finding enough food, especially in the winter months. That is why I have a feeder which I fill with seeds daily. If more people would feed birds on a regular basis, fewer birds would starve to death. That is a simple action which everyone can take to help some wild animals.

해석

Lee Anne과 Anthony의 아이디어는 모두 훌륭하지만 그들의 해결책은 정부만이 취할 수 있는 조치이다. 나는 나와 같은 평범한 사람들도 동물들에게 도움을 줄 수 있는 한 가지 방법을 제안하고자 한다. 나는 사람들이 동물들에게 먹이를 주고 깨끗한 물을 제공해 주기 위해 노력해야 한다고 생각한다. 예를 들어 우리는 수많은 조류종이 서식하는 지역에 살고 있다. 또한 철새들도 이곳을 1년에 두 차례 지나간다. 이러한 새들 중 일부는, 특히 겨울에 충분한 양의 먹이를 찾는 데 어려움을 겪는다. 바로 이러한 이유 때문에 나는 매일 모이통에 모이를 채워 놓는다. 더 많은 사람들이 주기적으로 새들에게 먹이를 준다면 굶어 죽는 새들이

줄어들 것이다. 이는 모든 사람들이 일부 야생 동물들을 돕기 위해 취할 수 있는 간단한 행동이다.

Sample Response 2 Supporting New Ideas: Restricting Land Development

Lee Anne and Anthony propose good ideas which I support. My solution is also one in which the government would need to act. I believe governments need to pass laws stating that people are not allowed to develop land if animals use it as breeding or nesting grounds. For instance, near the university, there are some wetlands in which all kinds of animals live. I heard that a property developer wants to drain the land and put up apartments there. The government should prevent something like that from ever happening by passing a law. Additionally, when people break the law regarding land development, violators should be prosecuted, fined, and jailed. This will punish wrongdoers and convince others to leave the land alone. By taking these actions, we can save wild animals.

해석

Lee Anne과 Anthony는 훌륭한 아이디어를 제시했으며 나도 이들을 지지한다. 내 해결책 역시 정부가 취해야 하는 것이다. 나는 동물들이 번식을 하거나 둥지를 짓는 지역이라면 해당 토지의 개발을 허용하지 않는 법안을 정부가 통과시켜야 한다고 생각한다. 예를 들어 우리 대학 근처에는 온갖 종류의 동물들이 서식하는 습지가 존재한다. 나는 한 부동산 개발업체가 이곳에서 물을 빼내어 그곳에 아파트를 세울 것이라는 이야기를 들었다. 정부는 법을 통과시켜서 그와 같은 일이 일어나지 못하도록 만들어야 한다. 또한 사람들이 토지 개발과 관련된 법을 위반하는 경우에는 법 위반자들을 기소해서 벌금형이나 징역형에 처해야 한다. 이로써 범법자들은 처벌을 받게 될 것이며 다른 사람들도 그러한 부지를 그냥 놔두어야 한다는 점을 깨닫게 될 것이다. 이러한 조치를 취함으로써 우리는 야생 동물들을 보호할 수 있다.

Actual Test

Task 1

Reading

해석

옛 건물을 보존해야 하는 몇 가지 명확한 역사적인 이유가 있을 수도 있지만 이러한 점 때문에 대다수 건물의 철거가 중단되어 새 건물을 짓지 못하는 일이 있어서는 안 된다. 오래된 건물을 보존하는 관행은 즉시 중단되어야 한다. 오래된 건물은 새 건물에 자리를 내 주어야 한다.

역사적으로 중요하다고 여겨지는 건물은 일반적으로 보호를 받고 있으며 심지어 정부 기금으로 재단장되기까지 한다. 대통령의 생가와 같이 정말로 역사적 중요성을 갖는 장소에는 그러한 관행이 필요할 수도 있지만 많은 오래된 건물들은 정부에서 중요하게 생각하는 현재의 기준을 충족시키지 못한다. 이들 관리에 불필요한 정부 지출만 발생하고 있을 뿐이다. 그 대신 정부 기금은 범죄 소탕과 학교 및 병원 시설의 개선을 포함하여 보다 명분 있는 일에 쓰여야 할 것이다.

많은 오래된 건물들이 미적으로 아름답지 않고 실제로 아무런 실용적인 기능도 수행하지 않는다. 대다수 사람들은 현대 건축 디자인으로 지어진 건물을 더 좋아하며 자신들이 원하는 활동을 할 수 있는 장소를 원한다. 오래된 건물들은 쇼핑 센터 및 오락 시설과 같은 현대식 건물들에 자리를 내 주기 위해 철거되어야 한다. 이러한 건물들이 오래된 건물보다 훨씬 더 대중의 요구를 충족시켜 줄 것이다.

여러 해에 걸쳐 건축 법령과 기준이 극적으로 바뀌었다. 오래된 건물들은 이러한 기준을 충족시키지 못한다. 수도관은 유해한 납으로 만들어져 있고, 전기 시설은 낡고 구식이며, 단열재로는 발암 물질인 석면이 사용되었다. 이러한 오래된 건물들을 모두 교체하고 보수하는 일은 엄청난 비용을 요구하며 많은 시간을 필요로 한다. 실제로 철거를 하는 것이 더 안전하고 경제적으로도 이익일 것이다.

Listening

Script 🎧 02-03

W Professor: Historical buildings are a part of our heritage. Many important events in our city, state, and, of course, country took place in these buildings, so they must be preserved. There are several ways that we can guarantee they won't be blights on their neighborhoods but will in fact improve them.

Preserving, modernizing, and making buildings safer does not require government money at all. People can raise money and ask for donations to help preserve them. Remember that just last year, the old post office down on Fifth Street was saved thanks to a local fundraising campaign started by an elementary school class. By raising private funds, we can do the same for other buildings.

Take a look around this city. Like many others, it's dominated by steel and glass structures, strip malls, and fast-food restaurants. While some people may enjoy these places, I know many others who don't. The architecture of the past . . . the wood, brick, and concrete buildings, the art-deco style from the thirties, the brick townhouses . . . they're all parts of our heritage. And they're much more pleasing to the eye than many new structures being erected.

And let's not forget that historical buildings can generate money through tourism. The birthplace of an important figure or a building where a historical event took place can attract many paying customers. For example, Virginia makes millions of dollars a year off of tourism. Why? Well, it's the birthplace of at least eight presidents, it has the building where the Civil War ended, and it contains many battlefields from both the American Revolution and the Civil War. Old buildings and places really do have values beyond their historical importance.

해석

W Professor: 역사적 건물은 유산의 일부입니다. 우리의 도시, 주, 그리고 물론 국가의 많은 중요한 사건들이 이들 건물에서 이루어졌기 때문에 이 건물들은 반드시 보존되어야 해요. 이들이 주변에 해를 끼치지 않고 실제로 주변을 개선시키도록 만들 수 있는 몇 가지 방법이 존재합니다.

건물을 보존하고, 현대화하고, 그리고 더 안전하게 만드는 일에는 정부의 돈이 전혀 필요하지 않아요. 사람들은 건물 보존을 위해 기금을 모으고 기부를 요청할 수 있습니다. 작년에 한 초등학교 학급에서 시작된 지역 기금 모금 캠페인으로 5번가에 있던 오래된 우체국을 살린 예를 떠올려 보세요. 민간 기금을 마련함으로써 다른 건물들도 똑같이 그렇게 할 수가 있습니다.

이곳 도시를 둘러 보세요. 다른 도시들과 마찬가지로 철과 유리 구조물, 쇼핑 센터, 그리고 패스트푸드 매장들이 가득합니다. 어떤 사람들은 그런 장소를 좋아하지만 제가 알기에 그렇지 않은 사람들도 많아요. 과거의 건축 양식… 나무, 벽돌, 그리고 콘크리트로 된 건물과 30년대의 아르데코 양식, 벽돌로 지은 타운하우스… 이 모두가 우리의 유산에 해당됩니다. 그리고 이들은 요즘 들어서고 있는 신축 건물들보다 보기에도 훨씬 더 좋아요.

그리고 역사적인 건물들은 관광을 통해 수입을 가져다 줄 수도 있다는 점을 기억합시다. 중요한 인물의 생가나 역사적인 사건이 발생했던 건물은 많은 유료 관람객들을 유치할 수 있어요. 예를 들어 버지니아주는 관광 사업으로 매년 수백만 달러를 벌어들이고 있죠. 왜일까요? 음, 그곳은 최소 8명의 대통령이 태어난 곳으로, 그곳에는 남북 전쟁을 끝낸 건물도 있고, 독립 혁명과 남북 전쟁의 전쟁터도 많이 있기 때문이에요. 오래된 건물과 장소는 실제로 역사적 중요성을 뛰어넘는 가치를 지니고 있습니다.

Sample Response

The reading passage argues strongly in favor of tearing down the majority of older buildings. The professor, however, feels that efforts should be made to save many of them.

To begin with, the author of the reading passage feels the government money spent preserving these buildings would be better spent on law enforcement, education, and health services. But the professor notes that these buildings do not require government funds. Instead, they can be supported by private citizens donating money from their own pockets, as in the case of the old post office on Fifth Street.

In response to the reading's claim that many people dislike the appearances of older buildings, the professor states that she and many others believe most current buildings look awful. Rather, the varied architecture of older buildings is a part of the region's heritage.

The reading asserts that many old buildings could be dangerous since they do not meet current building codes and standards; however, the professor declares that many old buildings can actually be sources of income for the community. For instance, Virginia earns millions of dollars annually from tourists visiting its historical places.

While the reading passage's author writes against the notion of maintaining these old buildings, the professor advocates preserving them and making them valuable parts of the community.

해석

읽기 지문은 오래된 대다수의 건물들을 철거하는 것을 강력히 지지한다. 하지만 교수는 그들 중 다수를 보존하기 위한 노력이 이루어져야 한다고 생각한다.

우선 읽기 지문의 저자는 이들 건물을 보존하는데 지출되는 정부의 돈이 법 집행, 교육, 그리고 의료 서비스에 쓰여져야 한다고 생각한다. 하지만 교수는 이러한 건물이 정부 기금을 필요한 것은 아니라는 점에 주목한다. 대신 5번가의 오래된 우체국의 경우와 마찬가지로 자신의 주머니를 털어 기부를 하는 시민들에 의해 후원이 이루어질 수 있다.

많은 사람들이 오래된 건물의 외관을 좋아하지 않는다는 읽기 지문의 주장에 대해 교수는 자신을 비롯한 많은 사람들이 대다수의 현대식 건물의 모습을 흉물스럽게 생각한다고 주장한다. 오히려 다양한 건축 양식의 오래된 건물들은 그 지역의 유산의 일부이다.

읽기 지문은 오래된 건물이 현재의 건축 법령과 기준을 충족시키지 못하기 때문에 위험할 수 있다고 주장한다. 그러나 교수는 오래된 많은 건물들이 실제로 지역 사회의 수입원이 될 수 있다고 주장한다. 예를 들어 버지니아주는 역사적 장소를 방문하는 관광객들로부터 해마다 수백 만 달러를 벌어들이고 있다.

읽기 지문의 저자는 그러한 오래된 건물을 유지해야 한다는 주장에 반대하는 반면 교수는 건물들을 보존해서 지역의 중요한 일부로 만들어야 한다는 입장을 지지한다.

Task 2

Professor Wilkins

해석

다음 주에 우리는 중소기업에 대해 이야기할 것입니다. 중소기업은 수백만 명을 채용하고 있다는 점에서 국가에 매우 중요하죠. 많은 경우 사업을 시작하면 한두 명의 파트너와 함께 사업을 하게 됩니다. 따라서 여러분이 생각해야 할 문제를 알려 드리죠. 사람들이 가족과 함께 사업을 시작하는 것이 좋은 아이디어라고 생각하나요? 그 이유는요?

Melissa

해석

저는 가족들이 함께 사업을 하는 것을 전적으로 지지합니다. 보통 서로에 대해 잘 알기 때문에 각자가 어떻게 일할 것인지 잘 알고 있어요. 게다가 가족 구성원들은 기업을 성공시키기 위해 보다 기꺼이 노력할 것입니다. 저희 아버지와 삼촌께서는 함께 사업을 하시는데, 두 분은 좋은 업무 관계를 유지하고 계시죠.

Chris

해석

저는 가족들이 함께 사업을 하는 것이 좋은 아이디어라고 생각하지 않아요. 우선 문제가 생기는 경우, 특히 문제가 본질적으로 금전적인 것이라면, 다른 가족들에게 영향을 미칠 수 있습니다. 고려해야 할 또 다른 점은 일부 가족 구성원들이 사업 운영에 필요한 지식이나 기술을 가지고 있지 않을 수도 있는데, 그러면 사업에 도움이 되기보다 오히려 지장을 줄 수도 있습니다.

Sample Response 1 Supporting Melissa

I agree with the argument that Melissa presents mainly because it is true that family members will work hard to improve the fortunes of their families. I have seen many successful businesses which are run by multiple family members. These people all do whatever it takes to help their families prosper. While Chris makes a good argument that financial problems can cause harm to more family member than just the ones doing business together, this does not happen often enough to be a major problem. In addition, when family members work together, they are familiar with each person's strengths and weaknesses. As a result, they can have an easier time making their business successful than people who are not related to one another.

해석

가족들이 가족의 재산을 증식시키기 위해 열심히 일할 것이라는 점은 사실이기 때문에 나는 Melissa의 주장에 동의한다. 나는 여러 명의 가족들에 의해 운영되는 사업이 성공한 경우를 많이 목격했다. 이러한 사람들 모두 가족의 성공에 필요한 것이라면 무엇이든지 한다. 금전적인 문제로 인해 함께 사업을 하는 가족보다 더 많은 가족에게 피해가 갈 수 있다는 Chris의 주장은 타당하지만, 그러한 일이 중대한 문제가 될 정도로 커지는 경우는 드물다. 게다가 가족들이 함께 일하는 경우, 그들은 서로의 강점과 약점을 잘 알고 있다. 그 결과 서로 혈연 관계가 없는 사람들보다 더 쉽게 사업에서 성공할 수 있다.

Sample Response 2 Supporting Chris

While Melissa's argument appears logical, I cannot bring myself to support it but instead believe that Chris is correct. Family members absolutely should not go into business together. Chris is correct when he mentions that some family members may lack knowledge or experience. Yet they may still be permitted to help run a business because the other family members feel sorry for them or want to help them. This can have tragic results as some businesses go bankrupt due to incompetent workers. Something else to consider is that when there are problems in a business, these issues frequently affect the wellbeing of the entire family. For instance, my friend's parents were in business together, but when their business lost money, the parents wound up getting divorced. It simply is not a good idea to mix family and business.

해석

Melissa의 주장이 논리적으로 들리지만 나는 그러한 주장을 지지하기 힘들며 대신 Chris가 옳다고 생각한다. 가족 구성원들은 절대로 함께 사업을 해서는 안된다. 몇몇 가족 구성원들이 지식이나 경험을 가지고 있지 않을 수도 있다고 한 Chris의 말이 옳다. 하지만 이들이 사업 운영에 도움을 주는 것이 허용되는 경우가 있을 수 있는데, 그 이유는 다른 가족 구성원들이 그들에게 미안함을 느끼거나 그들을 돕고자 하기 때문이다. 이로 인해, 일부 사업체들이 무능한 직원 때문에 파산을 하는 것처럼, 비극적인 결과가 나타날 수 있다. 고려해야 할 또 다른 점은 사업에서 문제가 발생하는 경우 이러한 문제들이 종종 가족 전체의 안녕에 영향을 끼친다는 점이다. 예를 들어 내 친구의 부모님께서는 함께 사업을 하셨지만 사업에서 손실을 보자 그분들은 결국 이혼을 하셨다. 가족과 사업을 연결시키는 것은 좋은 아이디어가 아니다.

Actual Test 02   p.160

Task 1
Reading

해석

오랫동안 인쇄 매체가 뉴스원을 지배했지만 이는 빠른 속도로 온라인 매체에게 밀리고 있다. 실제로 가까운 미래에 마지막 신문이 발행되는 날을 맞이할 수도 있다.

인터넷에서 찾을 수 있는 뉴스는 빠르면서도 최신 내용을 다룬다. 전 세계 어디에서라도 뉴스거리가 되는 사건이 발생하면 거의 그 즉시 대다수 뉴스 제공 사이트에서 이를 찾아볼 수 있다. 예를 들어 스포츠 경기가 끝나면 몇 분 이내에 경기에 대한 완벽한 결과와 분석을 인터넷에서 접할 수 있다. 인쇄 매체의 경우 다음 날까지 기다리거나, 혹은 이미 인쇄가 진행 중인 경우에는 사건이 발생한 날로부터 이틀 뒤까지 기다려야 뉴스에 대해 알 수 있다.

온라인 뉴스는 다양한데, 이는 사람들이 어떤 분야의 어떤 내용이라도 읽을 수 있다는 점을 의미한다. 예를 들어 연예를 좋아하는 사람은 그와 관련된 수백 개의 사이트를 찾을 수 있다. 심지어 자신이 좋아하는 유명인에게 중요한 일이 일어나거나 자신이 좋아할 수도 있는 프로그램에 관한 소식이 있는 경우 이메일로 정보를 전달받을 수도 있다. 인쇄 매체의 경우에는 자신이 관심을 가지고 있는 내용을 찾기 위해 다른 모든 뉴스를 헤집어야 한다.

온라인 매체는 또한 지역이나 국내 뉴스에 국한되지 않고 현재의 전 세계 뉴스를 즉각적으로 제공할 수 있다. 사람들은 모든 곳에서 나온 뉴스를 읽을 수 있는데, 이는 인쇄 매체의 경우와 달리 삭제 당하지 않은 상태의 뉴스이다. 인쇄 매체 그리고 심지어 TV 뉴스조차 일반적으로 지역 및 국내 소식에 초점을 두며 그 내용도 심하게 편집된다. 인쇄 매체를 읽을 때에는 진실을 알기 힘든 경우가 많다.

Listening
Script 🎧 02-06

M Professor: While online news has many advantages over print media, I feel that we need both of them and that print media actually has several advantages over online news. Let me explain my reasons for thinking this.

Stories are often published on the Internet or even shown on television as they are actually happening. This can lead to, well, contradictory and confusing reports. For example, when there's a plane crash, the Internet and television are all over it even though they typically don't know much of importance since the story is still happening. Print media, however, has more time to absorb the story, to let it occur, and then to get all the details. When I want accurate reporting, I always read newspapers and magazines. They've had more time to get things right.

Some people hype the fact that online news is highly specialized. But you often have to pay for these services, including video fees for some major new services or websites that chart the lives of famous people. Or if you don't pay, your computer screen gets bombarded by advertisements and other pop-ups. Specialized services may provide more details for what people are interested in, but customers are definitely not getting these services for free.

While online media does a great job of providing international news, most people, myself included, are predominantly interested only in local and national news. This is the news, after all, which influences us daily. I don't really care about the price of gas in Japan or who won an election in France. I do, however, care about the price of gas locally and who is in office in this city. Print media can provide this information on a daily basis.

해석

M Professor: 온라인 뉴스는 인쇄 매체에 비해 많은 장점을 가지고 있지만 저는 이들이 모두 필요하며 실제로는 인쇄 매체가 온라인 뉴스에 비해 몇 가지 장점을 가지고 있다고 생각해요. 그렇게 생각하는 이유를 설명해 드리죠.

인터넷이나 TV에서 발표되는 이야기들은 종종 사건이 실제로 일어나는 순간에 발표됩니다. 이 때문에, 음, 모순되거나 혼란을 야기하는 보도가 이루어질 수 있어요. 예를 들어 비행기 추락 사고가 났을 때 인터넷 및 TV는 사건이 계속 진행 중이기 때문에 보통은 중요성을 잘 알지도 못하면서 그 사건에 큰 관심을 기울입니다. 하지만 인쇄 매체는 시간을 두고 사건을 다루며 사건이 진행된 후 세부 정보를 입수하죠. 저는 정확한 보도를 원할 때 항상 신문과 잡지를 읽습니다. 이들은 더 많은 시간을 들여서 올바른 정보를 전달해요.

어떤 사람들은 온라인 뉴스가 매우 전문화되어 있다는 사실을 과장해서 말합니다. 하지만, 메이저 뉴스 서비스의 시청료나 유명인의 생활을 싣는 웹사이트의 시청료를 포함해서, 그러한 서비스에는 종종 요금을 내야 하는 경우가 있습니다. 돈을 내지 않는 경우에는 컴퓨터 화면이 광고 및 기타 팝업으로 도배가 되죠. 전문화된 서비스는 사람들이 관심을 가진 것에 대해 보다 자세한 정보를 제공할 수 있지만 고객들이 그러한 서비스를 분명 무료로 받고 있지는 않습니다.

온라인 매체들이 훌륭하게 국제 뉴스를 제공하고 있지만 저를 포함하여 대다수의 사람들은 지역 뉴스 및 국내 뉴스에만 주로 관심을 가집니다. 어쨌거나 이들 뉴스가 매일 우리에게 영향을 미치니까요. 저는 일본의 유가나 프랑스 선거의 당선인에 대해서는 크게 신경을 쓰지 않습니다. 하지만 국내 유가나 누가 우리 시에서 재직하고 있는지에 대해서는 신경을 쓰죠. 인쇄 매체는 매일 그러한 정보를 제공해 줄 수 있습니다.

Sample Response

The reading passage's author believes online media is superior to print media; however, the lecturer thinks print media has several advantages over online news.

To begin with, the reading mentions that online news is fast and up to date. In fact, it often gets news out as it is happening or soon afterward while print media must wait at least a day to do so. However, the professor states that online coverage of breaking news events is sometimes confused and, in many cases, incorrect. He declares that print media, while slower, is more accurate than online media.

According to the reading, online news is more specialized, so people can get information on their favorite celebrities or anything they want without having to read news they are not interested in. The professor acknowledges this fact but states that these services are not free and often come with annoying advertisements and pop-ups.

Finally, in direct response to the reading passage author's claim that online media provides excellent coverage of international news, the professor declares he is not particularly interested in that. Instead, he prefers reading about local and national news, which print media provides much of.

While the reading passage's author feels that online news is the better version, the professor disagrees and thinks that print media is the much better option.

해석

읽기 지문의 저자는 온라인 매체가 인쇄 매체보다 뛰어나다고 생각하지만 교수는 인쇄 매체가 온라인 뉴스에 비해 몇 가지 장점을 가지고 있다고 생각한다.

우선 읽기 지문에는 온라인 뉴스가 빠르면서도 최신 정보를 담고 있다고 언급되어 있다. 실제로 종종 사건이 일어나는 순간이나 그 후 얼마 되지 않아서 뉴스 나오는 반면, 인쇄 매체의 경우 적어도 하루 정도를 기다려야 한다. 하지만 교수는 온라인의 속보가 때때로 혼란을 야기하며 많은 경우 부정확하다고 말한다. 그는 인쇄 매체가 더 느리기는 해도 온라인 매체보다 정확하다고 주장한다.

읽기 지문에 따르면 온라인 뉴스는 보다 전문화되어 있어서 사람들이, 자신이 흥미를 느끼지 않는 뉴스를 읽을 필요 없이, 자신이 좋아하는 유명인이나 원하는 것에 관한 정보를 얻을 수 있다. 교수는 이러한 사실을 인정하지만 이들 서비스는 무료가 아니며 종종 성가신 광고나 팝업을 수반한다고 말한다.

마지막으로 온라인 매체가 국제 뉴스 보도에 뛰어나다는 읽기 지문의 저자의 주장에 대해 교수는 자신이 국제 뉴스에 큰 관심을 가지고 있지 않다고 말한다. 대신 그는 지역 뉴스와 국내 뉴스를 읽는 것을 더 좋아하는데, 이러한 뉴스의 상

당 부분은 인쇄 매체가 제공하고 있다.

읽기 지문의 저자는 온라인 매체가 더 우수한 매체라고 생각하는 반면에 교수는 이에 동의하지 않고 인쇄 매체가 훨씬 더 나은 옵션이라고 생각한다.

Task 2

Professor Collins

해석

학년이 곧 끝날 것이므로 많은 사람들이, 특히 학생과 학생 가족들이, 여행을 떠날 계획을 세우고 있을 거예요. 여행을 할 때 어떤 사람들은 미리 계획된 활동을 하는 것을 선호합니다. 하지만 여행에 대한 아무런 계획이 없는 것을 선호하는 사람들도 있죠. 여러분은 어떤 유형의 여행을 하며, 왜 그러한 여행을 선호하나요?

Gregory

해석

저는 아무런 계획 없이 여행을, 특히 해외 여행을 떠나려고 하는지 이해할 수가 없어요. 저는 여행 기간 동안 매일 해야 할 일을 정확하게 알고 싶어하는 유형의 사람입니다. 그래서 저는 미리 준비를 하고 여행에 무엇을 가져가야 하는지 알 수 있어요. 저는 여행을 떠날 때마다 그렇게 하며 항상 멋진 여행을 하게 됩니다.

Carmen

해석

저는 여행을 자주 다니는 편은 아니지만 여행을 할 때에는 매일 깜짝 놀랄 일이 생기기를 바랍니다. 그래서 호텔을 예약하는 것 이외에는 아무런 계획을 세우지 않아요. 저는 호텔에 머물면서 휴식을 취하는 경우도 있고, 다른 여행객으로부터 들은 멋진 장소가 있으면 그곳에 가기도 하죠. 이러한 방법으로 저는 집에서 떠나 있는 시간을 즐겁게 보낼 수 있어요.

Sample Response 1 Supporting Gregory

Gregory and Carmen both make some valid points, but I side more with Gregory when it comes to traveling. I only take one trip a year, so like Gregory, I make sure to plan out all of my activities before I depart. I can therefore fill my days with great sightseeing, leisure activities, and dining experiences. Something else to consider is that by planning ahead, I have a rough estimate of how much the trip will cost. I am a budget traveler, so I cannot afford to spend an excessive amount of money. I wish I could be more like Carmen because it would be nice to make up my daily activities on the spur of the moment. However, for the time being, I have to travel like Gregory.

해석

Gregory와 Carmen 모두 타당한 주장을 하고 있지만 여행에 관한 내 생각은 Gregory의 생각과 더 비슷하다. 나는 1년에 단 한 번 여행을 하며, Gregory와 마찬가지로, 떠나기 전에 모든 활동을 계획해 둔다. 따라서 여행 기간을 멋진 구경, 레저 활동, 그리고 만찬으로 채울 수 있다. 고려해야 할 또 다른 점은 미리 계획을 세움으로써 대략적으로 여행 경비가 얼마나 들지 알 수 있다는 것이다. 나는 알뜰 여행을 하기 때문에 과도한 금액을 쓸 수가 없다. 순간적인 충동으로 하루를 보내는 것도 멋질 것 같기 때문에 나도 Carmen처럼 하고 싶다. 하지만 당분간은 Gregory처럼 여행을 해야 한다.

Gregory's method of travel seems like it will provide him with the most efficient trip. However, I like traveling the way Carmen does much more. I prefer to be spontaneous when I travel, but if I have already planned various tours and made bookings, acting impulsively is impossible. On my last trip, I heard about a fascinating cave from another traveler, so we decided to go together. It was definitely worth the effort. If I had already planned out my trip, I never would have seen that inspiring place. I also make friends easily when I travel, so I like to do activities with the people I befriend. Because I do not make any plans ahead of time, I can join my new friends and see and do various things with them.

해석

Gregory의 여행 방식으로 그는 가장 효율적인 여행을 하게 될 것 같다. 하지만 나는 Carmen의 방식으로 여행하는 것을 훨씬 더 좋아한다. 나는 여행할 때 즉흥적인 것을 좋아하는데, 내가 이미 다양한 투어를 계획하고 예약을 했다면 충동적으로 행동하는 것이 불가능하다. 지난 여행에서 나는 또 다른 여행객으로부터 환상적인 동굴에 대한 이야기를 들어서 우리는 같이 가기로 결심했다. 그곳은 확실히 노력을 기울일 가치가 있는 곳이었다. 내가 미리 여행 계획을 세워 두었더라면 결코 그처럼 황홀한 장소를 보지 못했을 것이다. 나는 또한 여행할 때 쉽게 친구를 사귀기 때문에 친구가 된 사람들과 함께 활동하는 것을 좋아한다. 나는 계획을 미리 세워 두지 않기 때문에 새로운 친구들과 어울려서 그들과 함께 다양한 것들을 보고 경험할 수 있다.